GEORGE CURTIS
Training Greyhounds

JULIA BARNES

To Bill Peters, who gave me my first job in Greyhound Racing. And to my brother Charlie, a fellow trainer who was tragically killed when returning from an open race at Crayford. **F.G.C.**

First published 1987.
This revised edition published 1991 by
Ringpress Books Limited, Spirella House,
Bridge Road, Letchworth, Herts SGF6 4ET

Printed and bound in Great Britain by
Mackays of Chatham PLC

ISBN 0 948955 66 X

Contents

Foreword	1
Introduction	4
Early Days	6
The First Division	22
The Champion	40
Choosing a Greyhound	65
Breeding Winners	69
Whelping	84
Rearing	91
Schooling	95
Diet	106
Exercise	112
Grooming and Massage	117
The Kennel	131
The Open Racer	136
Problem Dogs	147
Common Ailments	157
Racing Injuries	169
A Star is Born	186
World-beater	198
Last Goodbyes	215

Foreword

PUBLICATIONS on greyhound personnel are extremely rare, so I applaud this commendably bold decision to write a book on George Frederick Curtis. But if ever a subject warranted such an undertaking then it was the former champion trainer, who was such an ambassador to greyhound racing during his star-spangled career.

He retired on December 31, 1986 after 48 years in his beloved sport which saw him rise from the happy bread-and-butter life at Portsmouth to an equally enjoyable post at booming Brighton and Hove.

During his near half-century term, which meant a 6 am start and often a near-midnight finish six days a week, caring for Man's Best Friend, George fostered a string of close and happy relationships with greyhound owners, staff and fellow professionals. Affectionately known as 'Gentleman George', few in this sport have attained so much genuine respect.

George's affinity with the hounds he trained — and particularly world-record beater Ballyregan Bob, as this delightful book has chronicled — became blatantly obvious during the latter years of his career, during which period he, at last, received the national recognition he so richly deserved.

His relationship with the greyhound Press was also something very special. In difficult circumstances, which would sometimes accompany any conversation or interview, he would go out of his way to explain 'the real story' about a subject, whilst also asking for discretion from the writer in any subsequent story.

The traditional annual Press Luncheon is held at the Cheshire Cheese in Fleet Street towards the end of January when the previous year's Greyhound Of The Year awards are announced. Ballyregan Bob lifted the title for 1985 and the wonder stayer retained the coveted crown the following year, when Curtis also received the Greyhound Writer's Association's special award for Services To Greyhound Racing in 1986.

George was chuffed for the first occasion, when he dined with the Press alongside his charmer of a wife Lily and Bob's owner Cliff Kevern and his good lady Jessie.

The quartet were so excited about 'Bobby's' award that they arrived at the Cheese two hours early and were promptly given an escorted tour of the premises by one of the management.

"This place is absolutely fantastic," declared George when the Press corps arrived. "It makes me feel so young when I visit historic places."

But his experience on that first visit was nothing to the following year's get-together. He was unashamedly embarrased by the special award and kept apologising to the assembled journalists. That luncheon lasted for close on four hours and it proved a particularly special function for the Press and certainly one which will linger in the memory.

There are other fond memories of gatherings with the Portsmouth-born maestro and the period when Yankee Express clinched a unique Scurry treble at Slough in 1982-1983-1984 is high on the list. I know the Scurry is a July competition and, even allowing for an English summer, it was odds-on to be warm. But for the fortnight during those three Scurrys, the climate seemed almost Caribbean. So while Yankee was burning it up around the delightful and much-missed circuit, Curtis maintained a hot pace in the bar area with memories of some of his former star trackers — Bad Trick, Upland Tiger, Glin Bridge, etc.

And as the great man whittled off star name after star name, Yankee's cavalier and mischievous owners, Sid Stenning, Bert Cusack and Ray Barnard kept up a barrage of light-hearted leg-pulls aimed at their trainer.

. . ."But none of them were as good as Yankee, isn't that right, George? And don't you tell the Press otherwise!" They joked.

It was at Slough where I first met George's head lad and successor Bill Masters: "I am putting Bill forward for my job when I retire," said George. "He's not frightened of hard work and I have taught him as much as I can. He is also a good man — and that is one of the most important things in life."

George Curtis's judgement about Bill Masters, as time has proved, could not be faulted and Curtis would probably have made it in most trades had he not decided to stay with training. I am certain he would have had few peers as a greyhound tipster. One of the first things he would do whenever I visited Hove would be to grab my racecard and tick-up those he fancied. More often than not, his selection would be trained by a fellow handler.

FOREWORD

I vividly remember the telephone conversation between us in July 1984. He told me: "I have just acquired two outstanding youngsters, son, Darkies Automatic and Ballyregan Bob.

"Ballyregan looks the better animal and he did a fast time around Tralee recently. He has the feel of a real good greyhound."

This book, by Julia Barnes, relates in super detail the life and times of Ballyregan Bob under Gentleman George and all the success which went with it. The world record triumph by Bob at home track Hove in December 1986, proved a fitting climax to both careers.

George remarked in early January, 1987: "It is nice now I have retired and scaled down on to a part-time basis. I honestly don't miss the long, daily routine, son."

"What is your working week now?" I enquired politely.

"Well, let me see. I do Mondays to Fridays and three nights a week at Hove, although I take greyhounds for open races on some of the other nights," he replied almost casually.

It mirrors the love the gentle-natured Curtis harbours for greyhound racing and the people who help make the sport tick. The fact that he was as happy as a sandboy when grafting at Portsmouth and a touch uncomfortable at the media exposure after he had hit the jackpot with Ballyregan Bob, speaks volumes for his unassuming character.

"None of this would have been possible without the help from my staff — they deserve the credit," regularly came from his lips whenever the personal accolades started flying around.

And when the *Life* asked him in early 1987 to contribute a regular monthly column, he answered: "I would love to, but do you think people will be interested in my life and experiences?"

Read on!

Bob Betts
Greyhound Editor, Sporting Life

Introduction

THERE is no mystery attached to training greyhounds, according to George Curtis. "Keep your dog warm in the winter, cool in the summer, feed him the best and he will run for you," he says.

That statement is 100 per cent typical of Curtis, the man who has been champion trainer three times in a career of unrivalled success. He is not over-simplifying in order to be devious. Following his retirement, he declared himself more than willing to reveal all he knew about training greyhounds. But he has never allowed himself to get caught up in any pretence. Commonsense has been the ruling force in all his decision-making and he believes that anyone is capable of training racing dogs.

"You need the facilities, the experience — and above all you need the right dogs," he said. "If you've got a kennel full of moderate dogs, you will be a moderate trainer — no matter how hard you work. You can feed them the best in the world but it won't make any real difference. You might improve them by a length — but that would be it. You can't make a grader into an open racer. It's all a matter of what they've got in them to start with.

"People used to ask me what was so special about Ballyregan Bob and I would say: 'Whatever it was — it was in him before I got him.' That was not being over-modest. I truly believe it. The job of a trainer is not to produce miracles but to bring out the best in a dog. No matter what standard he is, you should be able to make him fulfil his potential."

This philosophy has enabled Curtis to see every dog in his kennel as a challenge and he maintains that he has always had as much time for graders as for open racers. "To me, a greyhound is a greyhound. When it comes to the basics it's just the same. When I go to the kennels in the morning, I don't think — he's an open racer, I must do something special with him. You've got to get wins with all your dogs."

The real skill lies in discovering what each dog is capable of and then giving him the care and conditions that will bring out the best from him. "All greyhounds are different," said Curtis. "They come in all shapes and sizes. Some need more weight on them than others, some need more exercise. Some are nervous and excitable, others are calm and relaxed. You've got to know all your dogs and adapt to suit the individual.

"But the most important thing of all is consistency. Get a kennel routine organised and then stick to it. I have always listened to a lot of different people, picking up advice from everyone I could. But when it comes down to it, you must make your mind up and stick to your guns — or you will always be at sixes and sevens trying out different ideas. The object is to produce a calm, contented dog, who will always try his hardest for you."

CHAPTER ONE

Early Days

THE world's Press was gathered, the stadium was packed to capacity, live TV link-ups were set up — all for one man and his dog. Could George Curtis, the undisputed king of greyhound trainers, pull off his last and most spectacular feat? The maestro, due to bow out after 43 years as a trainer, did not disappoint his public. Ballyregan Bob's triumphant ran to victory, chalking up his thirty-second consecutive win and a new world record, earned a special place in greyhound racing history.

Any other trainer would surely have seen this unique moment of glory as the jewel in his own personal crown. But Curtis's first reaction was to say: "It's a wonderful achievement for the dog — and for the sport."

This degree of modesty might have had the ring of insincerity in any other man. But not from George Curtis, known throughout the sport as Gentleman George. His honesty, integrity and dedication are matchless — and he is always the first to praise others, shifting the limelight from himself. His success is the result of pure hard work — and yet you will hear him say countless times, how lucky he has been.

"The sport has given me everything. It has given me a life that I never dreamed was possible," he says. And certainly the ballyhoo that surrounded Curtis on that famous night in Brighton when Ballyregan Bob romped to victory, was a far cry from his early life in the slums of Portsmouth. "I think it is hard for some people to understand why I am so grateful to the sport," says Curtis. "But they do not realise what my life was like and I truly never expected it to be anything different. I was always hungry, I had no socks, the arse was hanging out of my trousers and I never looked for anything better."

George was born in 1923 — the third of nine children and his earliest memories are of his mother Ellen trying to find enough food to go round. "We had rice pudding for dinner and two slices of bread and marg for tea — with jam on it on Sundays," said Curtis.

His father Fred was a labourer invalided during the war and struggling to support his growing family on a 10-shilling-a-week pensions. "Times were hard," said Curtis. "There were the old soup kitchens and we had to queue up for stale bread. There were gifts from charity. We used to get boots on the cheap and at Christmas there were goodwill parcels. We used to hang out of the window and hope they were coming to us. We were one of the poorest families and so they usually did.

"All we seemed to think about was getting enough to eat. I think my only real ambition was to grow up so I could have as big a dinner as my Dad. I remember we all used to sit round the table and watch him eat — he got the most because he was the head of the family. My aim was to get out and start earning some money so I could get some proper grub."

Now George lives in comfort in a semi-detached house in Henfield, near Brighton, with his wife Lily. It is not a luxurious home — a fairly modest reward for reaching the top of his profession. But George and Lily are clearly proud of it. It is packed with paintings, photographs and trophies — mementos of his many triumphs. A focal point is the television and video, wired up for endless replays of greyhound races.

Another influential factor in Curtis's make-up is his amazement that he ever managed to survive to live a full and active life. When he was only five years old he was stricken with tuberculosis — a killer disease at that time. He was in hospital for some two years and underwent painful treatment which involved burning the affected areas of skin in order to stop the TB spreading. Curtis still bears the scars on his neck.

"It was a terrible time. We were only allowed to see our parents on Sunday afternoons and so I felt completely cut off from the family," he said. "And yet I was one of the lucky ones, compared with what other children on the ward were going through. They had to have all sorts of skin grafts and many didn't survive. All through my life I have felt that I was simply lucky to be alive. It's something I will never forget, even though I was so young when it happened to me."

When he was finally allowed to leave hospital he was sent to school. But as he is the first to admit, education more or less passed him by. "To begin with they said I was two years older than my actual age," he said. "You see, education was not considered as something important. The whole idea was to leave school as soon as possible so you could start earning some money. I didn't discover my real age until I was getting married. It said on my birth certificate that I was 25 and I had been going around thinking I was 27!"

Curtis managed to get through his schooldays without ever mastering the Three R's. "The best thing about school for me was the school dinner," he said. "I taught myself to read and write much later and that was so I could keep up with the daily paper the *Greyhound Express*. It was my Bible."

His great ally in those early years was his younger brother Charlie, who also went on to be a greyhound trainer. The two boys were only a year apart in ages and they were inseparable. "We used to do everything together," said Curtis. "Although I was older I always looked up to Charlie. He was bigger and stronger and I thought the world of him. We had a rough upbringing. Of course, there was no wireless or television and we just used to roam the streets like all the other kids in the neighbourhood. We had no real interests or hobbies. We had a dog at home but I was never especially interested. That all started with the greyhounds."

Curtis was 14 years old when he first went to a greyhound stadium. He was working as one of the Gordon Boys, a team of youngsters who were given uniforms and hired out to do odd jobs around Portsmouth. "We used to fetch and carry sailors' luggage, deliver bills, all sorts," he said. "One of the jobs was to go to Portsmouth Stadium between 7–10 pm and sell tote tickets. There were three of us and we each had our own booth. The pay was half a crown a night."

That represented good money in Curtis's book and so his first visit to the dogs proved decisive. It was the start of a lifetime's passion for greyhound racing and it paved the way for an escape from the poverty trap that was ensnaring him. But it still took nearly a year to find a way into the sport. "I went to the track on a regular basis doing the tote returns and eventually people got to know me," he said. "They started to talk to me, asking me about the various forecasts and the racing. I wasn't interested in the betting. I just used to watch the racing and I loved hearing all the greyhound talk. Whenever I got the chance I would go down and chat to the kennel lads. When I found out how much they earned I thought: 'I wouldn't mind some of that.' So I put my name down for the first vacancy that came up."

In April 1938 he joined trainer Bill Peters as kennel lad. The first morning he started work is one he will never forget. It was to prove the turning point of his life. "I walked into the kennels and was met with the smell of pine sawdust," he said. "I saw the dogs and that was it. I was hooked. There was something about the whole thing that got in my blood. I have lived and breathed greyhounds ever since. And I haven't regretted one day of it." Bill Peters was the first — and last — trainer Curtis worked for and he acknowledges a huge debt to his old Guv'nor. Peters was a kind and generous man — both to his dogs and to his staff.

"He treated me like a son," said Curtis. "He really cared about us

Above: At the starting traps at Portsmouth Stadium. Curtis (arrowed) is pictured with head lad Bob Staires in 1938, the year he joined Bill Peters as kennel lad.

Left: Curtis and his runners at Portsmouth in 1950. They are left to right: Queen Of Fairies, Proper Champion and Sailaway Mick.

lads. He wanted us to make something of ourselves. The pay was £1 a week, but it went up as soon as he started to do better. And it was the Guv'nor who advised me to open my first Post Office account. 'Save up your pennies lad,' he said. 'You'll need them later on.' He always offered to get an owner to put 10 shillings on a dog for us if he thought it had a real chance. But I was never interested in the betting side. I always argued that 10 shillings in my hand was better than risking it."

But temptations did come Curtis's way. Shortly after starting work for Peters, he was approached by two men who offered him £20 to take them into the kennel when the Guv'nor was away. For a boy earning £1 a week, £20 represented untold riches. But even then, Curtis's ingrained honesty and integrity came to the fore. He told them to wait until his boss returned and he alerted the Guv'nor of his suspicions. "He agreed to take them in but he told me to follow behind and keep an eye of them. They were asking the names of all the dogs and I saw the younger of the two slip his hand into some of the kennels as they went past.

"As soon as they left I got a lump of soda and gave it to the last dog they had been past — and a capsule came up. We vomited all the others but by that time the capsules had dissolved. I missed one — a bitch called Swift Stream and the next morning she could hardly stand up. We took her out to the track to see how badly she was affected and she fell over three times when she tried to gallop. In those days race cards were printed the day before racing and the men's aim was to find out the dogs' names so they could get two non-runners in a five dog race. But they were complete amateurs. They did the job so badly, it would never have got past the vet."

But Curtis's honesty and his swift thinking saved a lot of suffering among the dogs and it opened the eyes of the authorities to the faulty security. He was rewarded with a letter of commendation from Lord Denham, who was then senior steward of the NGRC.

It is a story that anyone would be proud to tell — particularly when you consider that Curtis was only 15 years old at the time. But he pushes it to the back of his mind, saying anyone would have done the same. His code of honesty is such that he did not question for a moment what was the right thing to do. But many boys coming from his background would have faltered when confronted with a sum of money they could only ever dream of possessing.

It was not long before Curtis's younger brother Charlie joined the Peters kennel at Tipnor and the two brothers became absorbed in a routine that was to dominate their lives. The work was hard and the financial rewards were meagre — but the Curtis boys thrived on it.

The kennel strength was around 38 greyhounds and with no paddocks each dog had to be exercised for one and half hours a day. They went out three times a day and the lads would cover a total of six miles — more if they had to go out with a second string. And then there was the grooming, a ritual that took up to two hours a day. "We were so competitive," said Curtis. "We took a real pride in the way our dogs looked. Each lad was allocated his own eight or ten dogs and we were always trying to out-do each other. And, of course, we were always trying to beat the dogs from the other kennels as well.

"Race nights were the highspot and I still feel the thrill and excitement as much as I did in those early days. I always shout them home — it makes no difference if it's a bottom grader or a classic winner. I just get so excited. People think I'm mad. But I think the day you lose that feeling of excitement is the day you give up. After all, it's what the game is about."

It is an interesting anomaly that a man who is renowned as a gentleman, can be so fiercely competitive. And although Curtis will always be the first to congratulate the winner, there is no-one who likes winning more. As a young lad Curtis used to talk to all the other trainers and get hints and advice. But he remembers Portsmouth trainer Jack Toesland saying: 'I'll help you as much as I can, but once we get to the track keep out of my way or I'll cut your throat.' "That sums it up," said Curtis. "You're good mates away from the track but once you're there at the business end you're in opposite corners and that's how it should be."

As Curtis got to know more about his job and the sport, his confidence grew. He began to feel a sense of importance for the first time in his life. "I felt so involved in the kennels. I knew all the dogs and their different ways. They would make a fuss of you and they seemed to appreciate what you were doing for them. When you got a winner it was fantastic. The owners would come along and the Guv'nor would point you out and say: 'That's the lad that looks after your dog.' The owner would pat you on the head, tip you a shilling and say: 'Well done, son.' It was magic."

But the outbreak of war shattered this happy existence. Trainers and lads were called up. Charlie was one of the first to go — but Curtis was left behind, exempted because of his TB. It was not a situation that he was altogether happy with. It is never easy being the one that is left behind. "I had to make the best of it," said Curtis. "I promised Charlie that I would save up all the money I could while he was away and we would split it fifty-fifty when he got back."

But to begin with, Curtis was almost the one without a job. When the news of the war broke, there was considerable panic. Many owners had their greyhounds destroyed thinking there would be no more racing. It was to prove a tragic waste. "We moved up to some kennels at Liphook and for a time the stadium was closed," said Curtis. "The racing boss Joe Childs, the former Queen's jockey, came to see us at the weekends. I remember him saying: 'As I see it we have two choices. Either you leave now — or you go on half-pay.' Well, none of us wanted to be without a job and so we agreed to half-pay. Fortunately it didn't last too long and within a month or so we were racing every Saturday afternoon. That went on throughout the war. I still remember the dogs that were destroyed. It was heart-breaking. There were some lovely animals. But I think when you're young you accept things like that more easily. The older you are, the harder you take it."

Portsmouth's coastal location made it the obvious target for German bombers and Curtis was enlisted for fire-watching duties at the stadium. One morning a bomb fell and the complex was within inches of being flattened. A fire started and, curiously, all the kennel doors were blown off. "It was pandemonium," said Curtis. "We were trying to fight the fire and the dogs were running loose." Undeterred by the panic, a couple of greyhounds came across the sandwiches the lads had brought in for breakfast. They set to, leaving a tell-tale trail of blood where one had nicked himself on some glass. "We found him wandering round looking very pleased with himself, despite a small cut on the nose," said Curtis. "He was a blue dog called Genial George."

War-time rationing presented new problems for the trainers who were faced with trying to get enough decent meat to go round. Bill Peters, who ran his kennel on the maxim 'Feed them well and they race well' — was not to be beaten. He sent Curtis down to the fish market and he came back with buckets-full of cods' heads. They also used sausage meal, soaking it first and inevitably ending up with tubfulls as it swelled up, almost with a mind of its own. At that time all the racing greyhounds came from Ireland. British breeding, still very much in its infancy, was at a temporary standstill. And there was no competing with the price of the Irish imports. Most dogs cost about £5 and if you paid £10 you expected something a bit special. They would arrive in a terrible state. Curtis remembers them coming over with a bit of old sack on their back and a chain round their neck. Their teeth were bad and their nails were long and uncared for. These dogs would have come straight from the farm, where agents picked them up for next to nothing. All they looked for was a couple of trials to see if they chased. It didn't matter what the times were — and no one cared about the breeding.

"But these rough old dogs presented a real challenge for us," said Curtis. "No-one had done any work on them and so we did all we could to get the best out of them. We would spend hours grooming and exercising and it was marvellous to see how a dog could improve. With luck, a dog that started off at £5 would be worth £50 by the time you had finished with it."

Unexpectedly the war gave Curtis his first opportunity to go open

The young trainer. Curtis pictured at the age of 22, soon after he took out his full trainer's licence.

racing. The open race calendar was drastically reduced and most of the events were in London. If any of the Portsmouth trainers had a decent dog they would send Curtis away with it — as the most senior lad at the stadium. He went to Wimbledon for the Puppy Derby and to Wembley. It was his first opportunity to see the best dogs racing and he was filled with ambition to get hold of one. Portsmouth was a track where virtually any dog could grade. Bill Peters was very much a track trainer and so there was no real prospect of competing in the big league.

But Curtis was content to bide his time and the good dogs they had at Portsmouth live on in his memory. He remembers Shady Rattler and Domino Dotter as the best two at the track and he has special affection for Tanmere — a top-class stayer who looked a world-beater at Portsmouth, though Curtis admits she would have been nothing elsewhere. He rates Clam as the best dog Peters handled — and sees the dog's success as a true tribute to his Guv'nor's qualities as a trainer. The dog would do fantastic times in trials but when it came to racing he did nothing. They took him coursing and put him in a trap on a swivel. When the hare came up they released him — and he tore after it. Clam came back to the track to win an open race and went on to clock a track record that stood for 10 years.

By now Curtis was gaining in experience and standing in for trainers when they were away. By the time he was 22 years old he had £120 saved up and was ready to make the jump to fully fledged trainer. He had been with Bill Peters for seven years and remains eternally grateful to his teacher. "He taught me everything and a lot of the lessons have stood me in good stead all my life," said Curtis. "He really cared for his dogs and went out of his way to make sure they were well fed, kept warm in winter and cool in the summer. He was always experimenting, trying different lotions and embrocations on the dogs. And if one died he would attend the post mortem. He believed there was something you could learn from every situation."

On the princely sum of £4 a week, Curtis set up on his own account. To begin with he ran his kennel very much in the Peters' mould but he admits to a certain degree of arrogance. "Of course, I thought I knew it all," he said. "It takes you 10 years to realise you don't — and another 10 years to realise you're stupid! You learn by your mistakes."

Through all the hard times, Curtis's boundless enthusiasm kept him going. "Every morning I would go to work whistling," he said. "I couldn't get there quick enough. I loved every minute of it and so the work never seemed hard. For me, there was always a challenge — a new dog to settle in, puppies to school, working on the racers, grooming and massaging. I was in my element." But Curtis also learnt a very sobering lesson. His greatest ambition was to train a really good dog and at last he thought he had got his hands on one when Singing Trail came to his kennel. He broke the track record at Portsmouth and Curtis thought that the time had come to take on the big league. He took the dog to London for an open race — and the result was disaster. Singing Trail was completely out-classed.

"I was so disappointed," he said. "I didn't think that the dog simply wasn't good enough. I thought it was me — I thought it was my training that had let him down. It took me a very long time to realise that you are only as good as the dogs in your kennel. You can work and work on a dog and you can finish up breaking your heart. If a dog hasn't got it in him to begin with, no amount of work can put it there. All you can ever do is bring out a dog's natural ability."

Curtis was now an avid follower of the open race scene and as soon as peace was declared the opportunities to travel, and for Portsmouth to stage open race competitions increased. This post-war period was a boom time for greyhound racing. The punters packed into the tracks — White City would have crowds of 20,000 on its big nights and even small circuits such as Portsmouth would get 3,000. The mood was buoyant and it was an era remembered for some great greyhounds and great trainers.

Curtis's hereos were the big London trainers — Leslie Reynolds, winner of five English Derbies in seven years, Sidney Orton, Jack Harvey and Paddy McEllistrim. The highspot of his working life was when Portsmouth staged an inter-track and he got the chance to talk to his idols. Charlie had joined the kennels of Stan Biss at Clapton and the two brothers spent hours swapping the training tips they picked up. "I was hungry for knowledge," said Curtis. "I would talk to everyone trying to find out the different ways that trainers did things. I talked greyhounds morning, noon and night — with anybody I thought I could learn something from."

Soon he notched up his first open race win with Lottbridge Win It — and when Charlie came back to Portsmouth to join him, the Curtis kennel gradually became a force to be reckoned with.

To begin with it was the graders that started to perform well for them. The secret was no real mystery. The brothers worked incredibly hard, getting to the kennels at five in the morning and not getting home until midnight on race nights. They fed their dogs on the very best — Curtis would even beg the powdered egg rations from his pregnant sister to overcome post-war shortages — and they would exercise their dogs endlessly. "Charlie was a big, strong man and he could walk and walk," said Curtis. "But what made a real difference was when we started taking them to Portsmouth football ground to gallop them. We used a straight about 400 yards long alongside the pitch and called the dogs up between us. The track at Portsmouth was often water-logged and this way we could always give our dogs a real good gallop."

But it was still a hard job to earn a decent living from the sport. To make end meet the brothers depended on getting winners and the resulting bonus from owners. "I was under a lot of pressure on the gambling side," said Curtis. "You knew that if you had a bad meeting, you had to wait a week before you could hope for another winner. And I was always conscious of trying to earn enough money for me and Charlie."

He recalls his biggest gambling coup, which occurred soon after he became a trainer at Portsmouth. A bitch won at 10–1 and the owner was upset because he hadn't had any money on her. Curtis promised him a win the following week — and that started a nightmare seven days for the young trainer. He worked and worked on the bitch, exercising her, grooming her and reserving the very best food for her. The day before the race she looked a picture and Curtis decided to take her out for a final gallop. The grass in the meadow was a beautiful lush green, but what Curtis failed to realise was that a sewerage pipe ran the length of the field, emptying its contents into the sea. Inevitably the bitch returned from her run covered in black filth from head to tail. "I didn't tell the owner," said Curtis. "I just cleaned her up and kept my fingers crossed. The owner backed her and I put £20 on her — and she came out and won at 8–1. That was the biggest win of my life."

But Curtis has always remained indifferent to the temptations of big-time gambling. He enjoys a speculation on a long-priced fancy. But he is a man who bets in fivers and tenners. He claims he never had the need to gamble after he became a full-time track trainer at Brighton. But more importantly, he is not someone to risk the things he has strived so hard for.

When he was 25 years old Curtis married Phylis Austin — he had worked with her brother Peter for many years. But tragically, their marriage was only to last for seven short years. Phylis had leukaemia and one day the doctor told Curtis that his wife only had three months to live.

"She was so young and we got on so well together. I just couldn't believe it," he said. "We didn't tell her she was dying, we just did everything we could for her in those last months. She had a couple of spells in hospital and the doctor was right. She died in three months time, almost to the day. It was a terrible thing, but I just had to accept it. Charlie and the rest of my family were marvellous to me and although I was on my own for the next 10 years I never spent a Christmas alone."

More than ever, hard work and greyhound racing — always inseparable in Curtis's mind — ruled his life. He lived for his dogs and became more determined than ever to train top-class greyhounds. But the breakthrough to open race success was slow in coming.

The tide turned with Bad Trick (Tuturama–Nifty Lady). One of

Above: Boreen Berry won the Cobb Marathon at Catford in 1965. Charlie Curtis is pictured right.

Below: The breakthrough. Curtis's first big race win came when Bad Trick won the Puppy Derby in 1964.

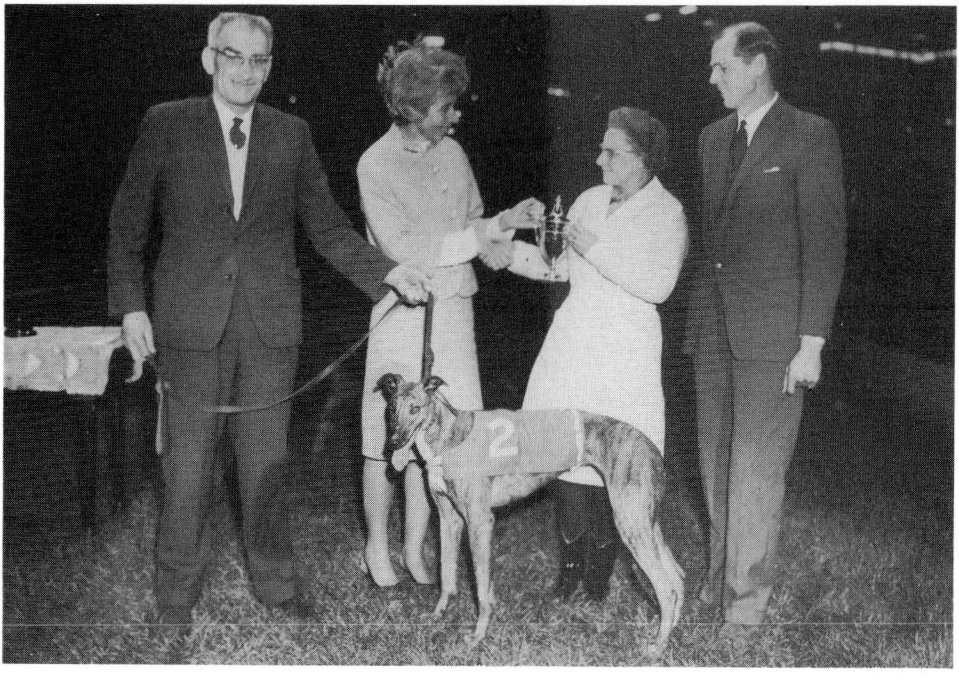

Curtis's owners, Morry Tucker, had been breeding greyhounds but had never had much luck with them. Curtis suggested that he got a couple of puppies over from Ireland and then try to rear them. "I picked them up from Portsmouth Station," said Curtis. "They were only 12 weeks old. Morry took them home and he did a good job rearing and schooling them. They were called Bar Ten and Bad Trick."

He was quick to realise that Bad Trick was a bit special. He started her off in open races but soon after her career she got knocked up at Portsmouth and jarred her wrist. Thinking she had recovered from the injury, Curtis took her to Wimbledon. But she checked on the bends, obviously still feeling the wrist. Con Stevens, racing manager at Wimbledon and one of the strictest in the game, was distinctly unimpressed. He told Curtis to take the bitch away and not return until she had produced some better form.

Undeterred, the young trainer still had total belief in the bitch and soon proved his point when she reached the final of the Trafalgar Cup. But the real vindication came when Curtis took Bad Trick back to Wimbledon and she won the 1964 Puppy Derby. The brindled bitch recorded 28.46 for the 500 yards and finished three-quarters of a length in front. She went straight on to contest the Junior Stakes at West Ham and got the verdict by a head, clocking 30.86 for the 550 yards course. Then it was back to Wimbledon for the Puppy Oaks and this time Bad Trick made it all look easy winning her heat by 11 lengths and then storming to a nine length victory in the final in 28.11. She completed a magnificent run by winning the Stayers Cup at Stamford Bridge clocking 39.79 for the 700 yards. "I must admit, I felt doubly good after what Con Stevens had said about the bitch," said Curtis. "In fact, Bad Trick turned out to be the best greyhound I trained during 29 years at Portsmouth. She had tremendous middle and final pace and was easily the best pup of that year.

"She started favourite for the TV Trophy and after being knocked out of that she won her heat for the Double Diamond at Wembley. She was odds-on for the final and she broke her hock. Even so, she still came back to win three open races on the trot."

The Curtis brothers also used to race their own greyhounds. Curtis remembers one in particular called Sliced Character. "We were going to sell her for £75 and she was all set to join Phil Rees at Wimbledon," he said. "But in the end he turned her down. He said she wouldn't grade at Wimbledon. That was fair comment because we were running over 470 yards and Wimbledon was over 500 yards. We decided to try her over the distance and discovered she was a good marathon bitch. Three months later we took her to Wimbledon and she won the Stayers Plaque. The prize money was £125 so we didn't feel too badly about losing out on the £75 we would have sold her for. Then the next year she went back to Wimbledon and won the race again. In fact, by the end of her racing career she had won £1,800 in prize money and that was enough to buy houses for both me and Charlie."

Right from the beginning, Curtis's chief love was training stayers and this has been reflected throughout his career. While he was at Portsmouth he won the Cobb Bowl at Catford twice, both times with dogs owned by Les Smith. Boreen Berry (Steady The Man–July Hawk) started at 20–1 in his heat for the 1965 competition but he was only beaten by a head. In the final he strode to a five length win, clocking 50.28 for the 810 yards.

The following year it was Breshen Crackers (Odd Venture–Pats Regret) who took the honours. The August 1964 whelp was beaten 13 lengths in his heat but in the final he got the verdict by a head at the rewarding odds of 16–1. His winning time was 51.71. Peculiar Way (Mad Era–Lottera Queen) came close to giving Curtis his first classic winner when the July 1964 whelp competed in the 1966 St Leger. He was runner-up in his first round heat, beaten a short head, but he came through in the second round to win by 2¼ lengths, clocking 40.08 for Wembley's 700 yards. In the semis he qualified in third place and started at 12–1 for the decider. In a tightly contested race, the favourite Summer Guest won in 40.03 and Peculiar Way was the runner-up — just 1¼ lengths adrift. The black dog continued in cracking form for Curtis when he won the Seymour Stakes at Portsmouth and then the Test at Walthamstow. In both these competitions Breshen Crackers also reached the final and finished third on each occasion.

"When you get a run of luck like that everyone starts scratching their heads and wondering what you are doing differently," said Curtis. "The truth of the matter is that you are getting the right class of greyhound. When I started training, I was nobody — I could only make a name by what I did. When you start winning, you attract better owners who can afford a better class of greyhound. It's all a matter of getting that first breakthrough."

Gordon Poole was one of his first big time owners. The property man has always taken his hobby seriously and money is no object when it comes to buying a good dog. "I remember him asking me if I knew of any good dogs for sale," said Curtis. "I said I had heard of one but it was a bit expensive. It was £215 which would be about £2,000 today. Gordon bought the dog and Crags Hope went on to win ten races on the trot." Curtis helped to make the Crags prefix famous in those early days at Portsmouth and he has trained greyhounds for Gordon Poole ever since. Gordon is unstinting in his praise for the trainer.

"I have known George since he was a kennel lad at Portsmouth and what I admire most about him is his complete integrity," he said. "There has never been a trainer who has given so much to the sport. I own race horses in England and America and the reason I prefer greyhound racing is entirely due to George.

"He has unending consideration for his dogs — 24 hours a day, seven days a week, the dogs are never out of his mind. And that's not just the top open racers — he cares about all his dogs. They are all there to win races. They are happy with him. If they are happy they look well, they feel well and they run well and with determination. You only have to watch George with his dogs to see how they respond to him. Recently I was in the restaurant at Brighton and someone wanted George to autograph his race card after one of his dogs had won. 'Don't ask me to write congratulations,' said George. 'I can't spell it!' This is the man who left school when he was 12 years old and has achieved everything through his own merit."

Gordon Poole is still deeply involved in the sport and has become increasingly interested in the breeding side. His bitch Evening Moon, who is litter sister to Ballyregan Bob, has a litter of pups by Yankee Express and he has high hopes for their future.

The sixties also turned out to be a lucky time in Curtis's private life. He met Lily on a blind date and three months later they were married. It was the second marriage for both of them. Lily had been struggling to bring up two children on her own — and Curtis had lived through ten lonely years following the death of Phylis. It was a match of mutual need — and has proved the most successful partnership of Curtis's career. Lily had never been greyhound racing before she met Curtis, although her mother used to do a bit of tic-tac. But she soon became swept up in Curtis's ruling passion and has shared his successes and disappointments whole-heartedly.

"I worked in the local cake shop when I first met George," said Lily. "When he went off open racing he used to pull up by the shop and I would run out and give him a bag of cakes. We got on well from the start and there was no reason to have a long engagement. We got married in the June and we had a lovely wedding with all George's owners and friends."

The only obstacle to their relationship was Lily's pet spaniel Ricky — who has earned his place in history as the only dog to bite George Curtis. Ricky had been given to Lily by her brother and he didn't take to his new master at all. He used to sit between them on the sofa, doing his best to protect Lily from George's advances!

"Everything was going well for me in those last few years at Portsmouth — and I look back on it as a very happy time in my life," said Curtis. As a direct consequence of his new-found success, Curtis was offered a job as full-time track trainer at Brighton. Strangely enough, he was reluctant to make the move. Portsmouth was his home and he had built up a good team of dogs and owners. He had recently married and was having improvements done on his house. "But I knew I had to move on," he said. "And I knew that if I went, it would give Charlie the chance to take over my job at Portsmouth. It seemed wrong to hold him back and so finally I allowed myself to be persuaded."

It was a decision he was never to regret.

CHAPTER TWO

The First Division

GEORGE Curtis felt at home from the first moment he arrived at Brighton and typically, 20 years on, he still can't get over his good luck at landing a job there. "I just couldn't believe the difference when I came from Portsmouth," he said. "At Target Road you had to work so hard just to survive. But at Brighton it is all made so easy for you. I loved Portsmouth. They gave me my start in greyhound racing and I will never forget what they did for me. But going to Brighton was like moving up to the First Division. The amenities are superb at the kennels. At Portsmouth they were very basic. There was a roof over the top but there was no front and if it snowed or rained it just blew in. Sometimes you had to literally break the ice when you arrived in the morning. But at Brighton there is central heating in the kennels, there are big paddocks and a proper gallop. You are given the best of everything — food, bedding, veterinary advice — you can't help but train top-class greyhounds."

Curtis arrived with a string of his best dogs from Portsmouth. They included Peculiar Way, runner-up in the 1966 St Leger, Breshen Crackers, winner of the 1966 Cobb Marathon and Ever Work, finalist in the 1967 Orient Cup at Clapton. And they got the new trainer off to a flying start. He began at Brighton in April 1967 and the first major competition at his new base was the Regency in May. Curtis showed he was more then worthy of his promotion when he ended up with three runners in the final.

Ever Work, a black bitch by Jungle Worker out of New Forever, stormed home to win her heat by 6¼ lengths clocking 40.70 for the 725 yards and then went on to win the final in 40.95, beating Small Ration, also trained by Curtis, by 3½ lengths. His third runner Breshen Crackers finished fifth.

That night, minutes after he arrived back at the kennels the telephone went. It was his brother Charlie desperate to know how he had got on. "He was over the moon when he heard I had got the first and second," said Curtis. "Even though we weren't working together we still shared each other's successes and disappointments. He was always the first person I wanted to talk to after a big race."

Owners Les Smith and Gordon Poole followed Curtis to Brighton and he remains deeply grateful for their loyalty. "I will always be grateful to the owners who moved over to Brighton with me," said Curtis. "It meant that I started with a dozen top-class dogs and they made all the difference. Gunner Smith was training alongside me and he would always help me out if I was stuck. I've learnt so much from him over the years. To me, he is the best living trainer in the game and he has the best knowledge of greyhounds of anyone I've met."

Curtis has always maintained that a trainer is only as good as the dogs in his kennel and at Brighton it was easy to attract new owners who had enough money to buy the best dogs. "When you have a track like Brighton with a beautiful running surface and first-class amenities for the public the owners come to you," he said. "If you have good dogs you get some success and so more owners with good dogs come to you."

He was also helped by breeder Marie Barwick who sent a number of top-class puppies to him.

Peter Shotton, general manager at Brighton, was racing manager at the Nevil Road track when Curtis first arrived. He left for a spell as general manager at Wembley and then came back as general manager.

He soon came to respect the young trainer and has followed his career with interest ever since.

"George has an open and enquiring mind," he said. "Even after all his success he still says he is learning his craft. His enthusiasm is undiminished and he pays great attention to detail in everything he does."

All racing managers know that it is no easy matter to get on with owners all the time. But Curtis, he says, had a gift for doing just that.

"He has an easy manner whether he is talking to artisans or the aristocracy," he said. "It is a blend of patience, natural diplomacy, and downright charming good manners. In all the time I have known him, I have only once heard someone say anything ill of him. The man who did so was a not only an acknowledged pain in the neck — he was, in fact, very lucky that it was George Curtis he maligned. For George has a capacity very rarely seen in successful people — he tolerates fools."

Curtis has never been afraid of hard work and as the kennel strength grew, there never seemed as if there were enough hours in the day. "Sometimes you can feel like you are dropping on your feet but there are still dogs that need letting out," said Curtis. "You can't pack up until all the work is finished. And even then Curtis would often come back to the kennels in the evenings to check on a dog that was ill — or if it was a nice night just to let the dogs out for a run. "I would bring the family down and kids always enjoyed it," said Curtis. "Lily took out a licence so she could help me in the kennels and she always comes open racing with me. It is a great help when we come back late at night and she can let the dogs out and give them their feeds. My step-children Roger and Yvonne always used to help out as well. The only thing I draw the line at is letting Lily parade the dogs for me. She's far too valuable. If anyone's going to get knocked up in the air — it might as well be me." But despite the pressure of time, Curtis has always been prepared to travel with his dogs to find the right tracks and the right competitions.

"I have always had my quota of graders at Brighton," he said. "They are the bread and butter living for any trainer and I have always cared about them just as much as the stars in the kennel. But over the years owners have come to me because they know I am prepared to put myself out. Travelling to open races can be an exhausting business when you have a big kennel to run, but its always been something I've enjoyed." Success was quick to come and in 1969 Curtis had his first Derby finalist with Hard Held. The fawn dog finished third and second in the opening rounds and won his semi-final by a short head clocking 29.26 over the White City course. "I didn't think I had much chance in the final and I wasn't disappointed when the dog finished fifth. It was a big enough thrill to reach the final," he said. That year honours went to the Irish trained Sand Star who won in 28.76.

It looked like being a golden summer for Curtis when Hard Held went on to create a new world record when he clocked 29.77 for Brighton's 550 yard course. But just as everything was going so well, personal tragedy struck Curtis a second time. Charlie Curtis took one of his dogs, Short Teddy, to compete in an open race at Crayford. He travelled with his lifelong friend Eric Naughton, and when they were within 20 miles of home the van skidded and Charlie was killed. "Charlie used to work so hard," said Curtis. "He was up at the crack of dawn and he said his eyes were playing him up. He asked Eric to drive and he went in the back with the dog.

"It was August and it had been very dry. Suddenly there was a downpour and it made the road greasy. The van skidded and hit a lamp standard and Charlie and the dog were both killed. He was only 44 years old and I had always thought he was so much stronger than me. It was a terrible blow and I have never got over it. We were so close, I thought the world of him. I think in the long run it made me more determined to succeed. We were both so keen and ambitious and we were in it together. I suppose, in a way, I wanted to make up for Charlie never having the chance to show how good he was. If he had lived, I have no doubt he would have been one of the top trainers."

The following year Curtis had his second tilt at the English Derby with Sirius, which was owned by Cliff Kevern. "Cliff paid £2,000 for the dog which was big money in those days," said Curtis. "He was a good dog and we got as far as the final and again finished in fifth place." That year the classic was won by British bred John Silver who clocked 29.01. "I thought I had a reasonably good chance with Sirius," said Curtis. "But there was no seeding and he was put in trap five. When I heard the draw I knew he couldn't win from there. He came out and collided with the dog in trap one. But there was compensation when Sirius, a June 1967 whelp by Shanes Legacy out of Jersey Queen, went on to win the Gold Collar Consolation at Catford and the Anglo-Irish International at Dundalk.

By now Curtis was establishing himself as a trainer of stayers and that side of the sport has remained his great passion. "I love to see them coming from behind," he said. "I have always tried to find puppies who will mature into stayers. I find there is more of a challenge in training for a long distance race than with the sprinters when it's a matter of out of the boxes and gone."

In February 1972 Curtis pulled off a one-two in the Ladbroke Marathon Championship which was televised live from Harringay. The race was over 900 yards and Real Darkie, a finalist in the Cobb Marathon Bowl two months previously, came to his best to win in 52.80. He beat the 16–1 shot Iver Flash by 2½ lengths. Iver Flash, a white and black dog by Winning Hope — Lions Rose was another of the Cliff Kevern string. He went on the show his run was no fluke when he went unbeaten through the Key at Wimbledon in June of that year. He won his heat by 6½ lengths clocking 54.59 for the 940 yards and then stormed to victory by 7 lengths in the final in 54.67.

Curtis has special affection for Leading Pride, the great staying bitch by Spectre out of Conigar Goddess who was owned by Ramsgate trainer George Ripley and his brother Absalom. She was undoubtedly the best bitch he trained during those early years at Brighton and established the trainer as a force to be reckoned with on the open race circuit. Her first major victory was in the 1973 BBC TV Trophy which was staged over Wimbledon's 880 yard course. She was strongly fancied as she came to the competition straight after setting a new track record at Brighton. She had been competing in an 880 yard open race and in an exciting finish she got the verdict by a neck, clocking 49.83. The first heat of the TV Trophy was run at Brighton and Leading Pride showed the same red hot form to win by 2½ lengths taking a further 21 spots off her own record. In the final at Wimbledon she justified her favouritism beating Yellow Escort by one length in a winning time of 51.16.

It looked as though Curtis's first classic victory was on the cards when the black bitch enjoyed two impressive wins in the opening rounds of the St Leger. But she finished fourth in the semi-final. Again, she came frustratingly close in the Grand Prix the following year. She ran unbeaten to the final and then finished fourth in the decider. Although she went on to win the 1974 Key at Wimbledon with a fine 54.49 run, Curtis felt that he was still failing to get the best from his dogs in the big competitions.

"The graders were doing well and we had our successes in open races — but we couldn't seem to pull off a major win," he said. "I took advice from everyone and tried all sorts of different diets and exercise routines to get the dogs keyed up, but we still missed out." The turning point came a year later when Abbey Glade won the Gold Collar at Catford. The brindled dog by Kilbeg Kuda-Abbey Groves had won the Sussex Cup at Brighton before she started her tilt at the classic. She won her opening two rounds and then just qualified in third place for the final. But then she made no mistake and stormed to victory in the decider beating Dancing Dolores by 7¼ lengths in 34.97 for the 555m.

Curtis was not even there to celebrate — he was away on holiday. And that proved to be the secret of his new-found success. "My trouble was that I had been worrying too much about the dogs," he said. "When I left everyone to it, with no major changes in kennel routine, it all went as smooth as silk." Curtis had now arrived. He had a flourishing strength of graders, open race contenders and a growing band of owners. "When you have a big kennel you have to have good staff," said Curtis. "You soon learn that you can't do everything yourself. You must be able to delegate — although ultimately you have the responsibility." He also learnt that owners must know who is in charge.

"I have been very lucky with my owners," said Curtis. "Many of them have become friends over the years. But you always get the odd one who thinks he knows better than you. He will come up to you on a race night and argue if the dog's weight is up or down by a few spots. I always say: 'See how the dog runs and then criticise.' There are others who think they can train the dog better than you. They come up with all sorts of suggestions and tell you what you should be doing. I just nod my head and carry on the same as before."

But behind his easy-going manner, Curtis has rigid principles and he makes no compromises when an owner wants to mess around with his dog. "You must get wins for your owners," he said. "That is part of the game. If they get wins it encourages them to buy more dogs, which is good news for you. But I have never messed around with a dog, it is not my way. I have always been honest and straight with owners. I tell them: 'No-one will work harder or try harder than me. But if that's not good enough, go somewhere else.'

"When I first started out, a trainer said to me: 'Feed the dogs the best you can and try your best — if the owner still isn't satisfied you're better off without him.' That is good advice. You can't please everyone and, as long as you know you have done all you can, that has to be enough. I always try to make an owner see sense — but equally you have to know when it's time to give up. The worst ones are those who have no feelings about the dog as an animal. All they want is a gamble. They'll say: 'Can't you give it this or that, or a couple of pounds of sausage meat.' But I say: 'I'll do it my way or not at all.' The other type of owner to be wary of is the one who comes in and thinks he can make a fortune overnight. You know he is certain to be disappointed."

Curtis has never trained a dog to race on the independent circuit and his record for straight dealing is legendary in the sport. "Don't think I'm little Lord Fauntleroy. I understand the problems of having a small kennel and needing to make it pay," he said. "You are under terrible pressure. I have been a track trainer all my life so I haven't had those sort of worries. I've been able to do things my way and come out on top. Of course, I have owners who like a decent gamble. Peter Carpenter had thousands on Sandy Lane, but I made sure I didn't know about it. She always ran to win and fortunately she was such a good bitch, Peter was rarely wasting his money."

Although Curtis is totally uncompromising in the way he runs his dogs, he tries not to fall out with his owners. "If the Duke of Edinburgh asked me to fiddle, I wouldn't," he said. "I would tell him to his face to take his dogs away. But equally I would say: 'My doors are always open. No hard feelings. If you go away and get fed up you can always come back.' " Curtis is also very firm in his views on when to retire a greyhound. In a career that spans close to half a century he cannot remember having a healthy dog destroyed. "At Brighton we all do a lot of fund-raising for retired greyhounds and they have a very good home-finding scheme," he said. "A lot of the kennel staff keep a retired dog at home and so do a lot of the trainers."

Ben, who raced as Ballymena Moon, enjoys a life of luxury in the Curtis household. In his track days he was a successful hurdler, reaching the final of the 1980 Springbok and Grand National. "I usually give owners the nod when it's time to retire their dogs," said Curtis. "I think when a greyhound reaches three-and-a-half-years-old, he has come to the end. A bitch may carry on a bit longer.

"Most owners know when it is time to give up. Sometimes people with graded dogs want them to keep running, but most don't like to see them fall in standard. I hate to see a good dog end up being beaten in the first race. I always advise owners to let a dog finish on top. When I saw Glin Bridge beaten by Westmead Champ in the 1976 Regency, I thought it was time for him to go. When you start getting the young dogs coming through and your dog is going to struggle to beat them, you should call it a day."

Glin Bridge (Spectre–Shore Susie) goes down in greyhound racing history as one of the finest six-bend dogs. And his reputation lived on as he became Britain's most successful stud dog. Curtis trained him when he first arrived from Ireland with a track record-breaking run of 33.50 over Enniscorthy's 600 yards on his card. "He was the cleverest dog I ever trained," he said. "He could run from any box, which is a tremendous asset. The first time he ran at Brighton he was in trap one and the conditions were terrible. The track was running about two seconds slow on the inside. Glin Bridge came out and made for the outside. As he came up the back straight he went dead wide and won by half a length. Peter Shotton, who was racing manager, rang me up later and said he had never seen a better performance from a pup first time out.

"Then I took him away open racing and had him seeded as a wide runner. Bill Mahon the bookmaker, who used to do the prices on the Derby, saw him run at Wembley and said: 'That dog of yours wants the inside. He hugged the rails all the way round.' I told him that Glin Bridge chose his own way. And a couple of races later he said: 'You're right. That dog's a computer. I've never seen another greyhound like it!' All through his career, he ran like that. If there were two or three dogs in front of him and he saw a gap he would make for it, whether it was on the inside or the outside.

"A dog is either born with trackcraft or he isn't. You can't teach him it. Glin Bridge was exceptional. He used to train himself. You'd let him out in the paddock in the morning and he would run round and round in track-shaped circuits." The brindle and white dog was quick to make his mark on the open scene and was soon competing at the highest level. His early victories included the 1975 Spring Cup at Wimbledon and in a spectacular open race at Wembley he beat Westpark Mustard coming from behind to win by 2¼ lengths in 40.68 for the 655m. He went on to run unbeaten through the 1975 Regency at Brighton and snatched final honours from Streaky Sheila by three-quarters of a length in 40.19.

"Charlie Coyle trained Streaky Sheila and he thought we were a bit lucky to win," said Curtis. "The connections organised a match race over the same course and Glin Bridge led from traps to line." Bridge was now becoming the dog to beat as he notched up a growing sequence of wins. Match races were organised and the November 1972 whelp kept romping to victory. He set a new track record of 39.77 for Walthamstow's 640m in a match against Dancing Dolores and then won heat and final of the Gold Cup at Wembley. He collected another track record over White City's 730m when he took on Lizzies Girl in a match race and won by 3½ lengths in 44.03.

The St Leger, the ultimate prize for a trainer of stayers, was looming and Curtis felt he had one of the best dogs in the competition. But Glin Bridge proved disappointing and made his exit in the second round. He was put away for a couple of months and in his last season he came back to win the 1976 Ladbroke Golden Jacket over Harringay's 660m. He ran from trap one in the final and won in 40.59.

"He was a wonderful dog and clocked up 15 wins on the trot in the highest company," said Curtis. "I think he could have gone on longer but he was such an excitable dog. He was on the go all the time, jumping up and down in his kennel, chasing round the paddock. He wore himself out. He was never as good in his second season and when Westmead Champ beat him in the Regency final we retired him. He went to stud and the first bitch he mated produced a crop of open racers and he was made. That is the sort of retirement you hope for when a dog has given so much on the track."

Bonzo, a big brindled dog by Silver Record–Clane Flint, was not one of Curtis's most brilliant stayers. But in a packed two years of racing he reached the final of numerous big competitions which certainly enhanced the trainer's reputation. He was in the decider of the 1975 and 1976 Cesarewitch, the 1976 Grand Prix and the 1977 Longcross Cup, Golden Jacket and BBC TV Trophy. At the end of his career his hard work on the track was rewarded with a win in the 1977 Regency Final, which he took in 40.03.

Stud dog Spectre, the outstanding sire of stayers, completed a hat-trick of top-class prize winners for Curtis when Langford Dacoit followed in the footsteps of Leading Pride and Glin Bridge. This May 1975 whelp out of Corboy Honey came close to giving Curtis his third classic victory when he reached the final of the 1977 Cesarewitch. The Brighton record-holder who set a new time of 43.58 for the 725m course, was eventually robbed of glory by his great rival Montreen who beat him on the line by a short head. It was again Montreen who took honours when Langford Dacoit reached the final of the Stow Marathon. But he also enjoyed his share of wins with credits in the 1978 Chingford Marathon over Walthamstow's 820m and the Key at Wimbledon. In this competition he broke the track record in the heats with a 53.75 run and then won the final by 6½ lengths in 54.25. He went on to break track records at Romford, recording 59.56 for the 925m, and Brighton where he clocked

58.46 for the 955m before winning the Harringay Marathon, by ¾ of a length in 52.30 for the 830m.

The Curtis kennel was now on the up and up and there was no shortage of owners wanting to place their dogs with the Brighton trainer. But in this matter, as in all others, Curtis has always been scrupulously fair. "The biggest worry is when someone comes to you and asks you to buy a dog for them," he said. "The agent I use, Mick Sylver, has done well for me over the years. But the risk is that if the dog doesn't live up to expectations you feel responsible. It's a different side of the business and there's certainly money to be made. But I've always preferred not to have the worry.

"Most people come to me with a dog and ask me to watch it trial. I think in this situation you must be totally honest. I am looking for a dog who is no more than 20 to 30 spots off grading time. More often than not, we are restricted for room in the kennel and if we take in a dog that is half a second adrift, he may be six weeks before he grades. All that time the owner is paying out the full amount for training fees. I always advise the owner to take the dog away and give it couple more trials around a schooling track until it finds that bit of extra time. There is no point paying bills for a dog that can't grade. The game is hard enough without giving yourself more heartache. But I always watch a dog trial before I make a decision. Equally, I don't take any notice of tales of fantastic times a dog has done. I want to see for myself. If I don't think a dog has it in him, I say so. But I always say: 'Come back if he gets closer to grading time.' "

Curtis admits his first love is open racing, but he doesn't only go for dogs who are potential open racers. "We have a range of abilities going right through the grades to open class," he said. "We take slow dogs that start in the bottom half of the card — and hopefully you can get some improvement from them. I've also had dogs who struggle to win in A5 at Brighton but when you take them away they become a different dog. That is the advantage of being prepared to travel. You can produce results that dogs would never have been capable of at their home track."

Open racing is a very expensive business and there is no way a trainer can bear the cost of transporting greyhounds nationwide when prize money is so modest. In the Curtis kennel they are usually able to share the cost between owners by making up the numbers with dogs competing in supporting open races or just going for the experience of running in a big competition. "You need owners who are prepared to put their hands in their pockets and pay the extra for the trainer taking a dog away," said Curtis. "We always try to share the cost. It makes good economic sense. And there has been more than one occasion when your main hope is knocked out in the first round and the dog you have taken along for the ride goes on to win the competition."

He believes the crux of the problem lies with the prize money that is on offer for open race competitions. "I could never afford to travel from Brighton to, say, Belle Vue for the amount of prize money they offer," said Curtis. "It has to come down to the owners paying out, and I don't see why they should. After all, the stadium is benefiting from staging the competition and having the best dogs racing there. They make their money on the tote and on the gate, but they don't even pay enough prize money to cover expenses."

Curtis feels this lack of funds particularly keenly for his kennel staff. "You are asking the youngsters to work terribly long hours," he said. "They start at the kennels at 7 am and if we are racing they don't finish until 11 pm. If we are open racing it's much later than that. I have always paid my staff the best wage I could, but it is still far too low. It's okay if you are living at home, but you could never support a family on that money.

"The prize money goes to the owner — and he is under no obligation to give anything to the kennel. If they give £100 after winning a big race they think they are making a handsome gesture, but when you are sharing it between a staff of six or seven it's nothing. The best owners are the ones who are aware of the situation and make a special point of looking after the staff if they are travelling away with a dog. I have a lot of good owners and most will give the kennel a ten per cent share of the prize money. But they don't have to — and you can't rely on it."

Curtis has always seen his staff as an essential part of his success. "They are the ones you should look after," he said. "Without them, you are totally lost. And if you are talking about trying to keep the game straight, they are the last people you should short-change. If someone is short of money, they are obviously going to be that much more vulnerable to any wrong-doing."

As a former kennel lad who worked his way up through the ranks, it saddens Curtis that there is no real future open to kennel staff today. "When I was young I could set my sights on becoming a trainer," he said. "But now track kennels have more or less died out, this is no longer a possibility for most youngsters. At Brighton we are hanging on by the skin of our teeth. We are the last place where the stadium runs the kennels. Now trainers must have their own set-up, and you're talking about £200,000 for a decent place. It is the people who have money behind them who don't need to make the game pay that are our trainers of the future. There is no opening for a kennel lad living on basic wages who is trying to better himself.

"I always say to my staff: 'Come and work here and enjoy yourself. The moment you're not having fun, leave and find something else. There's no point in hanging on, hoping things will improve.' " In the past, some kennel staff have become trainers. Doreen Walsh was

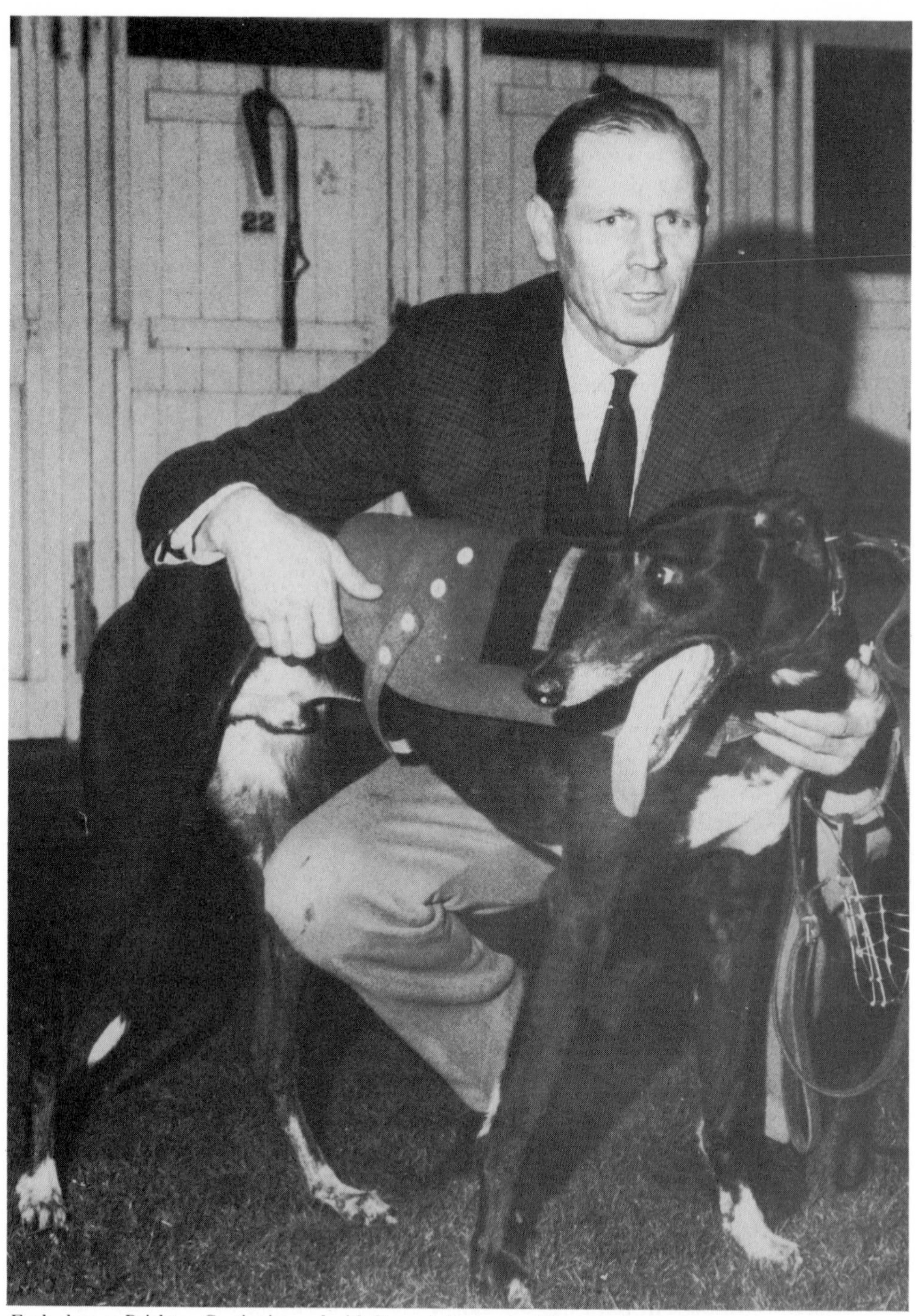

Early days at Brighton. Curtis pictured with George's Sam, a useful open racer.

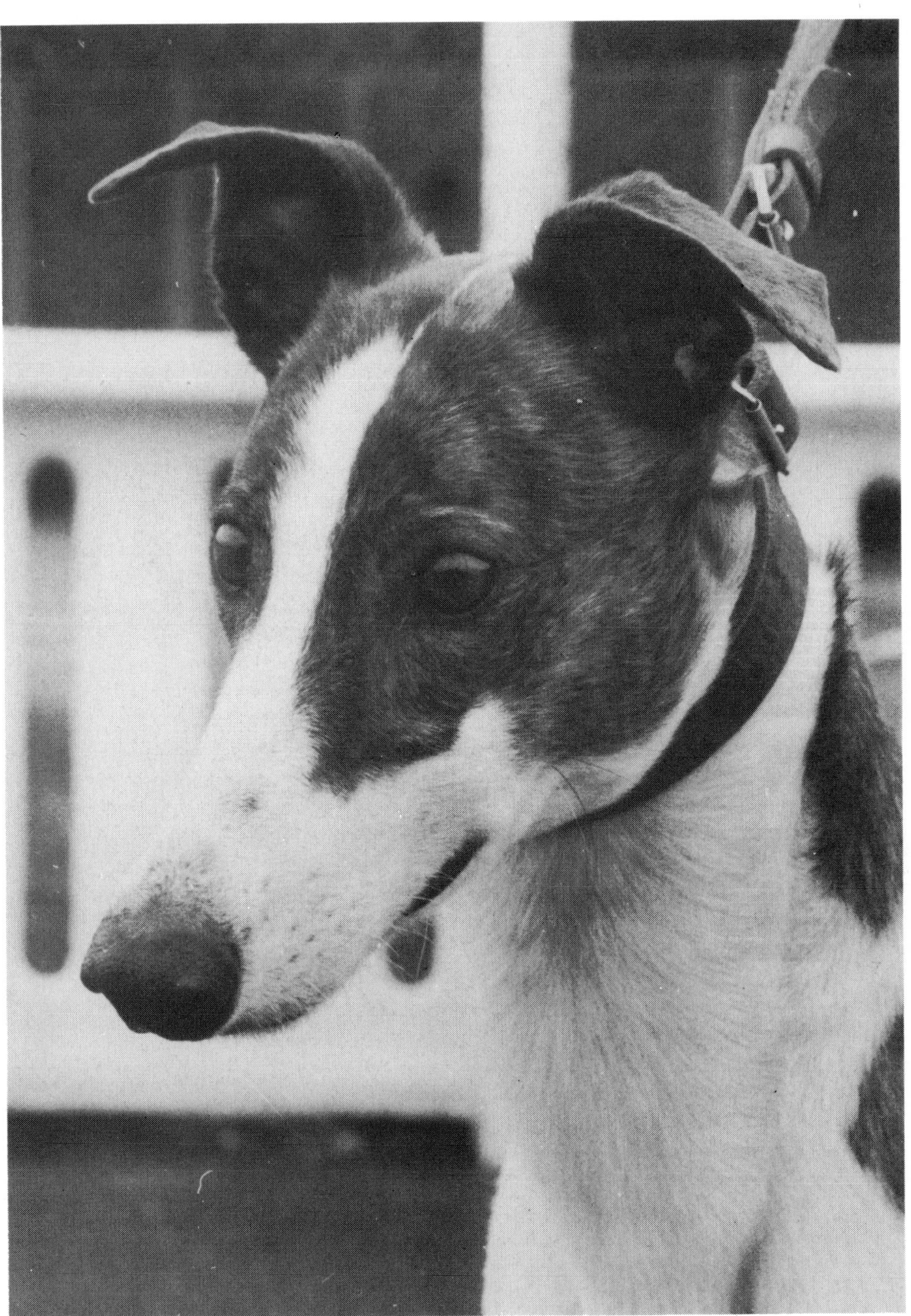

Glin Bridge. One of the cleverest dogs that Curtis trained. He won the 1976 Ladbroke Golden Jacket and notched up 15 victories in a row.

Wired To Moon gave Curtis his second classic victory when he won the 1977 Scurry Gold Cup. (A. W. Stubbs)

Above: Bonzo. Winner of the 1977 Regency at Brighton.

Below: Abbey Glade. Winner of the 1975 Gold Collar at Catford.

Curtis's head girl for eight years before getting her own kennel at Brighton. But now it is Curtis's owners who are making the move to become trainers. Bob Young, Peter Carpenter, John Copplestone, George Ripley, and Bill Tozer all used to have dogs with him.

"I have always given them all the advice I could when they were starting out," said Curtis. "I wish them all the luck. But it saddens me that the old days of track trainers with big kennels have gone." In fact it was Portsmouth trainer Bill Tozer who gave Curtis his second classic winner, in his days as an owner. "Bill brought Wired To Moon over from Ireland and he looked useful going round Brighton," he said.

The black dog by Monalee Champion out of April Atomic specialised over four bends and this gave Curtis a shot at the big money competitions. The 1977 Scurry Gold Cup at Slough was the first major target and in one of the best competitions for many years, the October 1974 whelp showed he was more than equal to the task. Carhumore Speech proved to be his main rival and there was little to choose between the two as the classic progressed. Wired To Moon beat him by 2¼ lengths in the first round, recording 26.93 for the old 434m trip. But in the second round Carhumore Speech got his revenge with a ¾ length win against him, clocking 26.70.

The two were separated in the semi-finals. Wired To Moon produced his best time of the competition with a 26.47 win but Carhumore Speech showed he was in blistering form when he also took his semi-final in a new track record of 26.37. This run was enough to make him favourite for the decider and Wired To Moon started at a generous 4–1. Xmas Holiday, winner of the classic the previous year, missed his break and White City runner Fiano briefly took up the lead. But by the second bend Wired To Moon took command and he was well in front going up the back straight. He won in 26.63 beating Carhumore Speech by 1¼ lengths. Xmas Holiday was in third place half a length adrift. Fiano finished last and sadly the Adam Jackson trained dog was killed in a road accident on his way back to the Northaw kennels that night.

Wired To Moon took over where Glin Bridge had left off for Curtis and in the next 12 months he was contesting all the major competitions. He missed out in the 1977 William Hill Lead at Hackney by just neck when Gaily Noble got the verdict, but a month later he made up for it by winning the William Hill Sixer final clocking 29.51 for Hackney's 484m. He looked all set for victory in the 1978 Pall Mall after running unbeaten to the final. He started as evens favourite but he was so badly baulked at the first bend, he lost the race and trailed home by 17 lengths.

"He was done so badly at the first bend that he went lame," said Curtis. "It was disappointing, but we had our share of wins from him. He was a useful dog and soon afterwards he retired to stud."

It was at the end of the Glin Bridge-Wired To Moon era that racing manager Jim Layton arrived at Brighton. This was the start of a useful working relationship, based on mutual respect. "Jim Layton is the man to go to if you want to know anything about breeding," said Curtis. "He has really promoted that side of the sport in the South of England and as a result we have a lot of good puppies coming through at Brighton."

Layton has always looked on Curtis as a true ambassador for the sport and has particularly admired the way he gets on with his owners. "I have never known him to say a bad word about anyone," said Layton. "He treats everyone with the same cheerfulness and honesty. He is not afraid to tell owners the truth about their dogs — and that is a vital ingredient for success. When it comes to the dogs his care is unstinting. He would sooner go without himself than see his dogs go short."

Life at the kennels had never been busier, but Curtis was struggling to keep pace as he was suffering increasingly from arthritis in his hip. "It got so bad I was like a cripple," he said. "I couldn't get in and out of my car, let alone exercise greyhounds." He was sent to hospital and given an artificial hip in an operation that transformed his life. "I was a couple of weeks in hospital and I was meant to take it easy for a month," said Curtis. "But I couldn't wait to get back to the kennels. We had a rotating washing line in the garden and I used to walk round and round hanging on to it, trying to get myself fit." In a couple of weeks, he was back at the kennels, although it took some time before he could walk easily. "If I hadn't had the operation I would missed out on the next nine years which were the best of my career. I'm so grateful to the surgeon, if it hadn't been for him I would never have trained the likes of Yankee Express and Ballyregan Bob."

Maplehurst Star (Tullig Rambler–Sparks Star), who went on to sire Curtis's great staying bitch Sandy Lane, proved a useful addition to the strength when he joined Curtis in 1979. He is, in fact, litter brother to hurdler Ballymena Moon, who Curtis now keeps at home as a pet. In a track career which lasted little over 12 months Maplehurst Star won the Take Your Place Tyrean Trophy at Brighton, the Inaugual final at Wembley and after finishing runner-up in the Sussex Cup at Brighton in 1979 he went on to win the competition the following year.

Curtis was well represented in the stayers' events in 1981 with Corboy Champion by Itsachampion out of Corboy Honey — the same bitch that whelped Langford Dacoit. The September 1978 whelp won the Mecca Bookmakers Stayers Stakes over 740m at Hackney, reached the final of the BBC TV Trophy and won the Cesarewitch Consolation at Belle Vue.

But it was when Upland Tiger arrived at the Brighton kennels that Curtis felt he had at last got his hands on a classic four-bend greyhound. The January 1979 whelp by Free Speech out of Bresheen was bought by

John Houlihan and arrived from Ireland with a few races on his card including a 30.60 win at Tralee. He soon proved that he was an exceptional dog going straight into Brighton's A1 grade. On his racing debut he clocked a lightning 29.09 for the 500m winning easily by 3½ lengths. The track record at that time was only 10 spots faster. He was immediately promoted to the open race circuit and Wimbledon soon became his favourite track. He took part in the 47th International and put in a brilliant run to go from sixth position at the first bend to win by three-quarters of a length from Lancia Q, breaking the 460m track record. A week later he again set a new time for the course when he beat Knockeen Warrior in 27.48 in the *Sporting Life* Juvenile Championship.

"He was the greatest puppy I have ever trained," said Curtis. "He was such a strong runner he would knock dogs out of the way. He would literally go through them as if they weren't there. His only trouble was that he was so excitable. He would run his race before he ever got on the track." After a winter's rest Upland Tiger came back in great style winning the Pedigree Petfoods Championship at White City and devastating a top-class field at Wimbledon when he won the Harris Carpet Stakes by 8¾ lengths from Corrakelly Air leaving future stud dogs Dans Arrow and Loch Lomond for dead.

The 1981 Laurels seemed tailor-made for Upland Tiger for there was no dog in the country that ran the Plough Lane track better. He had an easy passage to the final, winning his first round heat and his semi. When he was drawn in trap one inside five wide runners for the decider, the race seemed a foregone conclusion. But Upland Tiger missed his break and despite a brave effort he finished a short head behind Echo Spark. Curtis remembers this race as the biggest disappointment of his career and to this day he blames himself for letting down owner John Houlihan.

John Houlihan remembers the night well. "I was standing next to George when we were waiting fo the result of the photo-finish," he said. "When he realised we were beaten, he just froze. To be honest, my disappointment disappeared when I saw how upset he was. I thought it was just the luck of the game and I had forgotten it by the time I got home. But George was upset about it for weeks."

The Derby at White City gave Curtis a chance to make amends and Upland Tiger started as the 12–1 ante-post favourite for England's premier classic. "I have reached the Derby final three times with Hard Held, Sirius and later The Jolly Norman," said Curtis. "But I always thought Upland Tiger was my best chance of winning. He got through to the quarter-finals but he was badly baulked at the third bend and split his web. You have to accept these set-backs in greyhound racing, but it was a blow. Upland Tiger was undoubtedly one of the fastest dogs of the year." Tiger went on to add the Flying Four at Crayford to his tally of open race successes, but Curtis felt he never really trained on. "He was a brilliant puppy and was very unlucky that he did not win a major competition," he said. "He was never the same dog in his third year and I think that was because he took so much out of himself. He got so excited before a race and then he would thunder through the field. I think that is what finished him in the end."

Upland Tiger is now looked after by John Houlihan and is a much-loved family pet. Tiger was the first dog he had with Curtis but he has gone on to own a number of graders as well as open racer Cashen Son.

He finds it hard to highlight a particular quality he admires in Curtis as a trainer.

"I admire them all. I think he is quite brilliant," he said. "I have never met anyone who has such an instinctive knowledge of dogs. He can tell almost at a glance how good a greyhound is going to be. Yet he treats all his greyhounds the same from the bottom grader to the top open race star in the kennel."

Curtis was now universally respected as a thoroughly professional trainer of graders and open racers. He had his share of success but the big time still eluded him. The breakthrough was linked to two crucial factors — the arrival of Bill Masters and breeder Jane Hicks sending her first runners to the Curtis kennel.

CHAPTER THREE

The Champion

TRAINING greyhounds can be a lonely business. At its best you are surrounded by friends and fellow trainers and when everything is going well, everyone wants to talk to you. But the burden of responsibility when you have 70 racing dogs, kennel staff, owners and track management all making their demands, can be crippling. To this day, Curtis still misses his brother Charlie, the man with whom he could always share his problems. The two were so close they were a tremendous source of support to each other. It was not until Bill Masters arrived at his kennels that Curtis found someone else to share the load.

"I have always tried not to take my work home with me," said Curtis. "Lily has a fair idea of what is going on and she knows when something has upset me. But when Bill came, I had someone who could share the day to day problems." Curtis used to train dogs for Bill Masters, who had a farm and reared a few litters of greyhound pups on the side. "He decided to set up on his own account and he came to me for a few months to learn the game," said Curtis. That was in 1982 — and Bill is there still. He worked as head man until the start of 1987 and was an integral part of the team that made Curtis champion trainer three times in four years. "There was something in Bill that made him lucky for me," said Curtis. "From the time he arrived we started doing really well — and we never looked back. He made things so much easier for me. We worked well together and I had someone to discuss things with. I could trust him completely and that gave me more time to concentrate on the dogs instead of worrying about every little thing that was happening in the kennel."

When Curtis decided to step down, the two swapped roles and Curtis now works as Bill's head man. "Funnily enough, it was not a difficult thing to do," said Curtis. "It was much easier than I thought it would be. Bill and I think very much on the same lines and I am happy to give him all the help I can. There is nothing I want more than for him to succeed." When Bill first started, Curtis had 78 greyhounds in his range. "I couldn't believe how he had managed to look after them all," said Bill. "I loved the whole business of training greyhounds from the start but I soon learned what hard work it is. If there is one factor that has made George successful it is that he is such a tremendous worker. He is so dedicated he simply never stops working." Bill acknowledges a huge debt to Curtis. "He taught me everything I know," he said. "No matter how busy he is, he will always find the time to help people — and that has meant everything to me."

Bill's arrival at Brighton coincided with the first runners from the great Pecos Jerry — King's Comet litter bred by Jane Hicks. "The first litter she bred included Hackney Carriage and Status Quo," said Curtis. "They were good dogs, although they had niggling injuries. The turning point came with the second litter which included Yankee Express and Copper Beeches, which came to us, and Kings Merlin, which went to Arthur Hitch."

Right from the start Yankee Express showed he was a star in the making and according to Curtis he was a gift to train. "He was so easy," said Curtis. "He was a funny dog in the kennel, always a bit nervous of strangers. But he was a different dog on the track. Nothing could distract him. He trapped brilliantly and he had tremendous early pace. He was also tremendously consistent. He was the best sprinter I ever trained and the greatest dog I handled until Ballyregan Bob."

Yankee got his career off to a flying start, reaching the semi-finals of the 1982 Laurels. He then went on to compete in his first Scurry Gold Cup and showed an immediate liking for the tight-bended Slough circuit. He came second in the first round and then won his second round heat by 7½ lengths in 26.82 for the 442m and his semi-final in 26.94. He was made favourite for the classic final — and gave himself plenty to do. "He swung off wide and then nipped back inside," said Curtis. "It was certainly his luckiest Scurry win." The brindled dog got the verdict by a neck, clocking 27.19. But even with his share of luck it was a remarkable achievement for a greyhound that was only 20 months old.

Curtis always claimed that Yankee Express did not run the big galloping tracks so well and as a result he never showed his best form at Brighton. But that did not stop him going hot from his classic victory to land the Sussex Cup. He ran unbeaten through the competition and in the final he beat his brother Copper Beeches by 1¼ lengths, recording 30.06 for the 515m. He finished his first season's racing with a string of open race wins, reaching the final of the Take Your Place Trophy at

Brighton and the *Sporting Life* Juvenile Championship at Wimbledon.

In the same year Curtis also had the great staying bitch Paradise Lost running for him. The March 1980 whelp by Paradise Spectre out of Gerards Sally was a regular raider of the open race circuit. She won the 1982 Regency at Brighton in a record-breaking 44.65 for the 740m and then the following month she stormed to victory in a 740m open race at her home track and demolished the track record by a further nine spots. The GRA Stakes at White City was her next target and she picked up the £2,000 first prize after beating Alfa My Son by a neck, recording 44.67 for the 730m.

Kasama Trac (Butchers Trac–Lady Kasama) also joined the strength from Bert Barwick and put in a fine display to win the 1982 Cearns Memorial at Wimbledon. The brindled dog set a new course record of 40.70 for the 660m in his heat and then lowered the time by a further 13 spots when he won his semi-final. In the decider he clocked 40.83, beating Blue Torment by 2 lengths.

The year's successes were enough to make Curtis runner-up in the trainer's championship behind Wembley's Adam Jackson. But 1983 was the year that Curtis will always remember as the start of his real glory days. In that year Paradise Lost, Sandy Lane, Sammy Bear, Sir Winston, Copper Beeches and the great Yankee Express were all running at the peak of their form and there was no stopping the Curtis kennel. Yankee Express started the New Year on a winning note, running unbeaten through the William Hill Super Trapper at Hackney. He made it all look so easy, winning his heat by 5¾ lengths in 29.38 for the 484m, his semi by 6 lengths in 29.86 and then taking the final by 5½ lengths in 29.52. The Pall Mall at Harringay, acknowledged as the best test in the country below classic status, boasted a top-class entry that year, but Yankee hardly seemed to notice the opposition as he continued his unbeaten run through to the final.

He won his first round heat by 4 lengths in 28.73, his second round heat by 7½ lengths in 28.41 and his semi-final by 2¾ lengths in 28.47. The final was scheduled for Friday, April 8. But the Curtis camp had two other irons in the fire. Sir Winston (Myrtown–King's Comet) had reached the final of the Grand National at White City due to be run on Saturday, April 2 and Sandy Lane was in the final of the BBC TV Trophy at Walthamstow on April 6.

"We couldn't believe we had three runners in three major competitions," said Curtis. "I said to Bill Masters: 'If just one of them wins I'll be happy'." The first to run was Sir Winston. He was third in his first round heat — beaten 3¼ lengths. He won his second round heat in 30.92 and then qualified in third place in the semis. "I honestly didn't think he had much of a chance," said Curtis. "Alan Taylor had been taking him up to White City for me and he believed in the dog — but I didn't think he could pull if off.

"We were racing at Brighton on the Saturday night so I couldn't be there for the decider. But the result was announced over the loud-speaker. Gunner Smith also had a runner — Wolseleys Scout — and when they said: 'Home win for Brighton' I immediately thought 'Old Gunner's won it'. I couldn't believe it when they said it was Sir Winston." The brindled and white dog got the verdict by just half a length from Master Bob. His winning time was 31.09.

Four days later, Curtis's great staying bitch Sandy Lane, owned by Peter Carpenter who now trains at Reading, took her chance in the final of the BBC TV Trophy. The November 1980 bitch by Maplehurst Star out of Pla Irish Imp had been making a name for herself from the beginning of the year, reaching the final of the Mecca Bookmakers Stayers Stakes at Hackney and the William Hill Classic at Wembley. She was in great form at the start of the TV Trophy and won her heat from future classic winner Jo's Gamble by an impressive 8¾ lengths, clocking 52.40 for Walthamstow's 820m.

"I fancied Sandy Lane," said Curtis. "All she had to do was to keep out of trouble." Paddy Milligan's Minnies Matador started as 5–4 favourite but the anticipated match between him and Sandy Lane who started at 7–4, failed to materialise. Minnies Matador took an early lead but was soon challenged by Adamstown Miller the 33–1 outsider. Going down the back straight the two were still competing for supremacy as Sandy Lane swept past on the outside. By the finishing line she had gone 4½ lengths clear and recorded a winning time of 52.43. Adamstown Miller was second and Minnies Matador finished a further 1¼ lengths adrift.

"I was shouting her home and as she crossed the line I fell off the step, I was so excited," said Curtis. "When I went to collect the prize I could hardly walk." Two days later the crowd was buzzing at Harringay waiting for the start of one of the classiest Pall Mall finals in this history of the competition. The line-up in trap order was Hillville Flyer (4–1), Lannon Lass (8–1), Go Winston (33–1), Raceway Mick (66–1), Long Spell (4–1), Yankee Express (4–5 fav). "I walked Yankee round myself that night," said Curtis. "It was the hardest test because the competition was so strong. But I knew all he had to do was the same as he had done in the earlier rounds — get a flyer from the traps."

The lids went up and Yankee, ideally berthed in trap six, shot out like a scalded cat. By the second bend the race was his. Long Spell, the celebrated £50,000 purchase, tried valiantly to reduce the leeway from the third turn. But Yankee galloped on to win by 1¾ lengths in 28.55 for the 475m.

The Curtis kennel had achieved a seemingly impossible dream, winning three major competitions, including a classic, in seven days. "That is a week I will never forget," said Curtis. "Everything went like clockwork for us. We didn't seem to be able to do anything wrong."

He decided to miss the Laurels with Yankee and rest him in preparation for the Derby. But Sandy Lane kept the Curtis kennel in the headlines, setting a new course record over Wimbledon's 868m when she won an open race in 54.11 – a record which has yet to be bettered. She then went on to win the Key, staged at the Plough Lane circuit. Again, she was in unbeatable form and crossed the line 7¾ lengths in front of House Of Crystal in the final in 54.41.

Curtis started the 1983 Derby with his main hopes resting on litter brothers Yankee Express and Copper Beeches. Yankee came fresh to the classic, gaining a free entry with a record-breaking run in a Derby Trial Stake at Portsmouth. He flew round the 438m in 26.81, winning by 10¾ lengths. The Derby was run without seeding and despite being drawn in trap three, Yankee won his qualifying round in 30.37 for White City's 500m. He went on to win his first round heat in 29.28 and in the second round he beat Debbycot Lad and The Stranger in 29.44

Copper Beeches gave a surprisingly good show in the early stages. Berthed in trap three, he overcame the handicap of his draw with a fine win in 29.55. In the first round the wide runner was given trap one and ran a determined race to qualify in third place. He was rewarded with trap six in the second round and beat On Spec by 2¾ lengths in 29.59. The two brothers, who were kennelled together at the Curtis range, had five days to wait for the quarter final stage. But disaster struck — they both went off-colour.

"I don't believe in making excuses," said Curtis. "But two days before the race they both had a touch of enteritis. I didn't tell anyone – anything you say at Derby time gets in the papers. But I was worried. They weren't too bad. They were fit enough to run, but I knew it had affected them. I thought: 'If only I can get them through this round they're bound to improve.'"

The brothers were drawn in the same heat, Copper Beeches again being saddled with the red jacket. Yankee was luckier, drawn in trap six, but when the traps opened he failed to show. Copper Beeches inevitably got caught up in first bend trouble and the Curtis dogs finished fourth and fifth. Lisnamuck, Game Ball and Haymaker Mack went on to qualify for the semis. That year classic honours went to I'm Slippy, who won the final by a neck in 29.40.

"Yankee ran better in the Derby than I ever imagined he would," said Curtis. "He didn't like the big tracks like Brighton and White City. They were too big a gallop for him. He was brilliant at tight bends. But to begin with, he was coming out and doing the same things as Game

George and Lily.

The most memorable week in Curtis's career when Sandy Lane won the BBC TV Trophy, Yankee Express won the Pall Mall and Sir Winston won the Grand National. (Alf Baker)

Left: The Jolly Norman, finalist in the 1984 Derby. (N and B)

Below: Curtis and Bert Cusack celebrate after Yankee Express's Pall Mall triumph. (N and B).

Ball, who was favourite to win. Even so, I could never bring myself to believe he was going to win the Derby."

There was some compensation for Curtis on Derby final night when Sandy Lane won the Dorando Marathon by 6½ lengths in 60.06 for the 962m and Sir Winston set a new track record in the BBC 2 Chase recording 30.38 over the 500m course, which included seven hurdles.

A repeat raid on the Scurry Gold Cup was the next target for Yankee Express and Curtis also entered Sammy Bear (Mexican Chief–Lady Laurdella) as a second string. Yankee stormed his way through the rounds of the classic, making the opposition look like graders. He won his first round heat by 4½ lengths in 26.88 for the 442m and he crossed the line 4 lengths ahead in the second round in 27.13. In the semi-final he was drawn against Sammy Bear and the two turned the night into a Curtis benefit with a one-two finish. Yankee got the verdict by 2 lengths in a winning time of 26.90.

The line-up for the 1983 final in trap order was: Thor (5–1), Squire Cass (3–1), Ebony Chieftan (5–1) Yankee Express (8–11 fav), Adventure Kit (12–1), Sammy Bear (10–1). "It was a great day for the Scurry," said Curtis. "Whisper Wishes, who went on to win the Derby the following year, got as far as the semis and it was a cracking line-up."

It was a blistering hot night for the final and on the journey from Brighton to Slough Curtis had to keep sponging his dogs down in a bid to keep them cool. "But when it came to it, Yankee made it all look so easy," he said. "He hit the boxes and bang — he was gone." He was a length ahead of Ebony Chieftan at the first bend and then drew away to lead unchallenged to the finishing line. He beat Squire Cass, who had come through on the rails, by 4¼ lengths in a winning time of 26.84 – only 10 spots outside the track record. Thor ran on gamely after first bend bunching to finish third and Sammy Bear was fourth. Yankee, who had now been beaten only once in his last 18 races, earned a place in the record books as the third dog to win the classic twice in its 51-year history.

The Curtis team were now in such brilliant form, they were often competing against each other for honours. In the Essex Vase Copper Beeches and Kasama Trac both reached the £3,000 final. Copper Beeches won his heat and semi-final and started at 9–4 for the decider. Kasama Trac ran second in both opening rounds and was on offer at a generous 14–1. In the final, honours went to Winning Line with Kasama Trac in second place 1½ lengths adrift and Copper Beeches just 2 lengths behind in third place.

Yankee Express and Copper Beeches were both invited to compete in the Select Stakes at Wembley, although neither showed their best form and finished in the last placings as the youngster Whisper Wishes stormed to victory. But it was newcomer The Jolly Norman, (Knockrour Brandy–Breeze Valley), the latest product from Jane Hicks' range, that provided the opposition for Yankee in the Sussex Cup.

"I knew Yankee didn't run Brighton that well but I felt we had a duty to show him to the Brighton racegoers," said Curtis. "He was the track's star and the supporters never got a chance to see him." Yankee did not disappoint his public in the first rounds winning his preliminary heat in 30.04 for the 515m and then beating The Jolly Norman by one length in the semi-final. But in the final The Jolly Norman showed his best form to win in 30.31, relegating Yankee Express to fifth place.

Jondy, litter brother to The Jolly Norman, was also showing promise, reaching the final of the British Breeders Forum Produce Stakes at Wembley after his brother was eliminated in the second round. And he was runner-up in the Produce Stakes at Wembley when Glatton Grange crossed the line 4¾ lengths in front, recording 29.25 for the 490m. The Jolly Norman finished in third place just ½ a length adrift.

In the Crayford Vase over 462m Curtis again had two runners in the final — Sammy Bear and Cashen Son and as it turned out there was nothing to choose between them. Sammy Bear, who had finished second in the Midland Grand Prix at Leicester started as 5–2 favourite for Crayford's £3,000 prize. But Cashen Son (Jimsun–Hinty Lady), on offer at 5–1, was the first to show as the traps went up. He steered a wide course at the bend allowing the John Gibbons trained Gentle Sentanta to take the lead. She looked an easy winner at the third bend but Sammy Bear came through with a challenge and Cashen Son rallied on the outside. The Curtis pair crossed the line together, dead-heating for first place in a winning time of 28.53.

Sandy Lane was continuing to plunder the open race circuit and notched up another track record, this time at her home track when she clocked 59.66 for the 970m – a record which still stands today. She then took her place in the 1983 Cesarewitch. But Jo's Gamble the dog she beat in the TV Trophy, had the edge over her in this competition. She finished third behind him in the semis and fourth in the classic decider when Jerry Fisher's runner took honours winning in 50.90 for Belle Vue's 815m.

Yankee Express was below par when he finished second to Creamery Cross in the Select Stakes at Leicester, but he went on to win the John Power Special Invitation race at Walthamstow. He was an automatic selection for the Anglo-Irish International team — but he failed to show his best either at White City or Shelbourne Park. He thrived on the tight circuits and at Harringay he set a new track record of 28.28 for the 475m when he beat Glatton Grange in the Classic Select Stakes — a time that will never be bettered.

It was an outstanding year for Curtis, capped by Copper Beeches reaching the final of the Gold Collar at Catford and Sir Winston ending his distinguished career by notching up ten wins in a row, including victories in the National Hurdles final at Brighton and the Oliver Humphries final at Wembley.

For the first time in his career, the honours were heaped on Curtis. He was Trainer Of The Year, Yankee Express was voted Greyhound Of The Year, Sandy Lane was Bitch Of The Year. And just to cement the Hicks-Curtis connection, Yankee's dam Kings Comet was Brood Bitch Of The Year. Certainly Curtis had his stars — but it was a year when the whole kennel performed exceptionally well. Curtis was getting the very best from every dog on his strength and his owners were receiving their rewards as the prize money poured in. Nine of his top dogs earned £2,000 or more in major competitions. It would have been a very different story in racehorse stables, but in greyhound racing circles it was a major achievement.

Amazingly, Curtis's run of success continued into the New Year. He had three in the final of the Coronation Cup at Southend — Shelton Song (Echo Spark–Candlemaid), Kasama Trac and Blue Shirt (Shady Monkey–Tour Tralee), and they finished in that order. Shelton Song got the verdict by ¾ of a length recording 40.58 for the 647m and Kasama Trac beat Blue Shirt by a further length. Just over a week later Blue Shirt and Kasama Trac were again lined up against each other — this time competing in the final of the £1,500 Mecca Stayers Stakes at Hackney. Kasama Trac was on offer at 11–2 after winning his heat in 43.12 for the 683m and then qualifying in third place for the final. But Blue Shirt was totally unfancied at 33–1 after coming third in his heat and then being beaten 8¾ lengths as Lisa King stormed to a 42.82 win in the semi-finals.

The final was marred by Paddy Milligan's charge Millers Corner breaking his hock, but Blue Shirt was a revelation. He flew the traps and hung on to win by ¾ of a length in 42.08 from the favourite Lisa King. Kasama Trac finished 1¾ lengths behind in third place. No-one was more surprised than Curtis at Blue Shirt's sudden show of pace.

"The dog had done nothing at Brighton so I suggested to the owners that we tried him at Southend in the Coronation Cup," he said. "Seeing how he ran there, we entered him for the Hackney competition. But he was disappointing so we took him back to Southend for a minor open race. After that he came out and won in style."

This story illustrates just how shrewd Curtis can be in his assessment of a greyhound. It took him no time to work out that Blue Shirt needed constant change to keep his mind on the job — and the trainer was prepared to put himself out in order to give him the stimulation he needed. "We were lucky that the dog had enough pace to go on the open race circuit," said Curtis. "That made all the difference to him."

The result was that the July 1981 whelp, who would have struggled in graded company at Brighton, picked up a handsome share of open race trophies and prize money. He reached the final of the BBC TV Trophy at Wimbledon, was runner-up in the Cearns Memorial, and won the Douglas Tyler Gold Trophy at Wembley. His best performance was in the Scot Grange Trophy at permit track Henlow. He won his heat in a record-breaking time of 45.50 for the 730m — a record that still stands — and then went on to win the final in 46.15, beating Decoy Alice by 9¼ lengths.

There are not many trainers with 70 dogs on their strength who would travel to a small permit track to take part in a competition – even when it was worth £1,000 to the winner. But Curtis has always been tireless in his efforts to find the right competition for his dogs.

"I think the permit tracks are under-estimated," he said. "Henlow or Rye House give you as good a run as anywhere. I would never hesitate to take a dog to those sort of tracks. The only way they fall down is not making a big enough fuss when they get sponsors to the track. They lack the style that is present at the bigger tracks." In fact Blue Shirt's career turned full circle when he returned to Southend the following January to win the Coronation Cup, and was then withdrawn lame after winning his heat and semi-final of the Mecca Stayers Stakes. At the beginning of April Curtis took his place in the Trainers Championship at White City and enjoyed a runaway victory. He accumulated a grand total of 51 points — nine more than his closest rival Jerry Fisher. He was represented by The Jolly Norman, Karinas Pal, Jondy, Cashen Son, Spiral Poysnash, Copper Beeches, Kasama Trac, and Shelton Song. He won three of the eight races, was runner-up in one, third in three races and fourth in one. This victory cemented Curtis's position as top trainer and at the annual prize-giving ceremony at the Hilton Hotel he was rewarded with a standing ovation from fellow trainers.

Curtis has never enjoyed the limelight and given the choice, he would prefer to be working at the kennels or away open racing rather than being the centre of attention. But within days the spotlight was on him again as he fielded his second successive Grand National winner. Just as Sir Winston ended his career, Kilcoe Foxy arrived at the Brighton kennels and was soon showing his ability over the sticks.

"I love hurdle racing," said Curtis. "I always think it takes more nerve than training dogs for the flat. I always worry about the hurdlers — but if nothing happens to them they can carry on much longer." Kilcoe Foxy was runner-up in the Crayford Hurdles final and the Daily Mirror Hurdles final at Harringay before trying his luck in the classic staged at White City along with kennel companion Champ Spa. Kilcoe was second in his opening heat and went on to win his second round heat in 30.96 and his semi-final in 30.54. In the decider Kilcoe, who had started as favourite throughout the competition, missed his break. But

Above: Kilcoe Foxy on the way to winning the 1984 Grand National. (N and B)

Below: After 43 years as a trainer, Curtis wins the St Leger for the first time with Lone Wolf. (W. A. Lewis)

Trainer Bill Masters and head man George Curtis with three of the kennel's staying stars, Thai King, Mines Kango and Lone Wolf.

he jumped faultlessly and took up the lead by the second bend. He finished in a fast 30.32, beating Oriental Express by 2 lengths. Curtis's second string Spa Champ finished in fifth place.

Curtis had been planning to try Yankee Express in the Pall Mall in a bid to win the competition for a second year. But a shoulder injury put paid to his chances and it was decided to wait for the Scurry Gold Cup for his comeback. Sandy Lane put in a strong challenge to lift the BBC TV Trophy for a second time — but in the end she had to be content with winning the consolation race. She was still a force to be reckoned with over the distance and proved that beyond doubt in the Key at Wimbledon which she won for the second successive year, this time finishing 9¼ lengths in front in 54.90. Although she raced until the Spring of 1985 this was her last major win. She proved a great servant to both Curtis and owner Peter Carpenter and is now enjoying life as a brood bitch. She has a litter of pups by Ballyregan Bob which Carpenter is rearing at his Sussex range and he is hopeful that the guts and determination shown by both parents will appear in the progeny.

The Jolly Norman was given a chance in the 1984 Derby — and much to everyone's surprise, he ended up in the final. He had started the year well, finishing second in the William Hill Super Trapper at Hackney. He then reached the final of the Blue Riband at Wembley, finishing fifth and ended in last place in the Olympic at Brighton. He did nothing spectacular through the rounds of the premier English classic. He was a slow starter which meant that he often found trouble but his strong finish always kept him in contention in the closing stages.

He came second in his qualifying heat and third in the first round before winning his only race in the run to the final. In the second round he beat Wyoming Ivy by 1¾ lengths, recording 29.67 for the 500m. He went on to improve on this time in the quarter-finals although Nippy Law got the verdict by ¾ of a length in the race which was won in 29.41. In the semi-finals he came second to Morans Beef, beaten 1½ lengths.

The brindled dog started as the 20–1 outsider for the decider and according to Curtis, the owners were the only people who believed The Jolly Norman could win. It was the first greyhound that Cliff Norman and Frank Jolly had ever owned and they couldn't believe their luck in ending up with a Derby finalist. "They were fantastic," said Curtis. "Frank would take his wife and daughter and they followed the dog everywhere he raced. They thought the world of him."

In the final the favourite Whisper Wishes ran a faultless race, leading from traps to line to win in 29.43, beating Morans Beef by ¾ of a length. Proud Dodger was half a length behind in third place and The Jolly Norman was by no means disgraced with his fourth place — 1½ lengths adrift. "I wasn't disappointed with the result — after all it was the closest to a Derby win I ever got," said Curtis. "The two other finalists I had, finished fifth. It was always going to be hard for The Jolly Norman as he had to do it all behind — but he ran a game race."

Curtis claims that he has no regrets that he did not field a Derby winner in his 43 years as a trainer. "I reached the Derby final three times and I never once thought I had a chance of winning it," he said. "The only time I was disappointed was when Upland Tiger went out. He was such a brilliant dog and I believed I could have won it with him." By now the greyhound racing world was on tenterhooks awaiting the comeback of Yankee Express. He was attempting to win his third successive Scurry Gold Cup — and he was coming up to four-years-old. "I knew we were asking a lot," said Curtis. "Truthfully, the dog had gone past his peak — but I knew there was some running left in him."

Curtis started Yankee's preparation with a solo trial at the Slough circuit and the dog recorded a fast 26.98. He followed this up with an open race win at the track in 27.00 and with a final solo trial in 27.04. Yankee was then ready to take on all-comers. In the opening rounds, he showed all his old fire and enthusiasm winning his first heat from Hot Sauce Feaver by 7½ lengths in 27.18 and then clocking 26.87 in the second round, beating Borna Slave by 3¼ lengths. But in the semi-final he squeaked into the frame by a short-head following a late burst of speed. The race was won by kennel companion Karinas Pal in 27.43.

Curtis made sure that his dog was back to his best for the classic decider. The line-up in trap order was: Fifth Column (11–4), Karinas Pal (3–1), Another Ronald (50–1), Decoy Star (16–1), Alone Sparky (10–1) and Yankee Express (11–10 fav). Another Ronald was the first to show, but the crowd were on their feet as Yankee Express soon caught the early pacemaker. They hampered each other at the first bend but then Yankee, spurred on by the cheers of the crowd, was unstoppable. He crossed the line ¾ of a length in front of Karinas Pal in 27.03 giving Curtis a one-two finish. He had become the first greyhound in the history of the sport to win a classic three times.

It was a magnificent achievement by the brilliant sprinter — and it spoke volumes for Curtis's skill as a trainer. The dog's ability is undisputed and his rearing obviously contributed to keeping him strong and fit over three seasons of racing. But Curtis's unique talent for consistently getting the best from a dog stands out in the success story. Yankee is owned in partnership by Bert Cusack, Ray Barnard and Sid Stenning, but Bert and his wife Irene have always been the most involved.

Bert missed only one race in Yankee's entire racing career — and that was when he was in hospital. "I went to every trial and every race," he said. "And we never missed taking him out on Sundays when he was at the racing kennels." As soon as Yankee won his triple crown, he was retired and now stands at stud with his breeder Jane Hicks. Bert's main reason for letting 'Wolfy' go back to Jane was because he knew the dog would have a good life there.

"I knew he would have all the freedom to gallop to his heart's content," said Bert. "After what he did for us, nothing could be too good for him." Bert has known Curtis for the last 35 years — but it was only when Jane Hicks set up her breeding kennels that he became an owner. His first dog was Holme Farm Boy — named after Jane's home — and he has had an interest in every litter she has bred. With uncanny luck, he picked Lone Wolf from Yankee Express's first litter — and so found himself in the enviable position of owning a classic winner, sired by his own triple classic winner.

During Yankee's track career, Bert could not have been more involved as an owner. But he left the decisions to Curtis. "I trust George's judgement completely," he said. "I soon learnt that there is no point pestering him and asking when a dog is right. He will always be the first to tell you. He is one of the few people who will never mess you about. He tells you the truth, if he thinks a dog is no good he'll say so. He does not believe in keeping people happy by only telling them what they want to hear." Bert remembers Yankee's third Scurry victory as his greatest because the dog was not 100 per cent fit. "He had a niggling shoulder injury which put him out of the Pall Mall. George did a very good job getting him back in time for the Scurry," he said.

Even though Curtis was established as champion trainer and contesting major competitions was becoming a way of life, he still suffered terribly on final nights. According to Bert, he worried non-stop and by the time the big race came along he was completely drained. "He is on edge all the time, he goes to the Gents about ten times before the race and his whole face goes rigid with nerves," said Bert. "It is some mark of the man that he cares so much after a lifetime in the game."

The Jane Hicks-George Curtis partnership came close to fielding another classic winner a couple of months later when The Jolly Norman reached the final of the Gold Collar at Catford. After his Derby campaign he had been invited to compete in the Select Stakes at Wembley where he finished fourth and he reached the final of the Sussex Cup in a year when Curtis had three in the decider. His dog Sammy Bear took honours beating Lulus Hero by 2¼ lengths in 29.28 for the 515m. Kennel mate Karina's Pal was 1¾ lengths behind in third place and The Jolly Norman finished fifth.

At Catford The Jolly Norman won his opening heat of the Gold Collar by 10 lengths in 35.13 for the 555m. In the second round he was runner-up to Rathkenny Lassie and in the semis he again finished second, this time beaten by Wheelers Tory.

The final was an incredibly tight race. Wheelers Tory led out, but he

Bill Masters.

Curtis at the Brighton kennels.

was strongly challenged by the favourite Aitch Bee. He managed to hang on to his lead and won the classic by a neck in 35.05. The Jolly Norman, coming through with a powerful finish, was only a neck away in third place.

The August 1981 whelp went on to contest the Grand Prix at Walthamstow along with kennel companions Blue Shirt and Sunrise Sonny. And this was one of the occasions when the least fancied runner sprang a surpise. The Jolly Norman came second in both the opening rounds and was eliminated at the semi-final stage. Sunrise Sonny got through to the semis where he was drawn against Blue Shirt after coming third in the first round and then winning his second round heat in 40.48 for the 640m. Blue Shirt had gone unbeaten through the competition and justified his 11–8 favouritism with a 40.32 win at the penultimate stage. The determined Sunrise Sonny overcame bad baulking at the first and second bend to qualify in third place.

In the decider Oakwood Lady, trained by Ken Linzell, who had three in the final with Glatton Grange and Lakefield Blue, started as favourite, Blue Shirt was on offer at 5–1 and Sunrise Sonny was completely unfancied at 25–1. But the May 1982 son of Armagh Rocket-Kerry Wedding was quick to show and although Glatton Grange got away at the first bend he could not withstand Sunrise Sonny's finishing pace. The Curtis dog got the verdict by just a neck in 40.00 from Oakwood Lady.

This victory was enough to cement Curtis's position as Trainer Of The Year — for the second year running. It had been another spectacular 12 months, with two classic wins and a host of major competition victories. Yankee Express had retired, but almost before Curtis could miss him, an interesting newcomer arrived in the shape of Ballyregan Bob.

The May 1983 whelp took his first title when he won the Cosmic Orbit Young Puppies Trophy at Brighton in November 1984. And for the next two years his name was on everyone's lips.

In 1985 he dominated the open race circuit and all Curtis's other open race runners were in his shadow. That is not to say that they did not have their share of wins, for Curtis never neglected his other runners in favour of his superstar. But all other achievements looked modest in comparison with Bob's escalating success.

There was a first for Curtis in 1985 when he added another classic title to his growing tally. Spiral Super (Cooladine Super–Spiral Mint) was brought over from Ireland specifically for the Oaks and Curtis guided her unbeaten through the competition, although the final was not without its nerve-wracking moments. She won her qualifying round by a neck in 28.91 but by the first round she had settled down to the task and led all the way to win by 4½ lengths from Sailing Maid. In both the second round and the semi-finals she again enjoyed traps-to-line victories, clocking 28.46 and 28.47 respectively.

Unsurprisingly, she started as favourite for the decider. But although she broke first Mick's Susie, trained by Mick Puzey, showed electric pace to head her in the run-up to the first bend. Running from trap three, Mick's Susie kept the pressure on up the back straight although Spiral Super did not allow her rival to pull away. By the last bend she got her head in front — but Mick's Susie came again and on the line Curtis's runner got the verdict by a neck in a time of 28.57. "I have trained a lot of the 'Spiral' greyhounds for the owner Vic Brooks and this was his first classic win," said Curtis. "The bitch had only been in my kennels for seven weeks by the end of the competition."

Curtis ended the year as runner-up to Ken Linzell in the Trainers' Championship. But an incident occurred with one of his runners that marred this triumph and was instrumental in his decision to step down as trainer. Supa Comet was running in graded company at Brighton and following a poor performance a urine sample was taken from the dog. After analysis it was found to be positive and Curtis was brought before the NGRC Stewards. He was cleared, but the experience left him shattered.

"Lily and I came back from the hearing in London and we sat in the kitchen and cried," said Curtis. "I've always tried to play the game straight and I've never messed around with dogs. But when that sort of thing happens you're really sick. People who know you would still believe in you. But others would read it in the papers and say: 'Oh George, he's just another villain.'

"If you talked to another 50 trainers they would probably say I was stupid to take it so seriously. But they are not me. If I had been younger I might have been able to take it. But I thought: 'It could happen again tomorrow'. I didn't want Lily or me to be that upset again. I had been up before the stewards before and cautioned over minor things. There was the time, earlier in the year when two of my dogs raced in the wrong jackets. The kennel lad had made the mistake. There was no reason for it. The dogs didn't even look the same — one was big and the other was small. It was just one of those things that happen. He came up and apologised and I told Jim Layton straightaway. In fact, it made no difference as both dogs were unplaced. But I was still fined £100.

"I didn't mind that. A mistake had been been made and as the trainer, I was responsible. You can say that is not fair and the blame lay with the paddock steward or the kennel lad. But the rules are the rules. The trainer is ultimately responsible for all his dogs even if he is not physically present. I don't argue with that. I don't think we'd be racing now if it was not for the NGRC. A lot of people would cry me down for saying that, but I believe in abiding by the rules."

The irony was that the most honest and genuine person in the sport had to suffer for something he didn't do. After the hearing Curtis gave notice that he would step down as trainer in 12 months' time.

He was also influenced by the new policy adopted by Coral, the owners of Brighton Stadium, which meant that all trainers were to be self-employed and employ their own kennel staff. "I was worried about the extra responsibility," he said. "It was not only the administrative side. If anything happened to the staff, you were responsible. Just after the changeover, a kennel lad was involved in an accident and a couple of dogs ran away. In that situation you've got the owners screaming at you. I thought: 'I'm too old for that'. I've enjoyed every minute of my time in the sport — but I thought after the hearing, that's enough."

Needless to say, Curtis was not the man to back-pedal, simply because his days as a trainer were coming to an end. He had some good dogs in his kennel and he was determined to do his best by them. Ballyregan Bob was aiming for the world record of consecutive wins and injury problems were a major headache. Curtis spent an incalculable amount of time in a bid to get his superstar right. He also had a fine string of open racers and he had the added satisfaction of training the first progeny of Yankee Express.

Raffles Nitepost, the result of a February 1984 mating with Raffles Bridge, was the first to win a major final. The brindled dog found his niche as a hurdler and won the Springbok Trophy at Wimbledon and then a couple of weeks later he got the verdict by a neck in the William Hill First For Prices Hurdles at Hackney when he clocked 31.41 for the 484m course.

Jane Hicks used her bitch Breeze Valley for the first litter she bred by Yankee Express — and the result was spectacular. She reared an all-winning litter with Lone Wolf as the star member. The June 1984 whelp started his career at the end of 1985, reaching the semi-finals of the Puppy Derby at Wimbledon and coming second in the Consolation final. He gained further experience on the open race circuit before being entered for the Coomes Test at Walthamstow over 640m.

He ran second in both his heat and semi-final and started at 6–1 for the decider. He made a moderate start allowing the favourite Fawn Lark to pull away and take up the lead, but this was cut away after bad baulking at the third bend. Lone Wolf was placed exactly right to take up the running from temporary leader Oriental Darkie and Curtis's dog crossed the line 1½ lengths in front in 40.31.

Lone Wolf is owned by Bert Cusack and once his dog had established himself as a top-class stayer, the St Leger was the competition that was always in sight. But, never one to miss an opportunity when a dog is running in form, Curtis picked up the Gold Cup at Wimbledon with his new star before starting his preparation for the classic.

Lone Wolf started the competition with second placings in the opening rounds and then he came good to win his semi-final in 40.02 for Wembley's 655m. Curtis's second string Windsor Ann was a surprise finalist after qualifying in third place in the opening rounds and then finishing second in the semis. But all eyes were on the Savvas' Irish import, Low Sail, which had won his semi-final in brilliant 39.74. This run was the more remarkable as conditions were appalling and the going was estimated at .30 slow.

The final six in trap order were: Low Sail (1–2 fav), Some Enchanter (50–1), Ballyhaden Queen (7–1), Lone Wolf (9–2), Windsor Ann (50–1), Mineola Aechena (8–1). Low Sail was inside five seeded wide runners and on form he looked a certainly. But at trap-rise he was left standing and Lone Wolf and Windsor Ann were the first to show with Some Enchanter coming through to challenge. Low Sail made a mess of the second bend and then roared into contention. But Lone Wolf never looked like being caught and he crossed the line ¾ of a length in front, recording a winning time of 39.99. Windsor Ann came through to take third place, giving Curtis two in the frame.

This victory was the sweetest in Curtis's long and distinguished career. His first love has always been for stayers and yet the elusive St Leger title had escaped his grasp in 43 years as a trainer.

He had come close with runner-up Peculiar Way in 1966 and he was tragically robbed of the classic in 1985 when Ballyregan Bob had to be withdrawn lame after winning his semi-final. Now in his final year as a trainer he had won the classic with the son of his great dog Yankee Express.

"It was like a dream come true," said Curtis. "I try to keep calm when it comes to a big final, but you wouldn't be human if you didn't suffer from nerves. That night I was standing at the first bend and I could see we were in front. My heart started pounding and I kept on saying: 'Keep out of trouble!' Then I thought if only he can keep going it is going to be our night. When he won I was jumping in the air. At first I thought we'd got beat and when it came over: Number four the winner, I simply couldn't believe it.

"But I know how Nicky Savva felt that night. It was so like the time I had Upland Tiger in the final of the Laurels. They were both drawn inside five wide runners and looked like certainties. I was always optimistic about our chances. I knew Lone Wolf had to come out in front and there would need to be some trouble to stop Low Sail — and that is exactly what happened. But Lone Wolf did everything right and was a worthy winner. To my mind, the most improved runner of the competition was Windsor Ann. I was delighted with her third place."

Jane Hicks also provided the dog for Curtis's last major competition triumph. Yankees Shadow is the result of a September 1983 mating between Cosmic Sailor and Kings Lace – and she soon proved herself as a force to be reckoned with over the distance.

Her first major target was the 1986 Regency at Brighton. She came second in her heat and started at 8–1 for the decider, with all the money going on Kylehill Heather. But Yankees Shadow came through with a great run to win by 2¾ lengths recording 46.03 for the 740m. The BBC TV Trophy was her next challenge in the year that the great Scurlogue Champ was attempting to make greyhound history by retaining the crown.

Ken Peckham's dog started the competition in blistering form knocking 36 spots off his own track record for Brough Park's 825m, recording a winning time of 52.26. Yankees Shadow was a little less spectacular when winning her heat and she was a generous 7–1 for the decider. But this was always going to be Scurlogue's benefit and he beat Sneaky Liberty by 3 lengths, relegating Curtis's bitch to fourth place. But Yankees Shadow was improving all the time and she raided the open race circuit over the next few months picking up wins at Poole, Portsmouth, Hackney, Harringay and Wembley, as well as at her home track, where she reached the final of the Stewards Cup.

She finally came of age in the Cesarewitch at Belle Vue. From the start of the classic, she didn't put a foot wrong winning her heat by 6 lengths and her semi-final by a massive 14¾ lengths. She started as favourite for the final in a line-up which read: Change Guard (20–1), Easy Rodger (9–4), Yankees Shadow (4–7), Father Ralph (66–1), Millrace Rose (100–1) and Raywee Delight (20–1). This time Yankees Shadow did not have everything her own way. Millrace Rose was the early leader with Easy Rodger in contention while Yankees Shadow and Change Guard were tailing the field. Easy Rodger took the lead and stayed in front until the last bend. But by this time Yankees Shadow had changed gear and came through to take the race by 1¾ lengths, recording 54.90 for the 853m course.

This gave Curtis his tenth and final classic winner. Yankees Shadow went on to win her next nine races from 10 outings. She broke Walthamstow's 820m track record with a time of 55.99 and then reached the final of the Key at Wimbledon which she won impressively by a huge margin of 10¾ lengths, recording 55.07 for the 868m. She proved to be a marvellously consistent bitch and Curtis used his magic touch to get a run of 12 wins on the trot from her. She then came third and went on to record another eight wins before retiring in the Spring of 1987.

Her exploits, along with Lone Wolf, Ballyregan Bob and the other open racers were enough to make Curtis Trainer Of The Year in his final year. "We didn't start the year that well and then the Savvas came through with a rush and were winning everything in sight," said Curtis. "But I think Nicky Savva must have felt a bit sorry for me because he knew it was my last year. He seemed to drop out of the competition and left me to win. Whatever happened, it was the most marvellous thing to go out winning. I had all the excitement with Ballyregan Bob breaking the world record and then went out with the trainers' title. Whatever else happens to me, I will always have the satisfaction of knowing I left when I was on top."

Of course, Curtis has not really left the sport — and there are those who doubt that he ever will. Greyhound racing has been his passion for half a century, and nothing will ever change that.

CHAPTER FOUR

Choosing a Greyhound

THE crucial step for a new owner-trainer is where to buy the first greyhound. This sounds fundamental — but it is an area where a lot of expensive mistakes are made.

George Curtis is an ardent believer in allowing the experts a free rein. Breeders and agents have spent years acquiring their specialised knowledge. To imagine you can take this on board, at the same time as trying to learn the art of training greyhounds, is foolhardy.

Money is obviously going to dictate your choice of greyhound to a large extent. But circumstances should also be taken into consideration. There is no point in spending a fortune on a top-class animal when you are feeling your way in the game. Curtis argues that it makes far more sense to start out modestly, learn by your mistakes, and then move into a bigger league when you have the ability to do the dog justice.

He strongly recommends picking up your first dog at the local track.

"The big advantage is that you will have seen the dog race," says Curtis. "You will know it chases, is genuine, and runs that particular track. If you go to a trainer with a good reputation, who you can trust, he is more than likely to have a dog he wants taking off his hands. There is no reason why this should be viewed with suspicion. There are always owners who are moving on or want to pull out.

"The greyhound to choose is one that is still a comparative youngster — two to two-and-a-half years old — who has won a race or two but still has the scope for improvement."

When you have built up a bit of experience, Curtis suggests the next step is to buy a pup. And sad though it may seem for British breeding, Ireland is the place to look.

"The proof of the pudding is in the eating and the best dogs consistently come from Ireland," he said.

"We have caught up a bit in recent years and the top British-bred dogs can hold their own, but Ireland is still the best bet."

Curtis warns all first-time buyers to beware. There are many pitfalls and there is no percentage in cutting out the middlemen and thinking that you are as likely to find a good a dog as an agent.

"Buying greyhounds is a game for the professionals who know what they are doing," he said. "An agent spends his time going round all the tracks and the sales and he knows what is value for money. He knows what times to look for and he will be able to match the dog with the track where you are planning to race.

"It can be very deceptive to look at a dog's form and try to analyse trial times. What the outsider will never know is the times the dog has been doing at the schooling track. You may be influenced by the times recorded by a so-called 'unraced puppy'. But believe me, that pup will have had a dozen runs round a schooling track and the owners will be well aware of its ability."

Curtis warns that sales can prove particularly hazardous for the uninitiated. The outsider may think he is seeing a fair representation of the dog's form — and he will also have any available race form to go on. But he will be competing with agents who have been scouting round the local tracks for months — and they will almost certainly know something he doesn't.

Buying a greyhound represents a major investment in anyone's book. There is little change from £2,000–£3,000 for a modest open racer. The bargain buys that turn out to be world-beaters are few and far between. They are certainly out-numbered by those who have got their fingers badly burned.

Curtis reckons that an agent is far more likely to pull off a good deal. For he is in a position to find a pup at an early stage, watch its progress and jump in when the price is right. But even so, professionals are doing business with professionals and Irish breeders are only too well aware of the market to give anything useful away.

Curtis has used Irish agent Mick Sylver throughout his career — and has found him to be an excellent judge of greyhounds as well as being totally honest and trustworthy. Most trainers will have their own agent and he suggests the beginner should go to a trainer and ask him to recommend the right person.

He remembers Peculiar Way, runner-up in the 1966 St Leger as a particularly good buy at £130, negotiated by Sylver who also bought 1969 Derby finalist Hard Held for £250. But the agent came into his own over the purchase of Monalee Customer.

A deal had been struck on the dog on behalf of one of Curtis's owners.

But at the eleventh hour, Sylver pulled out. He had discovered that the dog had two knocked up toes. Curtis discussed this with the owner and they decided to go ahead if Monalee Customer had recorded his best time of 34.20 over 600 yards at Shelbourne, when he had the injury.

"We made enquiries and found he had sustained the injury before he did that time," said Curtis. Mick got a £100 discount and bought him. Monalee Customer went on to win the Cearns Memorial.

This illustrates how vital the agent is in the wheeling and dealing that goes with buying greyhounds. If you have a good agent you can be confident that the dog you buy is 100 per cent sound — and injuries or persistent lameness in newly purchased greyhounds account for a very large percentage of hard luck stories.

George Curtis still is indisputably a first-class judge of greyhounds. But he still prefers to bow to the superior expertise of his agent. Although it certainly helps if you know what to look for when you see a puppy trial.

"I look first and foremost for keenness," said Curtis. "I want to see a greyhound that has his head down and is chasing the hare. You don't want one that is running into other dogs or looking for a bit of company. I like to see a dog that comes from behind and goes by cleanly. I don't care what they say about the pup being inexperienced. In Ireland they will have had so many runs round a schooling track that no dog is inexperienced.

"I always like to watch a dog to the trip. A lot of people take their eyes off the dog when it reaches the line. But I watch them to the death. That's how I have found my best long distance dogs.

"The other thing to steer clear of, is very excitable dogs. I don't like to see them jumping up and down and wearing themselves out. You don't want them dead quiet — but the ones that are too highly strung are always a risk. And I don't think they keep running as long as the calmer type."

With racing greyhounds, looks can often prove deceptive. Curtis describes his ideal dog as one with a deep chest, with plenty of lung-room, strong neck, short in the hock and one that walks high on his feet.

"Look at the hindquarters, that is where the power comes from," he said.

But he readily admits that this is no magic formula for finding the best pup of a litter. Copper Beeches was twice the dog to look at — but it was litter brother Yankee Express that won three classics.

"When you pick a puppy at the 12-week stage, you may as well look for needles in a haystack as for indications of a potential racer," he said.

"I like them to be bold and to come out to meet you and I like to see a bit of competitiveness between the litter mates.

"When they are saplings your chances of picking a winner are only slightly better. The most important thing to look for at this stage is keenness to chase. Watch the pups go after the lure and see if you can spot the ones that mean business."

But there are no safeguards and the trainer that attempts to breed his own pups or rear a litter is entering a completely different game.

CHAPTER FIVE

Breeding Winners

THE Irish are still responsible for the vast majority of racing greyhounds in this country, but British breeding is at last becoming a force to be reckoned with. George Curtis remembers the days when Percy Brown, rated as one of the greatest racing managers of all time, would select 48 greyhounds for the English Derby. If a couple were English-bred it was heralded as a major triumph. The Savvas made the greatest breakthrough some 20 years ago and have since set up a dynasty of top-class British-bred greyhounds. June and Stan Saxby made a major contribution and so has Geoff de Mulder.

In comparison Jane Hicks is a newcomer to the sport. She has been involved in the breeding business for only seven years but already boasts a matchless tally of major prize winners. In just five years she sent six classic winners and three classic finalists to Curtis and he attributes their partnership as one of the major reasons for his success.

The best greyhounds she has bred include Yankee Express, winner of three successive Scurry Gold Cups, Kings Merlin, 1983 St Leger finalist, Copper Beeches, 1983 Gold Collar finalist — all three dogs from the superb Pecos Jerry-Kings Comet litter. Sir Winston won the 1983 Grand National, The Jolly Norman reached the final of the 1984 English Derby and in Curtis's last year as a trainer, Yankees Shadow won the 1986 Cesarewitch and Lone Wolf gave him victory in the St Leger for the first time.

"A trainer relies on having good greyhounds in his kennel and Jane Hicks provided me with that — on a regular basis," said Curtis. "And she is continuing to do it for my successor Bill Masters. I honestly don't think it matters what pups she rears, they turn out to be top-class racing greyhounds."

Jane Hicks, in turn, acknowledges a huge debt to Curtis for bringing the best out in her puppies and training them on to such spectacular heights. Whatever the reason, it is a mixture of talents that has proved a great bonus to the sport.

Curtis's major preoccupation has always been with training greyhounds, rather than breeding. But it is something he has become increasingly involved with since Yankee Express and then Ballyregan Bob retired to stud.

He supervises all their matings and brings his unique understanding of dogs to this side of the business. But always a man to push others forward, he believes that breeding and rearing is a job for the experts — and should remain with them.

"If you want to breed top-class greyhounds, you have to have the expertise and the facilities," said Curtis. "It is no coincidence that year after year the best British-bred puppies come from the same places — the Savvas, Cobbolds and now Jane Hicks.

"I would honestly be reluctant to get involved in this side of the business, unless I was able to go into it properly. There are too many greyhounds that are bred for sentiment. People think they'll have a litter with their bitch when she retires and give no thought to the bloodlines or the rearing. The result is too many puppies that are too slow to grade, that no-one will give house-room to."

Despite this warning, Curtis is as anxious as anyone in the sport to see the growth of British breeding. He is also aware of the fact that not every breeder sets out to produce classic winners. They are simply trying to produce useful racing greyhounds as graders for the local track.

But he argues that no matter what your aim is — the cost will remain the same — with the exception of the size of the stud fee. It is a very expensive business to rear a litter of pups — at least £1,000 a pup — and so it is as important for the small-time breeder to do the job properly as it is for the Savvas or Jane Hicks.

THE STUD DOG: Confronted with a paper full of stud dog advertisements, it is no easy matter to select the right dog for your bitch.

Do you go for a top flight dog who has just retired from the track? Or do you choose an established sire who has proved that he can throw decent progeny?

When Ballyregan Bob retired to stud, he was literally swamped with requests for matings.

"We knew we were on the crest of a wave with him," said Curtis.

Curtis with Jane Hicks and triple classic winner Yankee Express, who sired a classic winner in his first litter.

"After his world record everyone was talking about the dog and wanted to have the first Ballyregan Bob pups. We restricted him to two matings a week, although that meant turning many bitches away.

"It might have been tempting to say the rush won't last forever and to cash in. But the last thing you want is the dog to loose interest and start performing badly. I think two bitches a week, with a minimum of three days between, is the most that any dog can cope with."

The majority of breeders who wanted to use Ballyregan at this stage were the ones that were looking to sell the pups at 12-weeks. They knew the stud dog's name was enough to attract purchasers and the asking price of up to £1,000 per pup proved no obstacle.

In this context Ballyregan Bob's stud fee of £600 is put into perspective. There is often a reluctance to go to the more expensive stud dogs. People fear they are being ripped off — often because the stud dog's part in the business is over so quickly. But when you are looking at an average size litter of seven to eight pups, the stud fee can often be re-couped by the first pup you sell. Equally, if you rear on, the size of the overall investment means that the stud fee is one of the lesser expenses.

According to Curtis, the Irish — the true professionals in the game — were not interested in using Ballyregan Bob when he first retired.

"The Irish will always go for a proven stud dog," he said. "They will wait until a dog has got some pups on the track which are performing well, before they will use their bitches.

"That is also true of the more discerning British breeder and so what every stud keeper hopes is that their dogs will produce a flyer in his first crop."

The problem is that it can be a long wait — a minimum time span of 15 months before the first pups can even race and realistically at least two years before they have had a chance to prove themselves.

Curtis has been very clever in reducing this time lag. He has allowed his best dogs, destined for stud duties, to mate a couple of bitches during their winter rest. This had the advantage of ensuring that the dog could do the business so could subsequently be advertised as a proven stud dog, and it also gave the opportunity for a couple of litters to reach the track relatively soon after the dog retired.

This short-cut has worked with spectacular results in a couple of cases and proved to be the making of two stud dogs.

Glin Bridge's first mating was to Galaxy Queen, during a spring lay-off in 1976. The resulting litter produced Princess Glin, Glin Fane and Watch It Buster who all held track records at Brighton as well as winning major open races.

These were the first of a fantastic line of Glin Bridge progeny which won graded, open races and important competitions nationwide. In fact, in the early eighties Glin Bridge has more runners than any other sire — English or Irish.

Yankee Express' first matings also paid huge dividends. He was given a lay-off following his second Scurry Gold Cup triumph and served a select number of bitches. Among them was Breeze Valley – coincidentally the result of a repeat mating between Glin Bridge and Galaxy Queen.

Breeze Valley's litter whelped in January 1984 included 1986 St Leger winner Lone Wolf, who triumphed in the Coomes Test and the John White Gold Cup and finished second in the 1987 St Leger. To produce a classic winner in the first crop is to have a dream come true, But this particular dream was very carefully stage-managed. Breeze Valley was a proven bitch — her first litter by Knockrour Brandy included The Jolly Norman, who went on to reach the final of the 1984 Derby.

Yankee's other early matings were all with quality bitches such as Grassmere Lass, who produced 1986 Stewards Cup winner Black Superman, and Raffles Bridge, dam of Raffles Nitespot who won the 1986 Springbok Trophy and the First For Prices Hurdles.

A stud dog must succeed on his own merits — initially on his track career and breeding, and eventually on the pups he sires.

But Curtis maintains that the dog is almost entirely dependent on the bitches that visit him. When a dog is launched at stud he must have quality as well as quantity. The period when he is sought after for his track record alone is very short — and it must be followed up by living proof in the shape of pups that win races in as short a time as possible.

For of course, not all great racing dogs make good stud dogs. The breeding game would be a great deal simpler if that was the case. And stud dogs will not necessarily re-produce the qualities that made them famous on the track.

"Yankee Express was the greatest sprinter I have ever trained," said Curtis. "Yet he produces a St Leger winner. Upland Tiger was the fastest puppy I have ever trained. He had real, genuine pace. Yet despite serving numerous bitches, including some of quality, he never really produced anything on the track." It all goes to show that no matter how much planning and research goes into breeding, there is no magic formula.

Curtis recommends going back at least three generations on the sire and dam's side when selecting a stud dog.

"I don't think you want the breeding too close," he said. "I wouldn't like to see any duplications between the sire and dam for three generations. There is a lot to be said for using a complete outcross. It certainly worked when Jane Hicks used the American sire Pecos Jerry with Kings Comet and produced Yankee Express, Copper Beeches, Kings Merlin and Blue Rover.

"I would go to a stud dog that has a top-class racing record. But if you can't afford that, go to a lesser dog who has the same bloodlines. Even if you go back a couple of generations to the high-class dog, it is still perfectly possible that the bitch will produce something decent."

Some people are suspicious of a stud dog that has suffered persistent injury in his racing career. But in fact, it is the type of injury that is significant. If a dog has suffered continuously from problems with his feet, there may be an hereditary weakness. But if he has broken a hock or a toe, it can be wholly atrributed to the strain of racing. Curtis remembers a stud dog that had a leg amputated because he was suffering from cancer. Yet he still proved a very effective sire and the cancer did not appear in any of his offspring.

Launching a dog at stud is not necessarily a straightforward business and any stud keeper will tell you, patience is essential. Some take to game immediately, but more often the beginners will need careful handling.

"We had a terrible time with Yankee Express," said Curtis. "He started off okay and then he lost all interest. It was very embarrassing when a bitch had travelled all the way from Newcastle and he just lay there looking completely bored by the whole business."

Fortunately Jane Hicks' vet tried him on a course of fertility injections which stimulate the testicles and ever since he has been working well. Jane Hicks attributes his unsettled period to missing the routine of the racing kennel.

"Although I bred Yankee and I had him here for one rest period, I think he found it very strange when he came back full-time," she said. "He had lived as a racing dog for three years and suddenly that was all taken away from him. Now he is completely happy, he loves the freedom of the place and he keeps extremely well. Mind you, he has never liked strangers and George and June Saxby are the only people he will allow to supervise the matings."

Both agree that the key to a successful dog is a contented dog — and it is a question of finding the right diet and conditions to suit the individual.

Ballyregan Bob and Yankee Express like to be kennelled with a bitch. They pine without the company and both thrive on having another greyhound to exercise with. Ballyregan Bob in particular loves to gallop — and he has been known to wear out his visiting bitches before the mating, because he is showing off getting them to chase him in the paddock. "You can almost hear him saying: 'Watch out I'm the champion'!" said Curtis.

He likes to see a stud dog kept at peak fitness.

"They can be a little heavier than racing weight but they should not be allowed to get fat and sluggish," he said.

He keeps Ballyregan Bob on more or less the same diet as he did when he was racing. But he cuts down on the raw meat as this can put too much strain on the kidneys. He also gives a daily supplement of vitamin E which aids sperm production.

He says ideally he would do two matings on a bitch — with a day's gap in-between. But when stud dogs such as Ballyregan Bob are so over-subscribed that bitches have to be turned away, it is simply not possible. For it is vital not to over-use a stud dog. It can lead to trouble with dogs losing interest or with bitches missing, although it is always hard to prove whether the fault in this case is with the dog or the bitch.

"Right from the start, you should take things step by step and ask advice at every stage," said Curtis. "There is no point in rushing in, spending money hand over fist and then ending up disappointed.

"And never be tempted to retire a mediocre dog to stud. He may have won a number of open races but the competition is so fierce these days you have to be sure the dog will keep himself. If you charge an average fee and then take advertising into account, plus the dog's keep, you will need to average one bitch a week. And the truth is, very few stud dogs get that many.

"You have to disregard sentiment."

THE BROOD BITCH: Following years of relative obscurity the brood bitch is now widely recognised as the principal influence when it comes to producing racing greyhounds. Curtis subscribes to this theory and believes that as much as 70 per cent of the hereditary genes come from the dam's side.

"You only have to look at the progeny of the top-class brood bitches to see this is the case," said Curtis. "A bitch such as Sarahs Bunny produced brilliant pups from virtually every litter."

Her best pups include Golden Sand, winner of the 1983 Midlands Flat Championship and the Winter Trophy — the result of a September 1981 litter by Desert Pilot. A mating with Special Account produced 1986 Blue Riband winner Fearless Champ and her February 1984 litter by Ron Hardy produced the great trio of Fearless Action, Fearless Swift and Master Hardy. Their combined haul of major open race competitions was spectacular. Swift won the 1985 Truman Puppy Derby, Manchester Puppy Cup and 1986 Oxfordshire Trophy. Action was a finalist in the 1986 English Derby, and winner of the *Sporting Life* Juvenile Championship, Northern Flat Championship and Select Stakes. And Master Hardy was second in the 1986 English Derby, runner-up in the Scurry Gold Cup and winner of the Mecca Bookmakers Guineas. Hardy Man, from the same litter, broke the sprint track record at Oxford. It was no surprise when Sarahs Bunny was voted Brood Bitch of the Year in 1986.

Her last mating to Mount Keefe Star has produced the brilliant puppy Fearless Ace.

Brood bitch Ka Boom, trained during her racing career by Natalie Savva, also displayed the same ability to produce top-class pups from every litter, when she retired to the breeding paddocks under the care of Joe Cobbold.

Her two matings with the Savvas' top stud dog Westmead County were the most successful. The first whelped in April 1978 included Decoy Sovereign winner of the 1980 Scottish Derby and Decoy Boom winner of the 1981 BBC TV Trophy. Her second litter whelped in January 1980 included Special Account winner of the 1982 Scottish Derby and runner-up in the 1982 English Derby, Decoy Ranch, winner of the 1982 Silver Muzzle, Decoy Ranger winner of the 1981 Mecca Bookmakers Guineas and finalist in the 1981 Scottish Derby and 1981 Blue Riband and Westmead Gem winner of countless open races including the 1982 Carling Test. This brilliant litter earned her the Brood Bitch of the Year award in 1982.

Her third litter by Westown Adam whelped in October 1980 resulted in Decoy Dorothy, winner of the 1982 Cock O' The North and Decoy Diamond winner of the 1983 Romford Stayers Stakes.

The Savvas have had great success with their damlines. Particularly notable is the one that has extended from Hacksaw, dam of the year in 1976 to her daughter — Westmead Satin, dam of the year in 1984 through to her daughter Westmead Tania.

Among the great greyhounds Hacksaw produced was Westmead Champ from an April 1974 mating with Westmead County. Champ won two classics — the St Leger and the Gold Collar in 1976 as well as reaching the Derby final the same year.

Hacksaw's daughter Westmead Satin, who is by Westmead Lane, whelped a total of 30 pups and 20 proved to be open class. They included Harringay track recordbreaker Westmead Alva, Westmead Dena, winner of the 1984 Ike Morris GRA Stakes and Westmead Tania, finalist in the 1983 Midland Oaks – all from her April 1981 mating with Glenroe Hiker.

In March 1982 Satin whelped a litter by All Wit and this resulted in the outstanding Westmead Milos — the star member of a brilliant litter. His wins included the Northumberland Puppy Cup, the 1984 International, Sporting Life Juvenile of the Year and the Olympic. He was ante-post favourite for the 1984 Derby.

Satin's daughter Westmead Tania was mated to Derby winner Whisper Wishes and she, in turn, produced an all-winning litter which included Westmead Call, winner of the 1986 Bedfordshire Derby,

Above: Kings Comet. Dam of the all-winning litter by Pecos Jerry.

Left: Her son Copper Beeches, litter brother to Yankee Express.

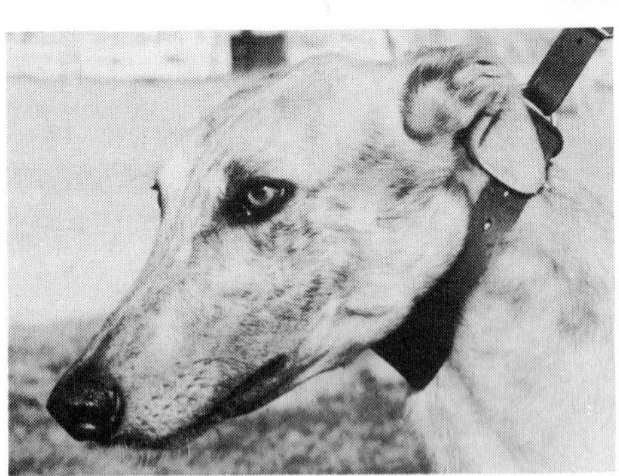

Above: Sarahs Bunny the 1979 Derby winner who has produced open racers from every litter she has whelped. Three of her most famous sons are Master Hardy (left) Fearless Swift (bottom left) and Fearless Action (below).

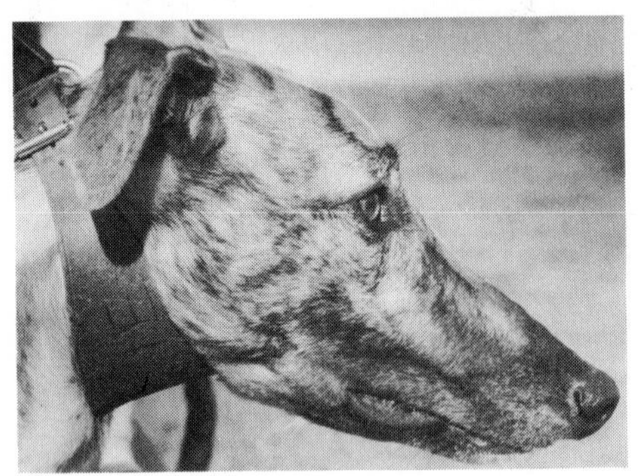

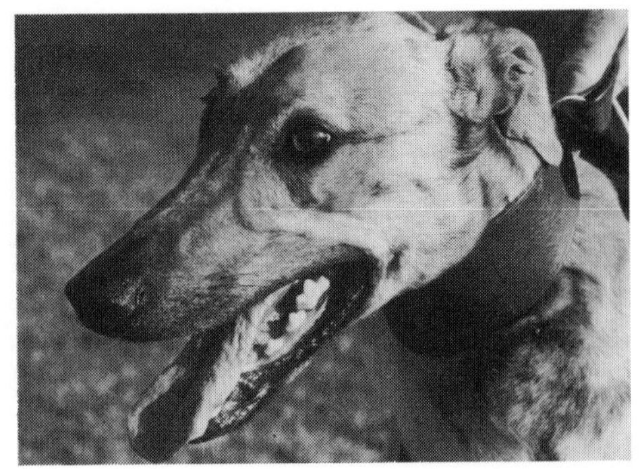

Westmead Move, winner of the 1986 Grand Prix and Gold Collar, and Olivers Wish winner of the 1986 Manchester Puppy Cup.

Curtis believes that most English breeders have got their priorities wrong. While the Irish have always kept a bitch with good bloodlines back from a litter to use specifically for breeding, the English have always put the emphasis on producing race winners.

"We are still chasing the glory," he said. "We want greyhounds to go on and on adding more and more titles to their tally — and only when there is nothing left, we will reluctantly retire them to the breeding paddocks. Then we are disappointed when they fail to live up to their reputations.

"If I had the choice of using a good-class bitch with 100 races on her card or a bitch that only had ten races — I would choose the one with ten races every time. Racing takes too much out of them.

"The ideal thing to do is to find a well-bred bitch that is 100 per cent genuine and has a bit of heart. Give her a few races and have a bit of fun out of her — and then put her by for breeding."

Jane Hicks likes to see some race form from a potential brood bitch as she believes this gives a good indication of temperament.

"I always think that if they have no form there maybe something suspect such as turning their head in a trial," she said. "Obviously if there is any hint of aggression it would be the last bitch you would want to breed with."

But it is equally important not to read too much into track performances. Breeze Valley, who proved an outstanding brood, was nearly ignored for breeding because she was no speedster.

"I honestly wondered whether I should use her," said Jane. "She had won graded races and trophy races but she was an out and out stayer and one of the worst trappers. But she was totally genuine. She had terrific guts and determination and she never stopped trying.

"She was out of a very good bitch and I felt that with an injection of early pace from a stud dog, she would be worth a try."

It was a decision Jane was not to regret. In her first litter by Knockrour Brandy, Breeze produced The Jolly Norman, finalist in the 1984 English Derby and Jondy, winner of the Fantasy Silver Sprint and runner-up in the 1983 Greyhound Breeders Forum Stakes with The Jolly Norman in third place.

And in her June 1984 litter by Yankee Express she produced an all-winning litter of eight, which included 1986 St Leger winner Lone Wolf and Breeders Forum Produce Stakes finalist She Wolf.

The one characteristic that Curtis would steer clear of in potential broods is nervousness.

"Temperament is one of the most important things you are looking for and if you get a nervous, scatter-brained bitch you get a good chance of passing that on to her progeny," he said. "There is no need to take the risk as there are plenty of bitches to choose from."

He likes to see an nice well-built bitch as a brood — not too big as this can cut down on the choice of stud dogs if you want to avoid producing enormous pups — and not too small as this can give the bitch problems when she is whelping down.

Injuries sustained on the track are not significant but Curtis warns of the danger of a hereditary weakness, such as calcium deficiency leading to weakness in the bones.

Jane Hicks discovered this with Kasama Tina — the first bitch she ever bred with.

"Tina had bad feet and she passed this weakness on," she said. "She had a brilliant puppy in her first litter called Hackney Carriage, but his feet let him down. He only raced as a puppy.

"I had a second litter from her and the same thing happened, the puppies were pretty unsound. Things would go wrong quicker, there was definitely an inherited weakness."

Curtis stresses that breeding is, at best, a high risk business.

"You can plan the perfect match of early pace with some staying ability — and there is no certainty that the pups will inherit these qualities — or certainly not in the proportions you might hope for," he said. "That is why it is so important to look back in the bloodlines so you can see what other influences might come through. But even so, luck still has its part to play."

It was Brighton racing manager Jim Layton who suggested using American sire Pecos Jerry with Jane Hicks' brood Kings Comet — and this was an instance where everything went according to plan.

The litter whelped in October 1980, which included Yankee Express, Copper Beeches, Kings Merlin and Blue Rover earned King's Comet the 1983 award for the best British bred litter.

Her guts and determination were characteristics inherited by all her pups. She had staying power too, and the fact that Yankee Express, who was famous for his early pace, continuously throws stayers, proves that Comet's influence is still making itself felt.

Kings Comet proved a great servant to Jane and was a much loved family pet before she died in 1986. But her career as a brood was by no means easy and in the end Jane was forced to retire her early as she suffered so badly during her pregnancies.

"From the moment she was in whelp, she went off her food," said Jane. "She was constantly sick and that lasted throughout her pregnancy. I used to cook her up delicacies like rabbit and chicken five times a day to try and tempt her appetite. But she could scarcely keep anything down. By the time she had whelped she looked terrible — painfully thin. But all the pups were fine and she picked up in a remarkably short time."

Kings Comet whelped four litters and the last proved the least successful.

"She was so ill during her pregnancies," said Jane. "Once you have found a good brood bitch the temptation is to keep breeding from her but you must safeguard the bitch's health and not treat her like a factory machine."

If a bitch comes into season every nine months, Jane recomends breeding with her alternately.

"Although this rarely works out for any length of time as the bitch may well miss," she said. "But if the bitch is healthy and hasn't been over-raced you can probably carry on using her until she is nine years old on this basis. If you are starting them at three to four years old this gives you a reasonable run."

Care of the brood bitch is all-important and Jane says that all too often people only start thinking about this aspect when the bitch is in whelp, rather than getting her into condition before she breaks down.

"I like to see a bitch in top condition when she comes into season," she said. "When you consider that over the next few weeks she will be carrying pups, going through the ordeal of delivery and then feeding the pups, she needs to be 100 per cent fit."

This involves getting the bitch wormed and checked over thoroughly. Jane uses a normal adult wormer — she recomends Lopatol — before the mating and then she worms the bitch again once she is in whelp using a much milder wormer such as Panacur which she uses on puppies. All vaccinations must be up to date — a recent parvo virus jab being a must. Jane is also a great believer in vaginal swab tests — a view that Curtis supports wholeheartedly.

"There's no sense in waiting nine weeks before you find out that something is wrong," he said. "It's a waste of time and money. You might think a bitch is perfectly all right — she seems well in herself. Nine times out of ten you're right. But it's not worth taking the risk. It's not good for the bitch and it's not good for the dog."

An infection can prevent a bitch coming into pup and in extreme cases it can result in malformation of the pups.

But if the swab test is found to be positive – there is no reason why the bitch should not still be mated if she is put on a course of antibiotics.

"If the infection is not severe, there is still time to get it cleared up," said Jane. "That is why the bitch should be tested the first day she breaks down. It normally takes three days to get the result, so you don't have too much time to play with."

A smear test, taken at 12 days can also be a useful indicator in working out when the bitch will be ready for mating. When the smear is mixed with a chemical it shows when the bitch should ovulate. This is a side of the business that frustrates many stud keepers for all too often a bitch is presented for a mating before she is ready.

Curtis, who supervises both Yankee Express and Ballyregan Bob at stud, has reason to lament the general lack of knowledge.

"I've had people bring a bitch along a week before she's ready," he said. "They are calculating from the first time a dog starts showing interest in the bitch. That is meaningless.

"They've got to show colour — a red discharge, not straw coloured – and then you count 12 days from then. It is best to phone the stud keeper and book the dog you want and take the bitch for the vaginal swab test on day one.

"The bitch should be ready for mating on day 12. This is a pretty reliable calculation, although maiden bitches can be a little more unpredictable."

Supervising the mating is a skilled business and the most important element is for the stud keeper to know his dog. Each stud dog varies and some need more help than others. And sometimes the bitch in uncooperative, which causes trouble for everyone.

A vet can tell if a bitch is in whelp within 26-28 days. It takes longer for a visible change to take place, although some show earlier than others.

Diet is an essential ingredient in care of the expectant mother and Jane feeds a meat meal twice daily throughout the pregnancy.

"You must feed them the best," she said. "I've heard of bitches whelping and then having no milk, which could well be attributed to poor diet."

Jane gives a mixture of raw and cooked minced beef with Vitalin which she uses in preference to biscuit or bread. If the bitch has poor digestion she cuts down on the raw meat, but the average meat intake for the day is around one pound. She also gives extra milk throughout the pregnancy and gives both vitamin and calcium supplements.

"Some people think that the extra milk is sufficient but I give extra calcium as I think this helps the pups' bone formation," she said.

The most frequent problem Jane encounters is the bitch going off her food in the early stages of pregnancy. And in this case she tempts them with any delicacy. But once they are eating normally again they should not be allowed to get too fat. For this reason she allows the bitch as much exercise as she wants. This goes against advice given by many breeders who would keep the bitch on the lead throughout the pregnancy.

"I think the bitch is a good judge of what she wants," said Jane. "Obviously you only allow them to go off the leash in a totally safe paddock which is properly fenced in.

"But most bitches enjoy a reasonable amount of exercise. It helps to keep them fit and their muscles taut. You don't want the bitch to get soft and flabby. Just remember not to force the pace. Let the bitch do as much as she wants to."

Jane prepares the whelping pen well in advance and allows the bitch to start sleeping there and getting used to it about five days before the pups are due.

"I used to let the bitches whelp in our big barn — but pups can make funny little noises and upset the other dogs, quite apart from the risk of infection. So now I use a special pen well away from the other kennels where the bitch can get plenty of peace and quiet."

Jane uses Marine Plywood for the bed and varnishes it a couple of weeks before the pups are due. She believes this is another way of cutting down on the risk of infection. She makes sure the bitch has plenty of room and avoids a drop from the bed to the floor.

"I know a lot of people worry about a bitch crushing her pups but in my experience the greatest danger is pups rolling off the bed on to a hard concrete floor."

She uses shredded paper for bedding and suspends two infra-red lamps over the bed to provide additional warmth.

"I've used hay and straw for bedding in the past," said Jane. "It sounds lovely. But when the bitch is cleaning the pups it can get caught up. And paper bedding is also much easier to burn."

The golden rule is to give the bitch what she wants and to keep her calm and contented throughout the pregnancy. If she is going away from home to whelp her litter, it is important that she gets to know the place and the person who will be attending her, so she feels relaxed and confident when the big moment comes.

CHAPTER SIX

Whelping

IN his early days as a trainer at Portsmouth, Curtis used to do a little breeding on the side with some measure of success. Yet he would be the first to admit that he is not expert and claims that he leaves this side of the business entirely in the hands of those who best know what they are doing. But as a true greyhound man, Curtis has an instinctive knowledge of what is right for the dog or bitch and his opinion has often been sought by top breeder Jane Hicks. Their relationship is based on mutual admiration and both have great respect for each other's opinions.

"I am always interested in the pups that are whelped at Jane's place," said Curtis. "I don't get directly involved — but I can't wait to go over there and see how the new pups are doing." In fact a typical day off for George is spent over at Jane Hicks' home and kennels. He takes Lily over and the hours are passed talking endlessly about dogs and puppies — a true busman's holiday. Jane's background before she went into greyhound breeding was principally with horses and then cattle.

"I've kept animals all my life," she said. "I learnt most from breeding pedigree Hereford cattle but I turned to greyhounds because they are smaller and much easier to keep than prize bulls and herds of cattle. I used to worry about my inexperience in the early days but the late Phil Rees once said to me: 'You're a stockman and you understand animals and that is all you need to know.' "

The first litter Jane bred was a bumper crop of 13 out of former racer Kasama Tina so she was plunged in at the deep end. "To be honest it was a great strain on everyone," she said. "I would always prefer to have a litter of six to eight pups. It's better for the pups and for the mother."

The pregnancy lasts for 63 days, although a couple of days early or late is by no means unusual. The majority probably tend towards the 64–65 day mark. If the bitch is up to a week late a check by a vet would be advisable. The real time to worry is if the bitch is showing signs of distress and the labour fails to get underway. "Bitches all have their own ways of showing they are ready to whelp," said Jane. "The tell-tale signs are general restlessness often accompanied by loss of appetite. I find they don't do much bed-making at this stage. They keep getting up and down off the bed, acting as if they've got stomach ache. When they start panting, you know it's imminent and when the waters go — you're away."

If the bitch continues in the preliminary stage for a couple of hours, the vet should be called. The largest pup is often born first and it could be blocking the birth canal. This will obviously cause problems for the bitch and it could also affect the other puppies. Jane thinks it is very important to have ready access to a vet so you can call on him the moment you sense there is trouble. A bitch will usually cope perfectly well on her own but Jane advises that the vet should be alerted as soon as labour starts and that you have a contact number for him over the next 24 hours.

The length of time a bitch takes to whelp can vary enormously. Jane remembers Breeze Valley starting at 7 pm one night and going on until 3 pm the next afternoon. "That was exceptional," said Jane. "It was an exhausting ordeal for her — and for me, as I always stay with them throughout the whelping. I think they should have somebody they know and trust with them the whole time. There are gaps between the arrival of the pups — they tend to come in twos and threes. It is nature's way of giving the bitch a rest and giving her a chance to clean the pups. It is very apparent when one is imminent as the bitch contracts. Never be tempted to pull one out if it seems to be taking a long time — you can do more harm than good.

"The only thing I do is when they are clear of the bitch is break the bag over their nose to start them breathing. If they gurgle a bit, tip them down to get rid of the liquid. Then let Mum get on with it. Most bitches know instinctively what to do — even if it is their first litter." The bitch will clean the pups thoroughly and her licking will stimulate them to feed. A guiding hand to help them to a teat is often useful.

There is an awful lot of mess after whelping and when Jane was supervising for the first time she took away the after-birth. "But I would never do that now," she said. "The bitch got so worried she thought I was taking the pups away. So now I let them eat it if they want to. Others don't mind if you take it away. You might not think it looks very nice, but eating the after-birth is the natural way. It is full of protein. It can give them extreme diahorrea, but that doesn't matter."

During the whelping period Jane keeps a ready supply of milk and glucose, which the bitch has access to. This is easy to digest and prevents dehydration. No bitch will actually want to eat during whelping down — no matter how long it takes.

"Breeze got through six pints of milk while she was whelping," said Jane. "It sounds like a lot — but you don't have to worry about the bitch needing to empty. She is losing so much fluid and she is under the heat of the infra-red lamps so that dehydration is more of a problem. Never attempt to get the bitch to leave the whelping pen until you are certain that all the pups have been born. Even then, she will be reluctant to go and you will need to use a collar and lead." A vet is best qualified to judge if there are any pups left. But failing that, Jane suggests leaving a three hour gap before you take the bitch out for a couple of minutes just to empty.

In Jane's experience, most bitches are very careful not to crush the pups. It is only if there is a sudden disturbance, which could upset the bitch that trouble occurs. "You do get cases when the bitch will attack her new-born pups or even eat them. I know of a bitch called Pecos Queen who had eight pups and ate four of them. The only way the others were saved was by putting a muzzle on her. What I think happened was that the owner, who was a huntsman, came back from a day's hunting to find the bitch whelping down. He looked in to see if she was all right and then went to change his clothes. As soon as he turned his back she started eating them. I think it must have been the smell of the other dogs that upset her. But she was a funny, nervous bitch. In fact, she went on to have another litter by Mathews World and was perfectly okay."

But this story backs up Jane's policy of keeping the doors firmly closed while whelping is in progress.

"I don't let anyone in — even the family — while the bitch is whelping. She needs to be with one person that she can trust with no outside interference."

As soon as the whelping is over Jane advises that the bitch is checked over by a vet. "I like them to have an antibiotic injection," she said. "This is a safeguard in case any of the after-birth is left inside which could set up an infection. Then once you are confident that all the pups are warm and feeding well, you can feel safe to leave them."

For the first three days, the bitch will be reluctant to leave her pups for any length of time. She will go out to empty and feed and then she will want to go straight back to them. "But it's amazing how quickly they get back to normal," says Jane. "After whelping they look a very funny shape, all their muscles have gone. But after three days or so they look better, they will be ready for some exercise and they will relish some time away from the pups."

Jane puts a second bed in the whelping pen for the bitch to use if she chooses. "I think it is important to give her a chance to stretch out and have a proper rest," she said. "If the bitch is in with the pups all the time there will always be one that wants to feed from her." Keeping the pups warm is important, especially if they are born in winter. Jane keeps the infra-red lamps on all the time if necessary for the first couple of weeks, and always at night.

The sign of a contented litter is one that you will hardly ever hear. If there is a lot of crying and whimpering, the most likely problem is that they are not getting enough food. Then you have to supplement. Jane has never needed to help the bitch before the two-week stage but sometimes a bitch will fail to cope with a big litter and bottle feeding will be necessary.

This is often done with a syringe which is a fairly straightforward method of feeding the pup without making too much mess. There are a variety of powdered milk formulas on the market. These should be made up to the prescribed instructions and served warm. Make sure the milk is not lumpy as this can cause indigestion. When the pups are three-weeks-old Jane uses milk formula, she finds Litter Lac the best, and adds Farex or Readybrek along with glucose or honey. To begin with, she lets the pups lick it from her fingers and then they get the idea of lapping from saucers.

"I don't rush them on to solid food," said Jane. "You're not going to beat Mum's food so you might as well leave her to feed them for as long as possible. I usually leave it for three weeks — I have even left it as long as four weeks. The most important thing is to feed the bitch enough so you can keep the production line going. Fresh water should also be available for her at all times to keep her liquid level up." Jane feeds the Farex and milk three or four times a day spreading out the meals as much as she can. Then, at four to five weeks she adds a little lean cooked mince. The pups won't want too much to begin with and it can cause more problems if they are overfed. In a week or so they will be ready to take the meat with a little well-soaked puppy meal. This should be given twice a day and the Farex and milk three times a day. Again, the more you spread out the times of the meals, the better they will do.

Another important job in the early weeks is trimming the puppies' nails. "This is sheer murder," said Jane. "But it has to be done. Their nails grow incredibly fast and they can make the mother's tummy very sore with scratching. If you allow that to continue unchecked there is a danger that she will get aggressive when she is hurt and turn on one of the pups. I use rounded edge baby scissors and trim the nails every five days."

The puppies will also need worming for roundworm and occasionally they may have hookworm. Jane uses a puppy wormer called Coopane

Above: Most bitches will know instinctively how to care for their pups.

Below: The litter of eight by Yankee Express out of Evening Moon — pictured at 13 weeks.

when the litter is two weeks old and then changes to Panacur at six weeks. This is administered by a syringe and differs from other wormers in the length of time before it takes effect. When tablets are used the worms will be excreted live within a few hours. But with Panacur it takes three to four days for the worms to emerge — but by this time they are dead, as a result of starvation. The advantage of this is that it cuts down on the risk of re-infection if the puppies have a tendency to eat their own dirt. "Puppies pick up all kinds of rubbish so I worm them every two weeks until they are six months old," said Jane. "Then they can move on to an adult wormer which does not have to be administered so frequently."

Immunising the puppies within their first 12 weeks has always been a vital part of rearing a litter. But since the purge of parvo virus has swept through the greyhound breeding industry it has achieved new realms of importance. Jane has had parvo in her kennels once and now takes every available precaution. She used to allow shooting parties to use part of her land but she has stopped this as she believes it was the source of the infection. A litter of seven pups was affected and one puppy was put down after it became unconscious. The others were on saline drips.

"The smell is unmistakable," said Jane. "The moment you walk into the kennel you know that something is very wrong and within 24 hours the transformation is amazing. The pups literally become skin and bone. They can't keep anything down. I tried to get fluid down them every two hours as the great danger is dehydration. The only fortunate thing about the whole business was the pups were 12 weeks old when they caught the virus and so they had more strength to fight with. I had had the bitch immunised when she was six weeks in whelp and that immunised the pups so their first injection failed to take effect. We were lucky to lose only one out of the seven — but I seriously wondered if they would ever make racing dogs."

In fact, Jane's fears proved groundless. The litter included 1984 English Derby finalist The Jolly Norman and prolific open race winner Jondy. But Jane suspended all breeding at her kennels for the next 10 months to make sure the virus was completely eradicated.

Now she gets the bitch immunised before the mating and the pups get their first parvo virus jab at seven weeks. This is repeated at nine weeks with the first phase of the distemper inoculation which includes protection against viral hepatitis and leptospira. The final parvo and distemper injections are given at 13 weeks.

NGRC regulations say that the puppies must have completed the first part of their inoculations before the earmarking is done at approximately 10 weeks. "This is an unpleasant but necessary task," said Jane. "It is better to get it over with at this stage when the pups don't seem to mind so much." But this is the only outside contact she allows with the pups until all their inoculations are completed and they have absolutely no contact with other dogs. There is a run attached to the whelping pen which the pups can use until they are ready to venture into the outside world. Within four weeks of the whelping, the litter must be registered with the English Greyhound Stud Book. It is registered under the sire and dam's name and the puppies are listed by sex and colour.

Jane always rears the litters that she breeds and although they are mostly sold at between 8–12 weeks she is against having pups taken away from the litter. "I don't like to see a pup reared in isolation," she said. "I have let some of my pups go in the past and they have not turned out as well as the rest of the litter. They get confidence from growing up with their litter mates and it breeds a healthy sense of competition when they feed and exercise together."

But Jane and George Curtis agree that there is absolutely no way you can pick out a potential star of a litter at the puppy stage. "I have often picked a pup for myself — and I usually pick the worst of the litter," she said. "You really can pick them out with a pin. The two best looking pups in the Pecos Jerry–Kings Comet litter were Copper Beeches and a blue brindle and white dog — who turned out to be the least promising. Yankee Express was never a particularly good looking pup and it certainly didn't do him any harm."

What every breeder hopes for, is an evenly matched litter that have enjoyed robust good health in the vital first three months of their lives. With a good foundation like this, the serious job of rearing can commence.

CHAPTER SEVEN

Rearing

GREYHOUND puppies need the space and freedom to run to their hearts' content. They are big dogs bred to chase and gallop and the start they get in life will prove vital when they get to the track. George Curtis firmly believes there is no substitute for the wide open spaces that breeders with extensive ranges can provide.

"The good dogs come from the same places time after time and there's got to be a reason for it," he said. "Of course, anyone can breed a litter in their own backyard but if you are trying to rear pups you must give them the freedom to learn to gallop. When they are growing they need everything of the best and, take it from me, you won't regret the money you spend."

The Irish have long had the monopoly in the greyhound breeding industry and their success is mostly attributed to their style of rearing. Pups are bred on farms and given the freedom to exercise from morning until night. They take the rough and tumble of running with their litter mates and the result is a tough, competitive greyhound with the stamina and build to stand up to track racing.

Jane Hicks, who has the spectacular record of getting every puppy she has bred to grade at Brighton, has an impressive set-up near Horsham in Sussex which rivals any Irish counterpart. But in fact, she has not based her ideas on the Irish style. "I have never seen any rearing in Ireland," she said. "I have kept animals all my life and I simply give the greyhounds what I think they need." She has two large fields — one of 12 acres and the other of three acres, which are used exclusively for exercising greyhounds.

"It looks enormous here," said Jane. "But the largest number of dogs I've had at one time was 25 — and some of those were very young puppies. I once did two litters very close together, but I would never do it again. I don't mind so much if I've got babies and pups at the schooling stage, but I'd rather concentrate on one litter. It's hard to compensate by taking pups out galloping if you haven't got room at home. They go so fast they might easily run on to a road or into a field of sheep. I used to take them up to the woods near here — but I lost one. I think the dog hit a tree and burst an artery in his leg. I heard him howling and fortunately he died very quickly. But I dare not take pups up there any more."

The fields at Jane's range are fenced three feet high all the way round, which is the major expense of the entire set-up. "It is vital to give them a place that is 100 per cent safe where they can gallop with no danger of hurting themselves," she said. "It is an on-going expense to keep the fields secure as we regularly have to replace the fencing when a fox or a badger burrows underneath."

The puppies are kennelled in a big barn and a small run leads to the gate of the field. They therefore have the freeddom to come and go as they please.

"I think this is the ideal set-up for greyhound pups," said Curtis. "The Irish way of rearing was always to let them run and it was the survival of the fittest. If one didn't make it, the Irishman would never lose any sleep over it. I was once over in Ireland and a farmer told me his greyhound bitch had just whelped down. I said: 'How many has she got?' And he didn't even know — he hadn't been to look. They were out in the field in a wreck of a car — it had no wheels, there was just the chassis and the bonnet and some straw — and she was in there, perfectly happy with her pups.

"When the English started breeding and rearing their own pups they would put six in a paddock with room to run for 50-60 yards. They couldn't afford the space to have just two pups in a paddock at a time. The pups would be running up the sides of the fence barking and tugging at each other. They were only playing. But it was no good when they came to the race track. The Irish pup is given the opportunity to run for half a mile at a stretch if he wants to. They may look a bit rough when they come over — but they've got the lungs, the wind and the pace because they've learned how to run. Jane Hicks can offer something along the same lines, although she also gives them special care in terms of diet. But what I like to see best when I go over there is the puppies running free and chasing the rabbits and pheasants that find their way into the fields."

Jane keeps the mother with the litter for as long as she can, as she believes the pups will learn to chase by watching her. "I take the bitch away from the pups' kennel as soon as she's had enough," she said. "But Mum often likes to go out to the field and play with her pups. If they try to start feeding from her, she'll soon tell them to cut it out."

At four months Jane starts reducing the number of meals from the five — three milk and Farex and two meat — she gives when they are tiny. The first thing to go is one of the milk-Farex feeds and by the time they are six-months-old they will just have plain milk in the mornings and then their two meat meals. "If they start losing interest in the milk I drop that too," she said. "They go back to it in the racing kennels because they only have one meat meal a day when they are there."

Jane feeds a mixture of cooked minced beef and chicken mixed with Vitalin. "I know some people use Vitalin as a complete food — but I would never do that, although I use it in preference to biscuit or bread because of the added nutrients," she said She cooks the meat right up to the time the pups are 12-months-old and only starts them on the raw if they are doing a lot of trialling work.

It is difficult to assess the exact amount each dog gets as Jane feeds in groups of twos and threes. "This helps to breed a healthy competitive instinct," she said. "I always watch them feeding so I make sure that no one is getting bullied and I can supplement if one pup is getting left out. If I have one pup that is a bit reluctant I use flat trays instead of bowls and this will give a better chance to watch the others and join in."

Jane keeps the entire litter together until they are six- or seven-months-old — sleeping and exercising together. "I only break them up when they start fighting and messing about with each other," she said. "The time to worry is if they start picking on one and you get bites that need stitching up. But on the whole it doesn't do any harm and it toughens them up. There are some dogs that will always have a nibble as they run alongside others in the paddock. But it does not mean they are going to turn their head when they are on the track — often quite the contrary."

She does not believe in mollycoddling the puppies she rears. "Our barn gets jolly cold in the winter," she said. "But I don't think that matters as long as they are kept out of draughts. The pups grow nice thick coats. I would only put jackets on them if the temperature really plummeted."

Jane aims to achieve a happy medium of getting the pups used to people, but essentially treating them as farm animals. She doesn't groom them, apart from when they are moulting, and waits until they are six-months-old before she introduces a collar and lead. "The only snag with this is if you have to take one somewhere like the vet's unexpectedly and they can prove a bit of a handful," she said. "They hate having the collar and lead put on to begin with. I used to spend ages coaxing and cajoling them. Now I find the best way is to walk a few steps in front of them and when they follow I praise them and move on to the next pup. If you do this at regular intervals it is more effective than making a big issue of it the first time.

"I don't think greyhounds are like other dogs. If you upset them, they never forget it. I treat the pups like children. They've got to have discipline and I smack them if they are naughty — biting or something like that. But I don't teach them to sit and stay or anything like that. As long as they will walk on a lead and settle in a car that's enough." The only specific treatment the pups need is regular worming. By the time they are six-months-old they can graduate to an adult wormer. Jane uses Lopatol and doses the pups every six weeks until they leave to go to the racing kennels.

Jane reckons that most puppies will have finished growing by the time they are nine-months-old, although they will muscle up and mature until they are 12-months-old. "I do think the structure of a greyhound is important," she said. "I always pay particular attention to the feet as if there is a weakness in this area it can lead to problems later on."

According to Curtis, trouble with unsound feet can result from allowing puppies to exercise on very soft ground. "I used to get puppies over from Ireland with dodgy feet because they had been allowed out for long periods in bad conditions," he said. "When the feet are forming the soft ground can have an adverse affect. Their feet will go flat and their toes will spread. For this reason some breeders like to keep puppies on hard ground or even concrete if the weather is bad for the first 10–12 weeks of their life."

Jane agrees that all greyhounds come in different shapes and sizes but there are characteristics she prefers. "I always like to see a nice depth of chest," she said. "I don't like in-breeding although I know a lot of breeders have done it with a lot of success. But I find with the outcross you get a good strong dog with straight bones, particularly in the leg. This is known as hybrid vigour and it certainly results in a healthier dog. My ideal is the 12-month-old pup who is as keen as mustard and chases everything that moves."

CHAPTER EIGHT

Schooling

GREYHOUNDS are born with the instinct to chase but the process of channelling this instinct to the demands of track racing is a skilled and specialised business. George Curtis gained most of his experience in this field when he was training at Portsmouth. The puppies sent over from Ireland were raw and unschooled. They knew nothing beyond the farm where they had been reared.

"They were completely bewildered when they arrived at the kennels," he said. "Some were in a pretty poor condition so you had to get some weight on them before you could start any serious work. But I always found it a great challenge. It was up to you to bring everything out of the dog. When people saw the improvement they thought you had done something wonderful. But it was simply that the dog had never been pushed before."

Curtis and Jane Hicks both agree that the most important maxim to bear in mind when schooling pups is not to rush. "People start schooling them at eight months and running them at private tracks and they're at least four months too early," said Curtis. "They'll have them coming out of the traps like rockets at 15 months and think they've got it made. But more often than not these pups don't train on. By the time they are two-and-a-half years old they are spent. I strongly believe that there are only so many races in a greyhound and there is only so much that you can get out of them. If you rush things at the early stages you will only be spoiling it for yourself later on."

But Curtis says there is no harm in getting a dog interested in chasing in its first 12 months. The best way to start is to put the pups behind a drag lure and see if they chase it. This can be done when they are coming up to one-year-old. Jane Hicks uses a half-gutted rabbit on a battery operated pulley. But if you don't have this facility a rabbit skin pulled on string over a 150 yard straight will do the trick. "All you are trying to do is to give them the opportunity to chase over a sustained distance," said Curtis. "They usually take to this straight-away and enjoy the competition of running against their litter mates. Again, you don't want to over-do it. Let them run behind it a couple of times, just to give them the idea."

It can also save a lot of time if the pups are introduced to a trap before they get to the schooling track. They have to cope with so many new experiences at once, it helps if this does not hold any unknown terrors. Jane bought a single handicap trap to use at her range when she had particular trouble with a pup. She took the front off and put it at the end of the run, making it the only way through into the big field.

"When the pup saw her litter mates disappearing through it, she got really worried," said Jane. "I left her for two days and she clearly didn't like the idea of going through on her own so I put her on a collar and lead and led her through. As soon as she realised there was nothing to be frightened of, she was fine and went in and out as good as gold." Jane now keeps the trap permanently in the gateway so the pups get used to walking through it right from the start.

"I would advise anyone rearing a litter to buy a trap," said Curtis. "But you can also start them off by using a cardboard box, which is open at both ends. Leave it out in the paddock and the pups will play about with it. At the same time, they will get used to walking through a confined space which will certainly help when it comes to starting them in traps." Another useful step to prepare the pups for trapping is to leave the front of the trap open and run the lure in front of it. This gives them the idea of coming out ready to chase.

When pups are reared in complete freedom, the muzzle can come as a nasty shock, so it is important to do some preliminary work. "I don't like to use the muzzle on them too young," said Curtis. "They go potty when you first put it on. I'd leave it until the pup was 12-months-old, although I might try him with a muzzle strap a couple of months before and let him run around with it. When the pup gets used to that, it makes it easier when you try to use a proper muzzle. Some dogs never get used to wearing muzzles and they are always pawing at them and trying to get them off. But the majority do get used to them. They are usually so excited when they get to the track they forget they're wearing a muzzle."

In fact, Jane Hicks operates totally on the policy that the pups will forget every other distraction once they start chasing. "I used to try to get them used to a muzzle in the field before I started schooling. But they've got nothing to distract them so they keep on worrying at it," she said. "Once they're at the schooling track and chasing, they don't worry. If you've got one that is causing problems you can make a special plea to let it run without the muzzle for its first couple of handslips."

Curtis recommends that muzzles should be fastened leaving enough room to slip two fingers underneath the throat. "I'd rather have a muzzle that's too loose than too tight," he said. "You have to find the happy medium. But you can do more harm with a muzzle that's too tight than with one that's flapping around a dog's ear. That won't make any difference to winning or losing. But if you've got one that's too tight over the nose and the dog can't open his mouth it is certainly not going to help him. I've had dogs winning with muzzles half off — and it really doesn't bother them."

Both Jane and Curtis agree that you should not expect too much from a pup when you first take him to the schooling track. "I would just let the pup have a look the first time," said Curtis. "Take him along when he's about 12-months-old and just show him what's going on. Let him look for about one hour — that's enough to see if he's keen.

"The next step is to handslip the pup. Always start them off on their own or they'll start playing with the other dogs. Then it can be a job to get them to stop doing it. In the old days I used to stand in the centre with the pup on a collar and lead and let him watch. Then when the hare came down the back straight, I'd run alongside. It doesn't take the pup long to cotton on." Curtis thinks a 100 yard handslip is enough the first time, graduating to two bends and then four bends. The best place to handslip is going into a bend, so the pups can course the hare round the bend and then have a full view of it going down the straight.

"Patience is essential," he said. "They don't all go the first time." Jane Hicks backs this up saying she isn't at all worried if a pup seems reluctant to begin with. "The most important thing at this stage is if they enjoy everything they do," she said. "If I have one that's a bit slow on the uptake, I let him watch his litter mates going round — and that usually does the trick."

Once the pup is chasing well, handslip him alongside the traps and allow him to run the full circuit. Then it is time to try him in the traps. It is easiest to start with the front open and when the pup is coming out confidently, try with it closed. The first couple of times the pup is put in a trap, he'll probably just stand there when the lid comes up. I've seen pups terrified the first time they are shut in," said Curtis. "Then they hear the bang of the trap swinging open and they walk out in a daze.

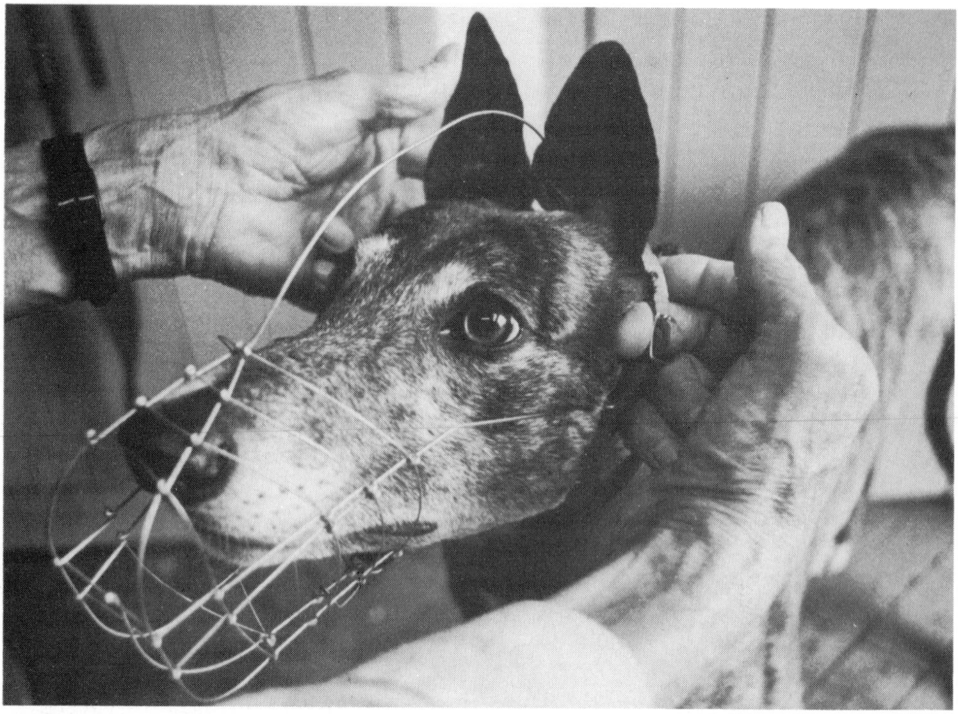

Above: The muzzle should allow enough room to slip two fingers underneath.
Below: The Curtis method of placing a greyhound in the trap.

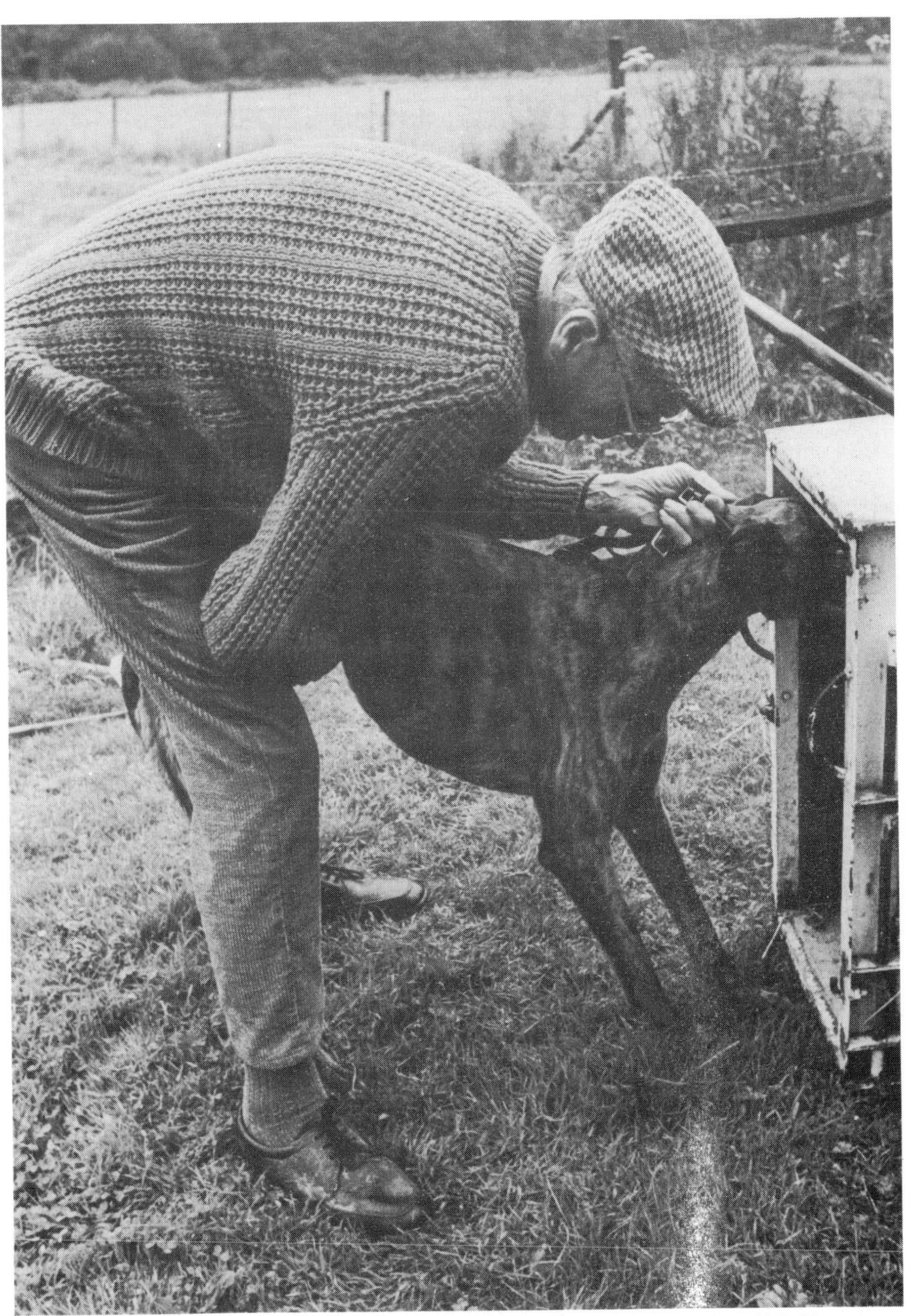

An alternative trapping method . . . but Curtis believes a difficult dog can wriggle free from this hold.

"The next time the pup will be slightly better and then all of a sudden it will click. But there is no point in taking any notice of times at this stage. The pup can lose as much as a second at the traps. When I am putting a dog in a trap I hold him between my legs and put my arm between his front legs and just ease him off the ground. This gives you a free hand to take off the collar. Some people put one hand round the neck and the other under the tummy — but if you get a difficult dog, he can wriggle out of this hold. The dog wants to be handled firmly and confidently and then he won't struggle so much. Everyone has their own technique and you learn with experience."

Curtis says it can take about six weeks to get a pup trapping reasonably well, although this time can be reduced if the dog is used to going through a trap at home. The best trappers are the dogs that really listen for the sound of the hare. "You see them standing in the trap and as they hear the hare approach, they crouch right down ready to spring out," said Curtis. "Yankee Express, who was a superb trapper, always used to crouch down and tense with concentration as the hare approached. That is something they learn for themselves. You can't teach them how to do it."

The most common obstacle to overcome is the pup that turns round in the traps. This can be fairly easily rectified at the schooling stage, although some greyhounds keep the habit throughout their racing careers. Curtis suggests getting someone else to put the dog in the trap while you stand in the front calling the dog's name or waving a rag in order to keep the dog's attention. Obviously, this method can only be tried at a schooling track. But if you get a dog that keeps turning round, Curtis has had good results with putting the dog in backwards so when he turns he is facing the right way.

Once the pup is trapping reasonably well, he can be tried in company. But Curtis warns of the danger of putting pups in together.

"I would never put two pups in at the same time," he said. "There's nothing worse than seeing them mess about all the way round. And the worst thing is to put a reluctant pup in with a couple of litter mates hoping that he will chase them and get the idea. Right from the start, you want the pup to chase the hare — not the other dogs."

He suggests putting the novice in with an older, experienced greyhound that is totally genuine. "The ideal schoolmaster is a greyhound of about five-years-old who still has a bit of early but will fade. This gives the puppy the idea of competitive racing — but you will also see if he is genuine if he goes by as the other dog slows. This has the added advantage of giving his confidence a boost at the same time.

"A lot of puppies course the hare to start with. They go wide and then cut in. You can't expect an old head on young shoulders. The most encouraging thing is if you see the puppy coming into contention down the back straight or home straight and then going by cleanly. Then you know you're on a winner. The last thing you want is the pup that gets up to the leader and then starts waiting around."

Patience and perserverance are essential and by starting the pups off at 12 months, it leaves a clear three months to work on them before they are old enough to race according to NGRC rules. In Ireland they are allowed to start racing at 13 months.

The NGRC regulations insist on three preliminary trials over a two month period in which the pup must achieve grading time at least once. Two of these trials must be run with a minimum of two other dogs.

Before official trials commence, it is important to get all the paperwork sorted out on the dog. For NGRC home-bred runners, the dog's racing name, which should contain no more than 16 letters, should be registered with the English Greyhound Stud Book before it is 12-months-old. An additional fee must be paid if the registration is made after this date. When the dog gets to the track, an official NGRC Identity Book must be issued. This book can only be issued by an NGRC racing manager or equivalent official and it contains a complete record of the dog's name, sex, colour and markings, including ear-markings. It must also include details of inoculations and the name of the licensed trainer who currently has charge of the greyhound. From that time onwards every official trial and race will be entered in the Identity Book. The owner's name must also be registered with the NGRC.

Curtis warns that it can be a gradual process guiding the pup through its initial trials.

"Some take to the game naturally and are ready to grade by the time they are 15-months-old," he said. "Others are more backward — particularly the bigger dogs. But you can ruin a good dog by rushing it."

Most puppies will run very green on their first few outings which can pose problems when it comes to seeding. More often than not, this is a matter of trial and error and after the first few races the pup will have decided on a definite course. When you are trying to seed a puppy, Curtis suggests the best place to stand is behind the traps or at the first bend so you either watch the dog coming towards you or from behind. "Use your commonsense and try to follow the pup's inclination," said Curtis. "Start him off in the middle and see which side he favours. Most will show a distinct preference. If this does not work out, try them back in the middle again."

This sounds straightforward. But Curtis is the first to admit that mistakes can be made. "I started Ballyregan Bob as a railer," he said. "I saw him trial at Brighton and he ran on the inside and won by seven lengths. I thought it was a brilliant performance and we made him a railer. But I was wrong. The more he ran, the worse he was going. I took him to Wimbledon and he ran straight off the track and I thought: 'Well, he's no dead railer.' At Brighton, when he got headed he would pull up and move out. After a few times I thought that he would get himself into trouble so I made him a wide runner."

There are few dogs who change their style of running and when you get a greyhound such as Walstone who was seeded wide in the 1985 English Derby and came back as a railer for the 1986 classic, it is the trainer who has made a mistake. "You can believe what you are seeing — but dogs can make fools of you," said Curtis.

He has always been an advocate of seeding and was one of the protesters when it was banned from the 1983 Derby. "I have always believed that seeding existed for the safety of the greyhounds," he said. "I ended up with Copper Beeches running from trap one and he was an outside runner — and to me that was an unnecessary risk. But White City was such a big galloping track, you could get away with it to some extent. The dogs had a chance to sort themselves out. When the Derby moved to Wimbledon they had to have seeding. It's a hard enough track to run in the first place. If they didn't have seeding there would be chaos."

But he agrees that the rule has been open to abuse. "I think a trainer should make his dog a wide runner or a railer and the dog should run from that position for his next six races," he said. "That would stop all the business of chopping and changing every week."

There are genuine middle of the track runners and Jim Layton, racing manager at Brighton puts these dogs in traps three or four. "But it is no real solution as no one wants to be in the middle all the time," said Curtis. If there is a genuine disagreement as to where the dog should run from, such as the row that erupted over Murlens Slippy in the 1986 Derby, Curtis believes the racing manager should have the last say. "Otherwise you've got the owner, the trainer and the Press all arguing about it," he said. "Someone must take the decision — but the trainer should always be given a fair hearing. If, in his honest opinion, he thinks the dog is either a wide runner or a railer, he should have the chance to prove it."

Even when the question of seeding has been sorted out, you should not expect anything spectacular time-wise from a puppy in its first few races. "They have so much to get used to," said Curtis. "They are running against four or five other dogs in front of a crowd with the added distractions of the noise and the lights."

For this reason, he keeps puppies on a basic diet while they are trialling and for their first couple of races. "You are trying to build the dog up gradually and give yourself something to work on. I keep the protein down for trial dogs. I feed something like minced chicken.

Then when they're ready to start in earnest, I change to a high protein diet introducing raw meat."

Curtis is also a great believer in cleaning a dog out. Before he changes the diet he gives the dog a lump of soda, first giving a pint of milk and water. When the dog has bought the bile up, he gives a tablespoon of milk of magnesia. "If you clean them out top and bottom and put good grub into them they're bound to improve," he said.

He also steps up the amount of exercise he gives the pups, introducing a couple of gallops a week. "But don't expect miracles," said Curtis. "A puppy is unlikely to come out and start doing fantastic times. What you have to bear in mind is that whatever times the pup has done in its first half dozen schooling trials, in six months he will be doing a second faster. Some may do it sooner. But there is no point in rushing. Let the dog race once a week. Hopefully you will start off in the lowest grade and you can gradually work your way up."

Curtis recommends that all puppies are confined to four bends in their first few months at the track. "I would wait until a bitch was 22 months old and a dog was two-years-old before I tried them over the longer trip," he said.

"When you're trying to judge a greyhound's best distance, watch him to the trip. You can see a dog beaten 2–3 lengths on the line and then he is ahead by the pick-up. He is putting in his best work from the last bend. Then I say: 'That one will do us for the distance next year.' You get experience by watching them over the years. Some people think that when a dog comes from behind, works his way through the field and then gets up and wins that he should go over the longer trip. But if he isn't any further ahead at the pick-up, this is not true, for the dog will already have done his best work.

"The ones I earmark for the distance are those that ping out of the box, drop back after 30 yards and tail the field. Then when they get to the third or fourth bend they start to make a move. They may leave it too late – but watch them to the trip and see if they are ahead. My favourite tracks to spot stayers are Walthamstow or Wembley when they run them up the back straight before the trip so you can get a really good idea of the dog's ability to stay."

A greyhound must be fully mature before a trainer decides whether he has the makings of a marathon runner. "These are usually the dogs with no early pace," said Curtis. "Some may come out of boxes okay and may run all right for the first 30 yards but they've got no middle pace. They drop back and then up the home straight they start to run. You have to take it one step at a time. You can see a dog with a flying finish over 600 yards but you don't know if he can reproduce it over 700 yards. And it is not until they run 700 yards that you can see if they have the makings of an 800 yards runner."

The best marathon runner Curtis trained was undoubtedly Sandy Lane, who notched up a formidable series of wins, including the 1983 BBC TV Trophy. "The owner, Peter Carpenter, bought her for £1,000 and I said straightaway that she wouldn't be any good over 500 yards – but when she graduated to 700 yards she would be different. She wasn't two-years-old then. When she was 22 months we put her over the distance and all of a sudden she started performing.

"The thing you should always remember with stayers and marathon dogs in particular is they are not going faster at the finish, it is the other dogs that are fading. I've only known one dog in my life who went faster and that was Scurlogue Champ. I've seen him 15 lengths behind up the back straight and still come through to win. You will never see another dog like that. He did great things for the sport and he will be remembered like Mick The Miller."

Curtis maintains that it is a myth that all hurdlers are dodgy. He has trained two Grand National winners – Sir Winston, who won the classic in 1983, and Kilcoe Foxy who triumphed the following year, as well as Spiral Sonny who notched up 2 wins over the sticks. "The dog I would choose as a hurdler would be a fair sort of greyhound, who never looked like doing anything wonderful," he said. "They are on the verge – but they are two to four lengths behind the good dogs. You think you are always going to be unlucky with a dog like that. But if he jumps, he could be the best in the country.

"Sir Winston was as straight as a die. He was a good little dog but he just lacked that bit of class. We tried him over hurdles and he was a natural. He jumped beautiful and low. He went on to do the track record at Brighton clocking 30.47 for the 515m. There was not much to choose between him and Kilcoe Foxy, although we knew that Foxy was a bit iffy from the start. The first time he went over hurdles he made a mess of it – but when he got the hang of it there was no stopping him."

The ideal hurdler is the fearless type who jumps clean and straight, and according to Curtis, most have the ability right from the start. "Most will take to it naturally," he said. "Some are a bit reluctant to begin with, and I wouldn't persevere with one that isn't keen and is jumping badly."

The first step is to take the dog — on a collar and lead over some easy obstacles. Curtis uses a couple of bales of straw covered in plastic sheeting. "The dogs who love to jump from the word go are the ones to keep your eye on," he said. "When they have got the idea, graduate to a hurdle and hand-slip them a couple of times.

"I don't like to see a dog jumping too high and swerving — that means trouble. Some come out like a bull at a gate and jump straight through. But that doesn't matter if they are keeping low. As long as they don't make too many mistakes, you've got the makings of a good little hurdler. If the dog is progressing well, the next step is to let him come out of the trap and clear a couple of hurdles. Then put him round the four bends. Don't worry if they check the first time they go round. What you want to see is low, fluid jumping."

The big advantage of hurdlers is, barring injury, they can often keep going longer than the average runner. "We've got one that is six-years-old and still winning races," said Curtis.

Obviously not every pup that is reared and schooled turns out to be a world-beater — far from it. Trainer Paddy Milligan reckoned that if a breeder got a third of each litter going, he would be doing well.

"If I had heard that when I was starting in the breeding business, I would never have got involved," said Jane. "I think that is a very depressing estimate when you are looking in terms of £1,000 to get a pup on the track." Jane charges a weekly rearing fee of £16 per pup. This is slightly higher than average — but there is no doubt that her pups get the very best food. And her results speak for themselves. She has defied Paddy Milligan's forecast with a vengeance and every puppy she has reared has graded at Brighton.

"My aim is to get the pups up to grading standard," she said. "If you end up with an open class dog, that is a bonus."

Said Curtis "We can't all be like Jane Hicks when it comes to rearing and schooling. But if you have the facilities, the time and the patience, there is no reason why you shouldn't end up with your fair share of winners."

CHAPTER NINE

Diet

GOOD food is of prime importance to the racing animal. Greyhounds are expected to race at least once a week, taking on fast and determined rivals and manoeuvring round the complexities of a track circuit. Compared with racehorses, the demands on their strength and stamina are enormous — and for this reason they need the very best nutrition. "Greyhounds are remarkably consistent animals," said George Curtis. "They can run again and again and produce near identical times. If a racehorse lost a second, no one would even mention it. If a greyhound lost or gained anywhere near that much, there would be a Stewards Inquiry."

Consistency has always been the hallmark of Curtis's training, along with the ability to keep a dog racing at its best over two or three seasons. He attributes his success in this area largely to the food he gives his racing dogs. "Right from the beginning when I worked for Bill Peters at Portsmouth, I was always taught to feed the best," he said. "There is no substitute for good grub — and it is a totally false economy to make do with second best."

Surprisingly, all his dogs get the same diet — whether they are competing in the first race at Brighton or in the final of a classic. "If you are giving a dog a well balanced diet he won't need a lot of extras, unless you are looking for something very special from him," said Curtis. The only major difference is that his open racers are given a daily dose of Orovite 7. This is an all-in-one vitamin supplement which is designed for humans.

"It is used as a tonic for humans and I have had great success using it with dogs," he said. "I have used Metatone which is an ascorbic acid with extra Vitamin C. But Orovite 7 includes all seven vitamins and when we tried it on our dogs they started running really well. I think its major asset is that it helps the open racer to keep going over a long campaign. It is expensive and I would only use it on top-class dogs. It simply isn't worth using it on graders when you know the expense is not going to pay dividends. You can't hope that by giving graders a few extra vitamins, they are going to start flying. If they are getting a good basic diet with fresh meat and vegetables they should be getting all the nutrition they need."

At the Brighton kennels breakfast is fed at about 9 am after the initial cleaning out has been completed. Each dog gets around one pint of milk which is made up from a powdered formula. "We use the type that is fed to calves," said Curtis. "It has all the nutrients and saves the problem of disposing of empty milk bottles." He adds cornflakes, brown bread and an egg to this. "If you are watching the pennies, dry out the brown bread in the oven and use that instead of cornflakes," he said.

A morsel of meat is given to any dog that needs building up in weight and glucose or honey is given to all the racing dogs. "We give a couple of tablespoons of glucose," said Curtis. "It helps to replace the energy that is lost during racing. Honey is more expensive. We would only use a teaspoon of that. But it is very good for the throat, particularly if the dog is a bit husky."

The main meal of the day is fed at about 1.30 pm. This is done more to suit the staff's hours than for any other reason. Many trainers prefer to feed later in the afternoon. But preparations begin immediately after breakfast. The Brighton kennels have a separate cookhouse at the end of each range — and although the meat is provided for each trainer according to the number of dogs in his kennel, it is up to the trainer to decide what amount and what proportion to feed.

Each dog is fed a pound to a pound and a half of meat, depending on its size. This is a mixture of raw meat — usually cow's meat or horsemeat — and cooked meat. "We buy frozen minced chicken and use it as the basis for soup," said Curtis. "We boil up the meat, along with some bones to make a stock. I add cabbage, onion and carrots, first putting them through the mincer. I put a handful of vegetables in early. But the majority we use raw.

"We use two big handfuls of Dog Diet or rusk per dog and soak it first. Then we add the soup, which is served warm, a couple of tablespoons of raw vegetables and then the meat, the raw making up about half of the meat intake." There is a big range of dried food and complete diets on the market — but Curtis remains largely unimpressed. "I have been lucky enough to have some of the best dogs in the country in my kennel and I believe they should be fed the best," he said. "To me, there is no substitute for fresh meat." Curtis ensures each meal is fed very moist. At least a pint of gravy stock makes up the total weight. "A greyhound always gulps his food and if there is dry biscuit, he'll tend to cough it back," he said.

To cut down on potential trouble, the dogs are fed separately, one in the kennel and the other on a lead outside. "Greyhounds should always be supervised while feeding," said Curtis. "Food is the first thing they will fight over." He reckons that each feed weighs three pounds — going up to three and a half pounds for the big dogs, although he doesn't weigh them individually. In fact, it is an education to watch Curtis at work dishing out the dogs' feeds. He doesn't use a list — but remembers each dog in the right order going right through the kennel. When you consider this includes racers, resters, injured and even stud dog Ballyregan Bob, each with their own requirements, it is quite a feat of memory.

But Curtis recommends the novice trainer should weigh out each individual feed to begin with. "A pair of kitchen scales is perfectly adequate for the job," he said. "You learn to judge it with experience but when you are trying to keep a dog's weight stable it is important to know exactly how much food you are giving. If you are feeding the same food every day and keeping to the same routine, the dog's weight won't vary a lot. And no one is going to worry about a couple of spots either way.

"To find the right racing weight it is easier to start off underweight and gradually work your way up. Watch how the dog is running and the times he is doing. Greyhounds are incredibly consistent and you can see the improvement. When the dog puts in a really good performance and does his best time — that is his racing weight. It can vary a couple of spots either way — but that is the level to aim for."

Curtis always takes individuals into account and believes that some dogs race better heavier and some will never put weight on. "It is easy to get obsessed with weight," he said. "But if the dog is performing well, that should be your yardstick. We weigh our dogs before breakfast the day prior to racing and on race days. This gives us the opportunity to make the necessary adjustments. If one is up in weight we can cut down on the meat or take a handful of rusk out of the main meal."

But all trainers vary. Gunner Smith weighs his dogs twice on race days and Gordon Hodson never weighs his at all. "He does it all using his own judgement," said Curtis. "And he is rarely wrong when he gets his dogs to the track. But it can be a problem for trainers who do not have access to scales. It means you don't know until you reach the track how much the dog weighs. You can weigh yourself and then pick the dog up. But that is obviously fraught with problems.

"The other method is to use skilliers and a harness. If you don't lift the dog too far off the ground you can get a fairly accurate reading."

Curtis says he finds it remarkable how quickly a dog's weight can be reduced. "I've had one that was 14 spots up the day before he was due to race. He was a tall, skinny dog and we had been trying to put weight on him for ages. In fact, we had done nothing different but his weight suddenly shot up. But on the night he was only 7 spots up because we had a chance to adjust his feed. You also have to take into account the dogs who retain water. If I weigh one and he is well up, I always take him down to the paddock again and give him a chance to empty. Sometimes they have a tightened muscle and they can't get rid of their water straightaway. It may take a couple of hours, but when you weigh them again, they are often all right."

Trainers have different opinions on how much weight an individual greyhound should carry and some consistently run their dogs heavier than others. "I don't like a dog to be too thin," said Curtis. "I like a fair back on him. The muscle should cover the bone. If you've got a sprinter you're looking for power and you want big back legs and a strong back. For distance runners you want them a bit leaner."

At Brighton the greyhounds are weighed after racing — and this can be useful if a dog has lost too much weight through dehydration. The vet is informed if any dog has lost over 2 lb in weight. "It is amazing how much some dogs can loose," said Curtis. "I remember Miss Taft ran against Spectre in the 1967 BBC TV Trophy at Brighton. She ran a blinder. After the race she was 3½ lb down in weight. In a case like that you have to get the liquid back in them without delay."

On race days Curtis feeds the same breakfast and cuts down drastically on the midday meal. "The racers have a good breakfast, the lunch is just to stay their appetite," he said. "If you missed the meal altogether they would get so disappointed, particularly if they know other dogs in the kennel are being fed. It is better to give them a little rather than let them fret. And as soon as they get their reduced rations, they know they are going racing."

Curtis gives each dog just a few morsels of raw meat in gravy with two tablespoons of glucose. The meat content weighs no more than a couple of ounces. After the meal the dogs are kept on a lead when they go out to empty in the paddock. "This is to guard against accidents and to make sure they don't pick anything up in the paddock," said Curtis. "Dogs will always pick up any rubbish that is lying around. It is no good for the dogs and it could affect their weight. If you want to be on the safe side, put a box muzzle on the dog as well."

The meals are made up for racing dogs at 1.30 pm and kept for them until they get back from the track. By the time they have travelled back from Brighton, this usually allows a two hour gap after they have finished racing. Curtis recommends a minimum gap of one hour. "You have to be careful leaving the food in the summer," he said. "It should always be covered and kept in a cool place. If it is very hot, a fresh batch will have to be made up.

"The meal is very much what they would get for their normal midday feed. At the racing kennel we wash their feet and then give them about half a pint of milk — some prefer water. I don't like them to drink too much at this stage, but I always leave water in their kennel overnight after they have been racing." Curtis doesn't believe in leaving water in kennels overnight as a rule, although fresh water is always available in the paddock.

"The dogs get so much liquid in their feed that they don't need a lot of extra water on a normal day," he said. "I leave water in the paddocks but in the winter they rarely touch it. In the summer it's a different matter. The dogs dry themselves out and drink a lot after they've been running in the paddock."

When Curtis goes open racing, he follows exactly the same routine as when he is running dogs at Brighton. "We don't feed the dogs until we get back home," he said. "If we are going as far away as Birmingham, I would give the dog a pint of milk after racing. And if I had to travel back from Manchester or Newcastle, I would take half a bowl of meat for the dog to have with the milk."

The golden rule for resting dogs is to knock out the raw meat from the diet. "We don't feed any red meat and we make up the weight with cooked chicken," said Curtis. "We put them back on the racing diet after they've been through their trials and had a couple of races. That gives you something in hand when it comes to looking for improvement."

Bitches returning from seasonal rest can pose a problem with being overweight. This is often because they are still carrying milk. Each bitch varies, but as a general rule most will come into milk about eight weeks after the start of their season. They are in milk between the eighth and tenth week and are ready to trial back from ten weeks and race again at twelve weeks. Some bitches scarcely show any milk, others struggle to get rid of it and go on until the fourteenth week.

"You have to get the milk moving or they will run sour," said Curtis. "Most overweight dogs will lose very quickly once they are on a reduced diet and the exercise is stepped up, but it takes time with these bitches. You can't over-do them and you certainly can't race them. Exercise is no real solution as if the bitch is not feeling right in herself she won't be bothered with running about."

Curtis suggests the bitch is kept on the basic diet until the fourteenth week and then the protein is stepped up to the proper racing diet. If the milk fails to dry up he suggests a tablespoon of milk of magnesia. "It cleans the bitch out and hopefully after a couple of doses she will be clear," he said. He is a great believer in keeping his racing dogs cleaned out. Open race dogs are dosed every week to 10 days with a tablespoon of milk of magnesia and the same treatment is given to the graders once a month. "Some dogs are okay, but others make a lot of bile and it is best to be rid of this," he said.

Greyhounds like routine and Curtis thinks consistent performances are produced by dogs who are kept in a stable environment with a stable diet. "Of course you can vary it from time to time with cooked fish or tripe instead of the cooked chicken," he said. "Sometimes a change can do them good.

"I remember making up the feeds and the gravy came out really strong. I don't know what I did. The next morning the kennels were in a terrible mess — and it was a race day. I thought we would be in dead trouble but that night we had four winners and Yankees Shadow won by 11 lengths. I think the clean-out did them all good."

Every trainer has his own theories on feeding and the Curtis diet might not turn every greyhound into a winner. But the experience accumulated in over 43 years as a trainer counts for a lot and results speak for themselves. "I would certainly say that feeding is the single most important job of a trainer," said Curtis. "If you don't get that right, you can't hope for success."

CHAPTER TEN

Exercise

PROFESSIONAL trainers are often the envy of the small-time owner-trainers because they have the best facilities at their disposal. But George Curtis maintains that anyone can take on the big boys — and win — if they are prepared to put in the necessary hard work. "If you are looking after half a dozen dogs, you must have the advantage over the trainer that has 60 to 70 greyhounds in his care," he said. "But you need to be dedicated."

When Curtis started to train greyhounds the top priority was exercise. All greyhounds were road-walked for a minimum of one and a half hours per day — and this was often supplemented by gallops. "But these days when greyhounds are running twice a week that amount of exercise simply isn't necessary," he said. "They go a long way towards keeping themselves fit."

As a result Curtis has had to adapt his training methods to suit the changed circumstances.

"When I first arrived at Brighton I was determined to stick to my own methods," he said. "I had the kennel staff trudging up and down the road. We all worked really hard. Then I used to see Gunner Smith whistling his dogs up and down the paddock — he never took them out at all. And on race nights his dogs would be flying. Eventually I was forced to admit that I was on the wrong track."

Curtis gave up road-walking his greyhounds and has subsequently relied entirely on the kennel paddocks for exercise.

"It makes life much easier," he said. "But to me the real art of training was lost when the amount of racing was stepped up to such an extent that you had to cut down on exercise. Instead of working out what each dog needs, the emphasis is to keep them fresh enough to race twice a week."

There are two paddocks attached to the range — measuring about 120 yards in length and 100 yards across. "We paddock our dogs as much as possible," said Curtis. "From first thing in the morning until we go home at night it is a constant procession of getting dogs in and out."

The first job of the morning at Brighton is to take the racing dogs out for a 20 minute walk round the gallop on leads. "We take four dogs per person and walk at a brisk pace, giving them the chance to empty," said Curtis. "Then as soon as we have fed breakfast the dogs are let out two at a time to run in the paddocks. Each dog varies as to how much he will exercise when he is in the paddock. They will do as much as they want to. Usually they have an initial burst of energy and then quieten down. But some, like Ballyregan Bob, just can't get enough exercise. He tears up and down, getting the bitch he is in with to chase him until they are both exhausted.

"Of course you can get lazy dogs. But most of ours shoot out of the kennel and can't wait to get to the paddock." Curtis aims to get his dogs in the paddocks five or six times a day for spells of about 10 minutes. "No dog likes being stuck in a kennel all day and this gives them the chance to enjoy a bit of freedom when they can run and chase," he said. "You have to be a bit careful in the summer when it's hot as they can easily get over-heated and distressed."

Fresh water is kept in the paddocks at all times and they are cleared up regularly to keep them as clean as possible. "With the number of dogs we have, the paddocks get used and used," he said. "So we do all we can to ensure that rubbish is not left lying around."

If you are keeping a couple of greyhounds at home, the space in an average size garden is sufficient for letting out purposes. Obviously you have to make sure the area is well fenced and 100 per cent secure. "Most people in this position are going out to work so you have to tailor the demands of the greyhound with the amount of time you have available," said Curtis. "I would suggest getting up early and giving the dog a brisk half hour's walk. If you keep up a sharp pace you can cover two to three miles in that time.

"Unless you live in the country, this will be road-walking exercise. This is perfectly okay as long as you choose a relatively quiet route without too much traffic and where you are not going to get into trouble with dogs fouling the pavement. We used to road-walk our dogs but even on a country road we found it was getting too difficult. If there is no pavement, cars roar past and you get dogs jumping out of their skins."

But there is a school of thought that positively favours road-walking as a method of hardening a dog up and keeping its feet in trim. "I think this really only applies to coursing dogs and possibly marathon dogs

At Brighton road-walking has been replaced with exercise in the paddocks. But on race days the dogs are given a brisk 20 minute walk around the gallop. Experienced handlers take four greyhounds at a time.

who need to build up their stamina," said Curtis. "But Yankees Shadow, who built up a winning sequence of 20 from 21 races, was never road-walked in her entire racing career. Road-walking does keep the nails short so if you are not doing any, you should make sure the nails are filed regularly."

Obviously the greyhound kept at home will have to be let out to empty in the middle of the day. But serious exercise can wait until the evening and Curtis suggests repeating the morning routine of a 30 to 40 minute walk. "If a greyhound is being kept at racing fitness, this daily quota should be supplemented by a couple of gallops a week," he said.

At Brighton there is an enclosed gallop which is about 240 yards long. But the dogs get so much racing it is mainly used for bringing resting and injured dogs back to fitness. "We also use it for open racers when there is a gap between the rounds of a competition and we are trying to keep them tuned up," said Curtis. In fact, life in the kennels is so hectic, this is often a job that Curtis and Bill Masters take on in their lunch hour.

"Ideally, you want a straight of about 300 yards so there is sufficient distance for the dog to start up and slow down," said Curtis. "That means they'll be hard galloping for about 200 yards. If the dog wants to go up and back — let him do it."

For trainers who do not have an enclosed gallop at their disposal, Curtis suggests going to the local football ground and using the land that lies alongside the pitch. "That is what we used to do at Portsmouth and we certainly got results," he said. "The advantage of this type of land is that it is flat and straight and usually well away from roads."

Curtis warns against galloping a dog on an uneven surface or on muddy water-logged ground. "But the worst danger is frozen ground," he said. "If it is frozen rock solid, you're better off not letting the dog out at all. I'm not talking about a superficial ground frost, that is no problem if the area is well grassed. But a dog can sustain an injury in no time on deeply frozen ground.

"It is best to go to a gallop with someone else and call the dog up from one end to the other. Remember, you are on public land so the dogs should be kept muzzled. Nine times out of ten it is unneceesary but if a stray dog comes up and picks a fight, you are liable."

Every greyhound has its own particular needs and Curtis is a great believer in adapting routine to suit the individual. "The worst thing is to rush it," he said. "Take it steady and find your way. You are in the best position to judge when you see how the dog is reacting to the work you give him. But you must judge each dog as you find him. You can tell if you're over-doing it as soon as you open the kennel door. If, instead of jumping out at you, the dog is yawning and stretching as though he's a bit stiff, you should cut down on the exercise until he starts bouncing again.

"A change can also help. There is always a good reason for a dog losing his sparkle so there is no sense in continuing regardless with the same routine. If you have been giving him a lot of road-walking, change your routine or give him the chance to run in a field." When a greyhound is racing once a week — say on a Saturday — Curtis suggests giving the dog a couple of gallops at the beginning of the week and then keeping to the two half-hour walks per day until the Thursday.

"Then you should start tapering off the exercise," he said. "Let the dog take it easy on the Friday with plenty of massaging — particularly if you've got a sprinter. If you're running 400–500 yards you are more concerned with stamina, so you can continue to exercise him the day before.

"On the race day you should keep the dog as fresh as possible. I would suggest giving him a couple of miles road-walking before breakfast, keeping at a steady pace. Then I would lay him up until mid-morning when I would give him a thorough massage. At lunchtime he should be fed his restricted rations and given a chance to empty — and that should be it until he gets to the track.

"The golden rule is to ease up with the sprinter the day before the race so he can preserve his energy and to give the long distance dog a bit more leeway. I would never be frightened of letting long distance runners off the lead on the morning of a race day. They will just do as much as they want to and this helps to loosen them up. When they get to the track, they seem to start running that little bit earlier."

But Curtis has never been afraid of breaking rules to suit the individual. Yankee Express, the greatest sprinter he trained, was allowed down the gallop on the morning of a race. "We wouldn't give him a serious gallop," said Curtis. "We just gave him the chance to scamper around a bit. He loved to stretch his legs — and that was what suited him best." And no one would dispute that Curtis got the very best from his legendary triple classic winner. "Trust your own judgement and give each dog what he wants," he said. "But I guarantee that if you are giving two half-hour walks morning and night, two gallops a week and feeding the best food, you will be training as well as anybody."

CHAPTER ELEVEN

Grooming and Massage

GREYHOUND racing is an expensive business for the professional trainer and it can prove a very costly hobby for the amateur. For once you have racing dogs in your kennel, the question is what equipment do you need? Faced with a baffling array of so-called essentials, it is far from easy to decide what is strictly necessary.

But Curtis, with typical commonsense, puts far more emphasis on the time you spend with each dog than on the equipment you use. "I love to work on a dog and get him looking immaculate," said Curtis. "I have always been a great believer in spending time grooming and massaging. In a big range, you have to cut corners but if you only have a couple of dogs you can really get them looking their best." He also advises working out a kennel routine and sticking to it. "The dogs like a routine — and more importantly, it helps to increase efficiency," he said. "All the jobs get done and if you have to go away, it is easy for someone else to substitute for you."

The first job of the day is to let the dogs out to empty and then Curtis suggests taking them for their first half-hour walk. "I would use walking out coats for road-work in the winter," he said. "But we scarcely ever use them in the paddocks. The dogs soon warm themselves up when they are running around. Good food also helps to keep a dog warm and ours get a good start with breakfast, which we always serve warm. The only time I would use a coat is on an injured dog whose movement is restricted."

The kennels at Brighton are centrally heated so the dogs do not need to wear coats when they are inside. "Paper bedding keeps a dog pretty warm. It is only in the worst of the weather that you would need to coat a dog if there is no other form of heating," said Curtis. But he strongly advises putting coats on greyhounds in transit in the winter, unless there is an efficient heater in the car. And once at the track the dog will need to wear a coat in the kennel.

"It can get very cold in racing kennels and the dog has no way of keeping himself warm," he said. "On really cold nights I would put two jackets on a dog and when allowed, I would take a blanket for the dog to lie on. You would not expect an athlete to come out and run his best if he had been shivering with cold and the same is true of a greyhound."

Once the dog is in his racing jacket, Curtis puts the walking out coat on again for the parade. It comes off just before the dog goes in the traps. He considers waterproof macs as non-essential items, except for parading purposes.

"We don't have anything like enough for every dog in the range," he said. "We have about a dozen which we use on race nights if it is pouring with rain. But we always rub the dogs down if they have got wet when they've been out in the paddocks. I would never bother with puppies. They will sit out in the rain or snow and be quite happy. They are used to it and it's all part of the hardening up process. But racing dogs get soft, particularly if they are kept in heated kennels. They'll be miserable if they are wet through.

"If it's really bad, don't let them out. We put a bale of straw at the end of the range and let the dogs relieve themselves there until it eases up. And if we can't let them out during the day, I come back in the evening to let them out."

Curtis grooms and massages his dogs every day. "The job takes as long as you have got," he said. "Obviously we spend longer on the dogs that are racing that day. But we probably average 10-15 minutes per dog.

"A racing greyhound's feet are of prime importance and the first job is to wash them thoroughly. We use a solution of water and Pevidine, which is a mild antiseptic wash used by surgeons. We use a nailbrush and scrub until the dirt is removed from the quicks. This is very important as the dog will pick up dirt and mud when he is exercising and this can set up an infection if it is left in the quicks.

The nails are inspected every day. They are filed twice a week and cut with clippers once a fortnight, if necessary. "I prefer to use a file and keep the nails short at all times," said Curtis. "I would certainly suggest a file for the novice as it is far easier to make mistakes with nail cutters." The aim is to cut to the bottom of the quick. This presents no problem on white nails as the quick will be clearly visible. But is can be a nightmare on black nails. For if you cut the quick, it will bleed.

"The trick is to look behind the nail and find the hollow and this locates the quick," said Curtis. "Then trim just below the hollow. Most dogs are pretty good about having their nails done. We have some which are complete babies like Leger winner Lone Wolf, who starts crying as soon as he sees a pair of nail clippers. But if in doubt, muzzle the dog. He might nip, just out of panic."

Ears are checked every day and are cleaned regularly with cotton wool. Curtis suggests using a solution made up of a tablespoon of peroxide or TCP in about half a pint of warm water.

The same mix is used for cleaning teeth, which also forms part of the daily routine. "We use an ordinary toothbrush and just give the teeth a good scrub," he said. "If they are particularly bad I use a scaler to scrape away the discolouration. Again, most dogs are perfectly docile when you do this. But if we get a bad one, I would give him a bone instead."

Giving a dog a marrow bone to chew on is often a preferred method of keeping teeth clean. But this is totally impractical in a big range. "You can't simply give each pair of greyhounds a couple of bones in their kennel," said Curtis. "In no time they would be taking lumps out of each other. You have to have a special bone kennel and let a dog in there for a couple of hours on his own.

"When I give a marrow bone, I cook it first and then the dog will clean his teeth as he tries to get to the jelly. But you can't have a racing dog full of bone and marrow. As soon as he's finished I dose him with a tablespoon of liquid paraffin or milk of magnesia to clear him out. Obviously you can only do this when the dog has a gap between races and I would only do it every couple of weeks.

"And I would always ensure that a dog was supervised when he has a bone. There is always an element of risk with choking."

Curtis believes the daily grooming routine is not only useful for keeping a dog in condition, it is also invaluable for picking up any problems. "If you give a dog a thorough going over once a day, you will be able to spot any soreness or locate areas of discomfort right from the start," he said. "That means you can give the necessary treatment without delay. Most dogs love being groomed. They enjoy the individual attention."

Curtis starts off by giving each dog a combing. "I use a couple of combs with different size teeth and then I go over the dogs with a hacksaw blade which helps to get the old coat out." If the dog is racing that day, he gives a complete massage using Curacho Embrocation. "In the old days we used surgical spirit, which was a lot cheaper," he said. "It is used in hospitals for bed sores. It gives the dog's skin a thorough cleaning as you massage. Now I don't think there is a lot of difference in price between surgical spirit and embrocation."

Curtis is a passionate believer in the benefits of massage and will go over a dog twice on the day of a big race. "Nothing beats massaging for

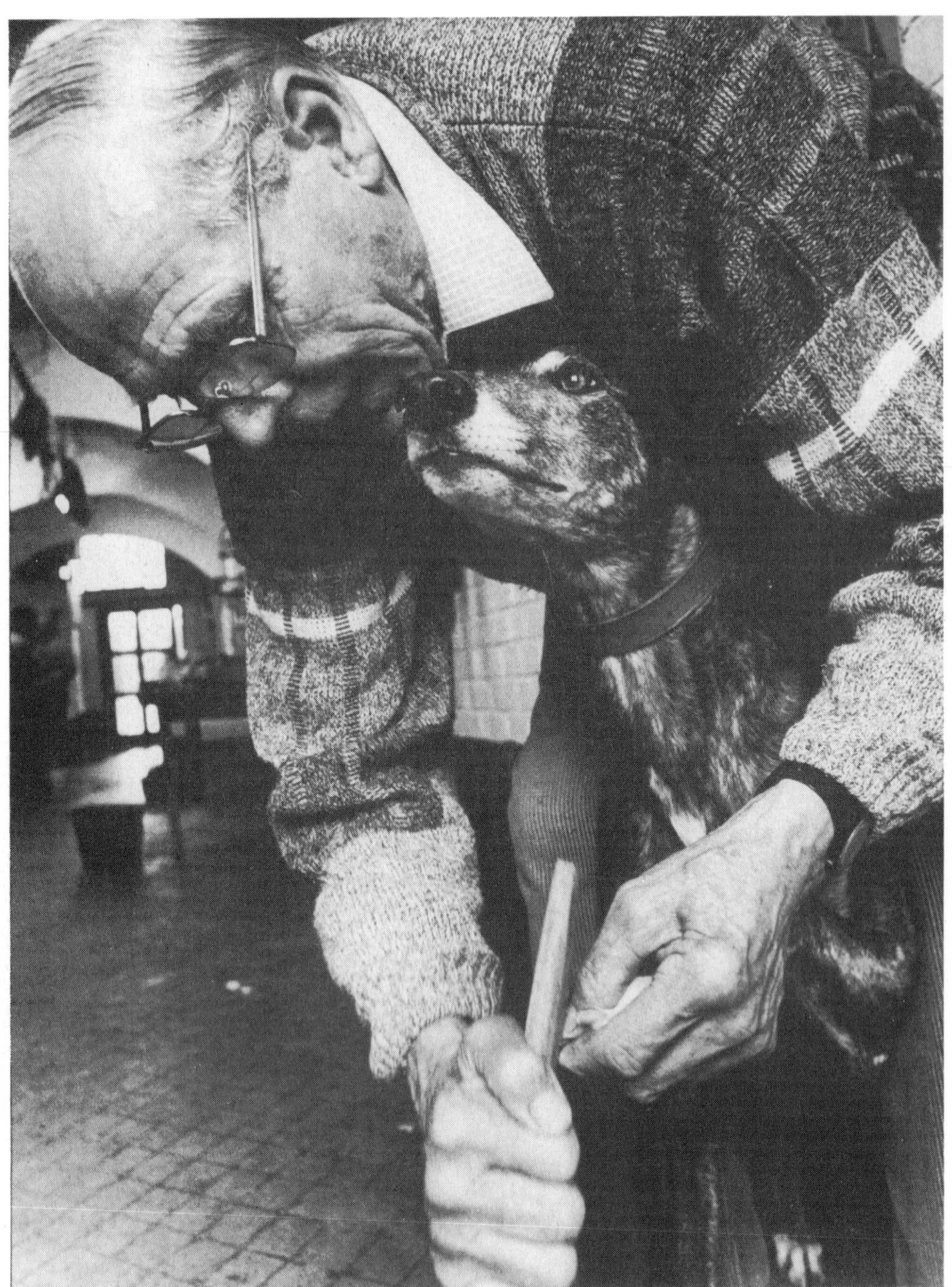

The greyhound's feet are inspected every day and filed once a week.

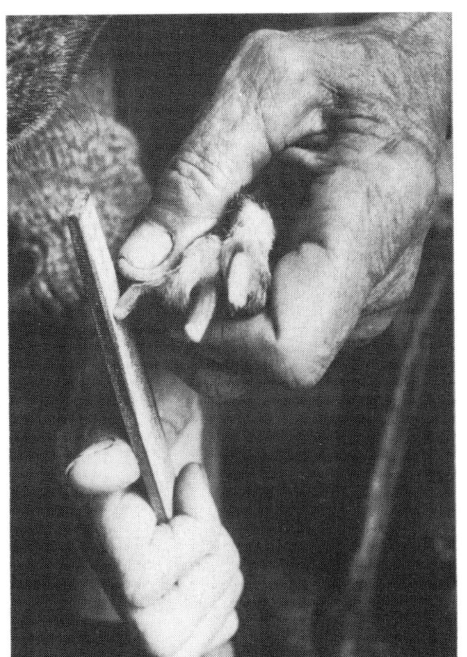

Above: The dog's paw should be held firmly and each nail filed using a brisk up-down action.

Below: The dog's foot after the nails have been filed.

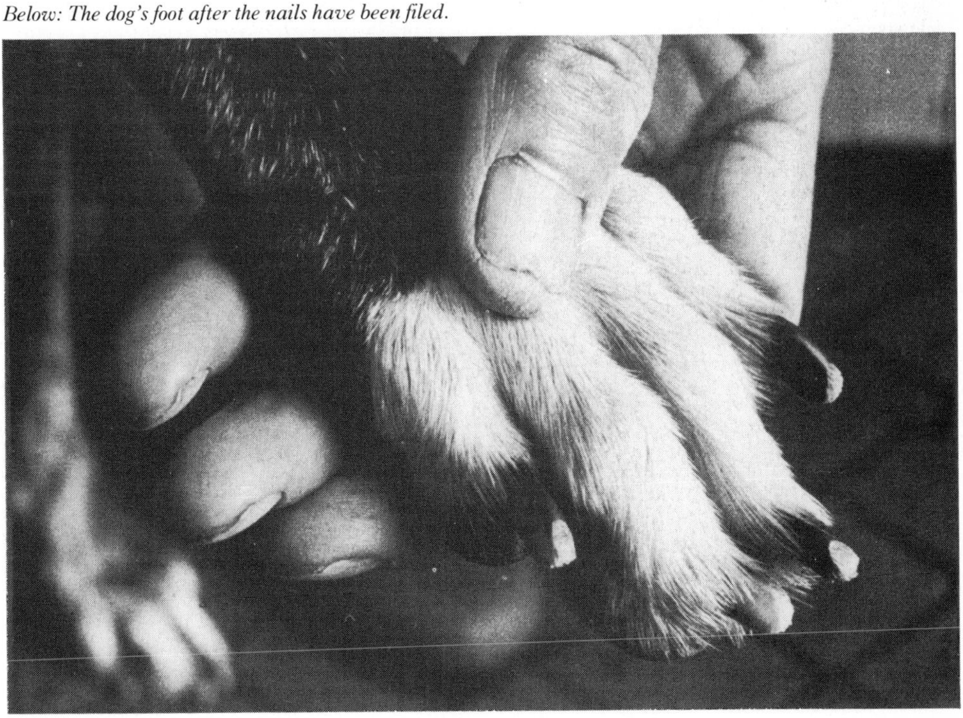

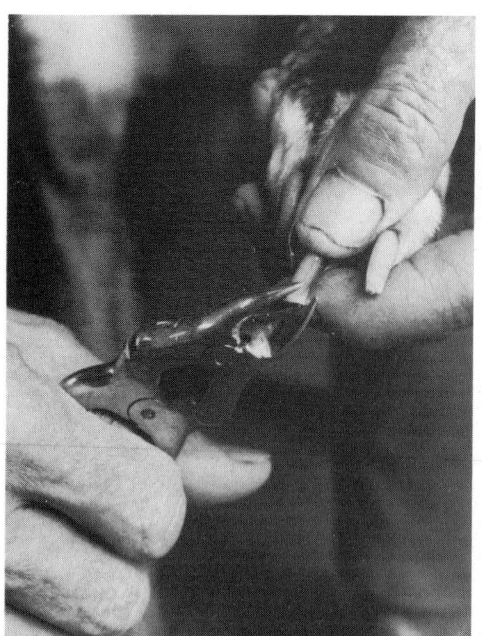
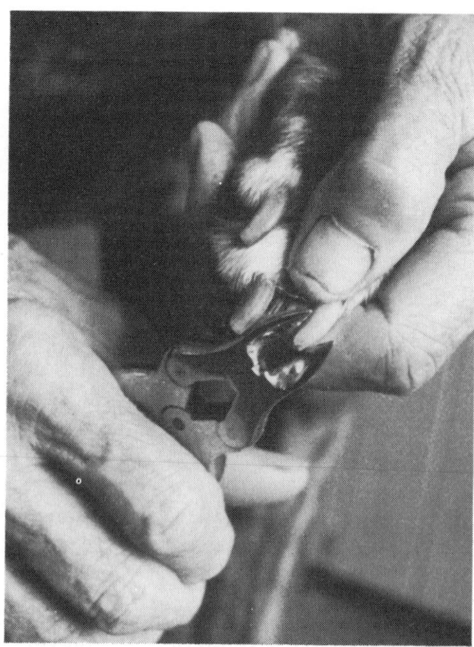

Above: Curtis uses nail clippers when the nails have grown too long for filing. The nail should be clipped to the bottom of the quick.
Below: A toothbrush is used to give the dog's teeth a daily clean.

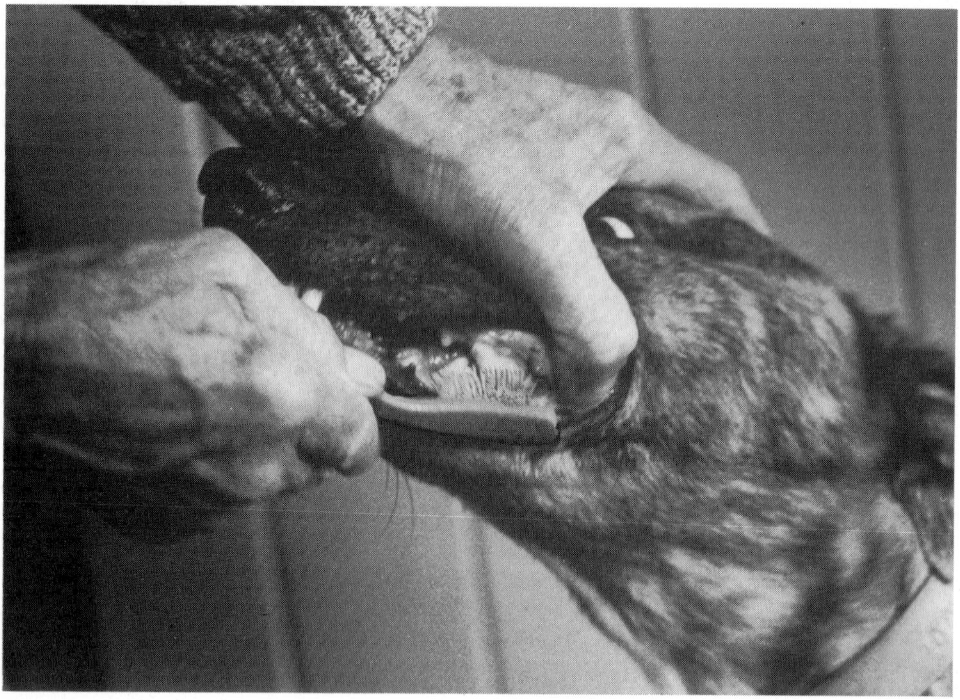

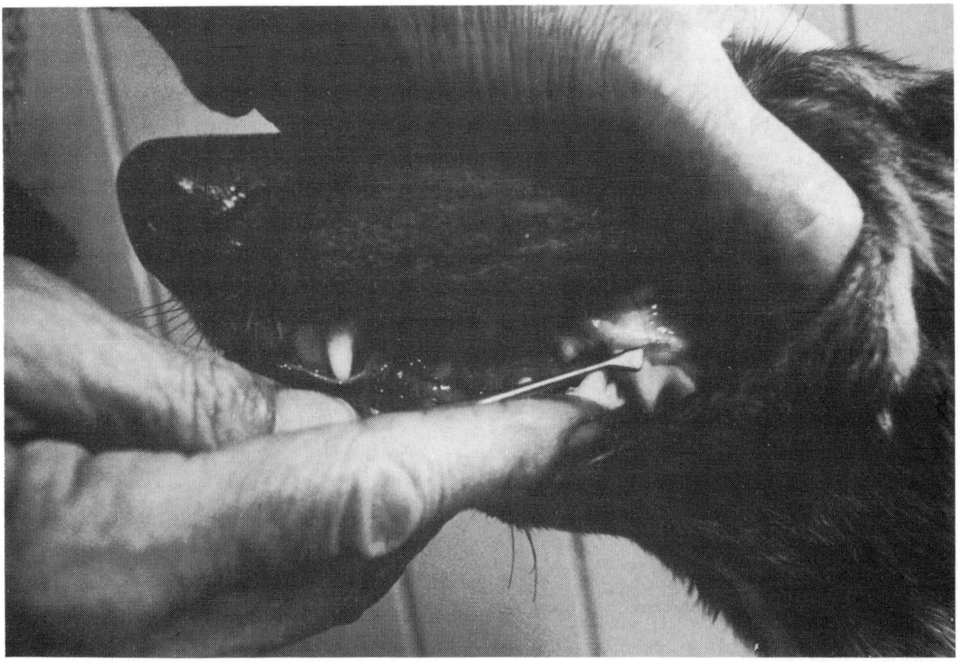

Above: A scaler is used to scrape away any discolouration.

Below: The dog is given a thorough combing every day. A hacksaw blade is useful for getting the old coat out.

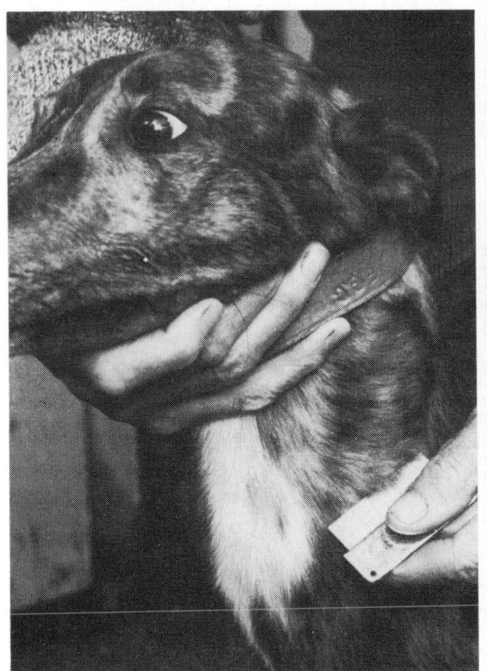

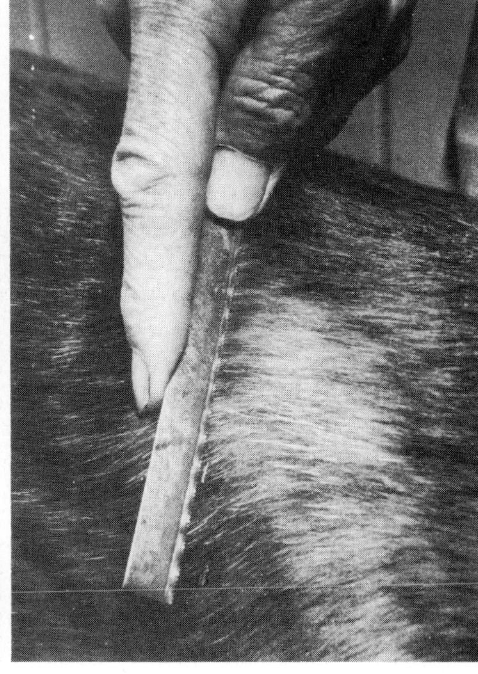

Curtis is a passionate believer in the benefits of massage.

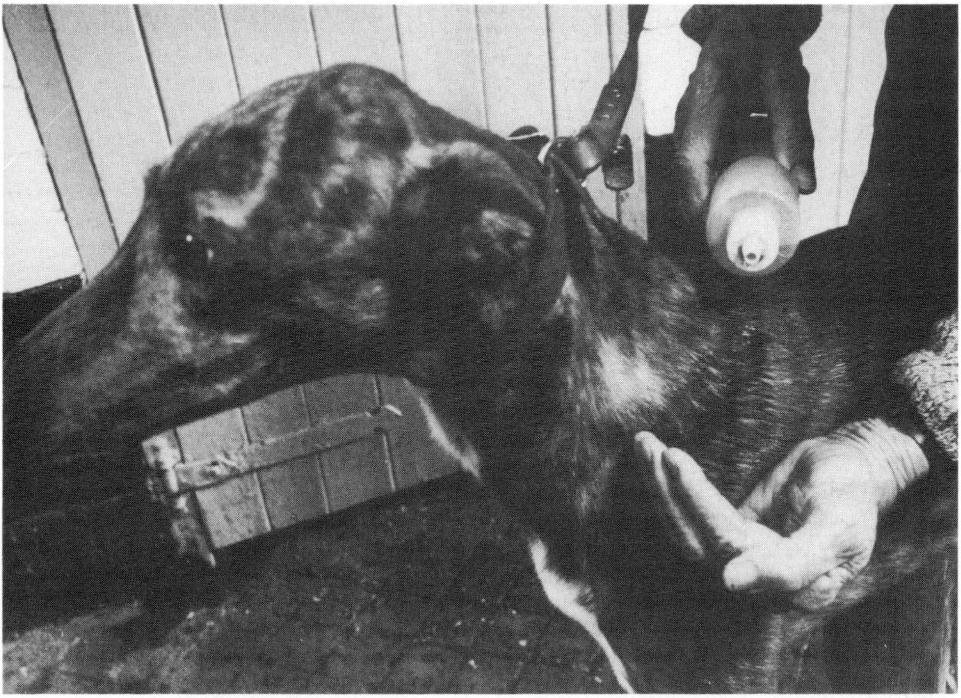

Above: Lone Wolf stands ready for his massage. Curtis uses Curacho embrocation.

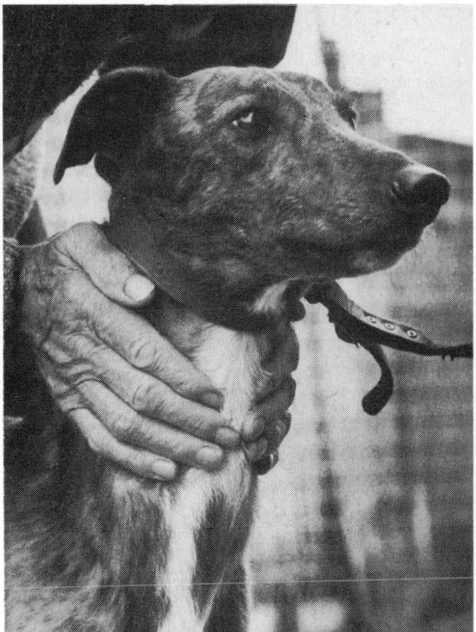

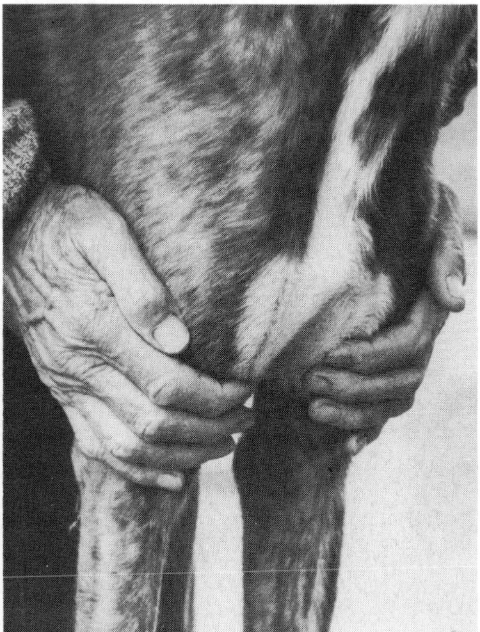

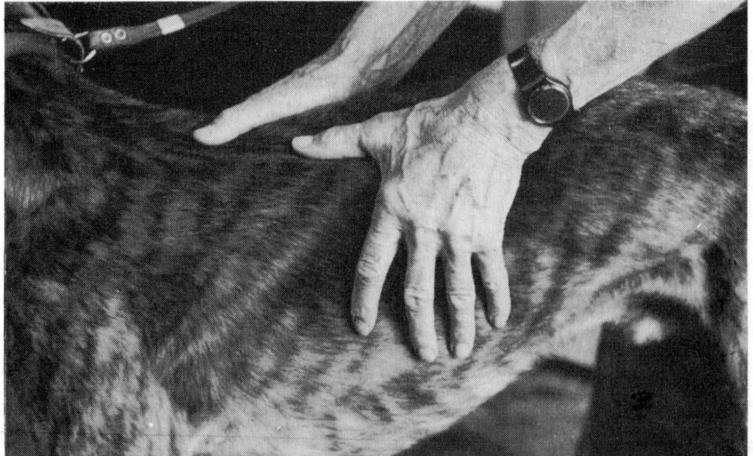

Curtis starts at the dog's neck and works his way over the shoulders, back and hindquarters. He uses strong, firm movements and follows the line of the dog's body.

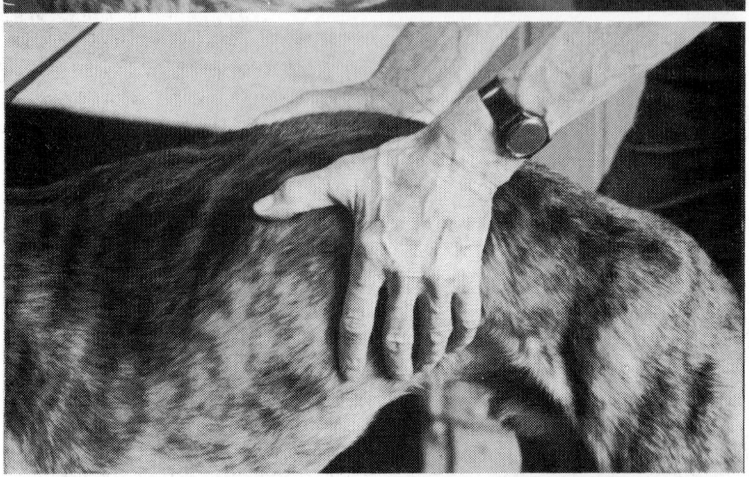

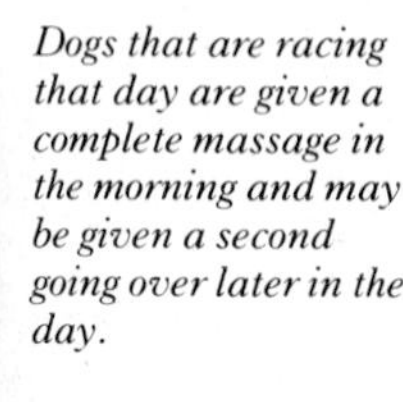

Dogs that are racing that day are given a complete massage in the morning and may be given a second going over later in the day.

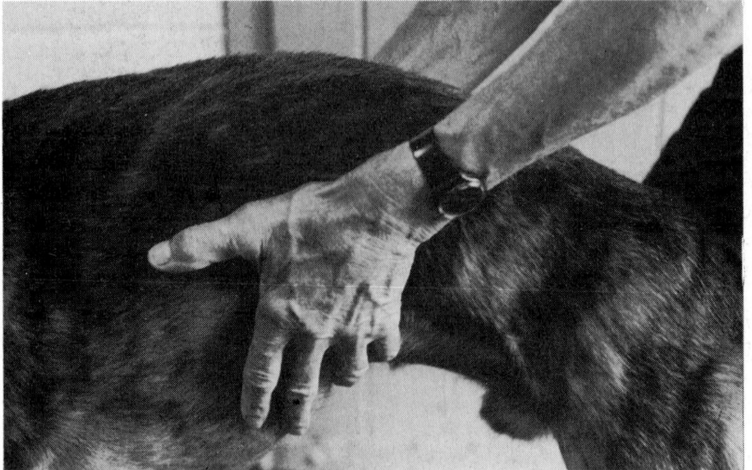

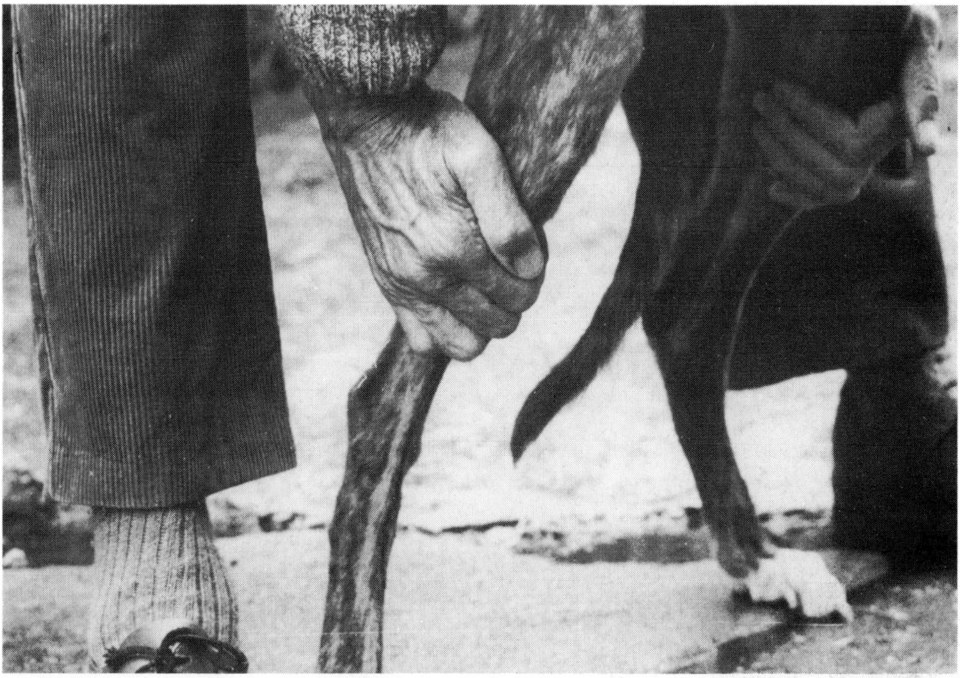

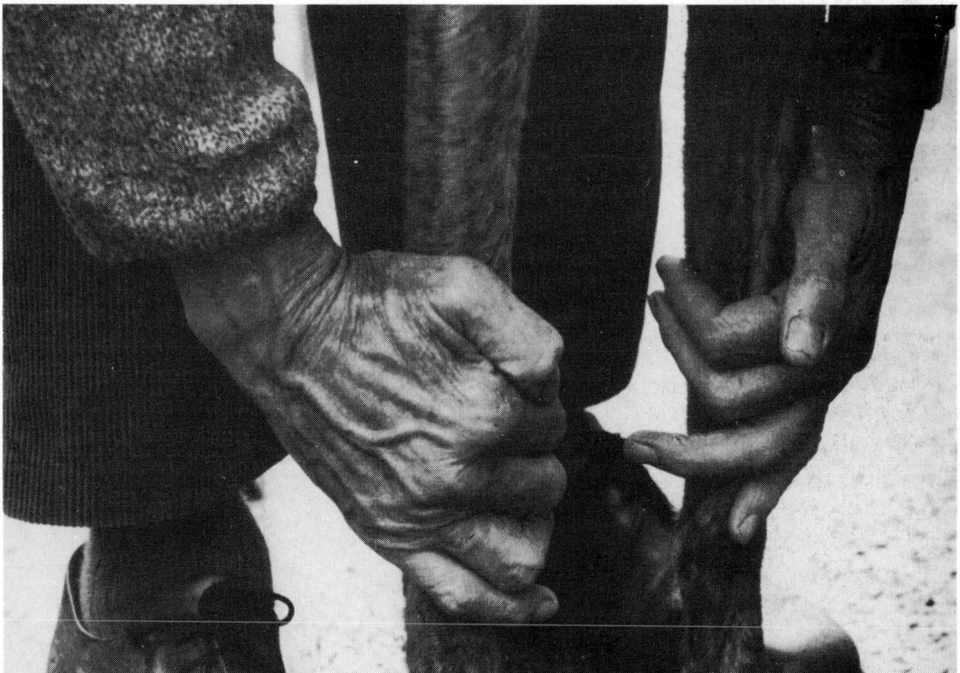

The dog is then given a stiff brush from head to tail.

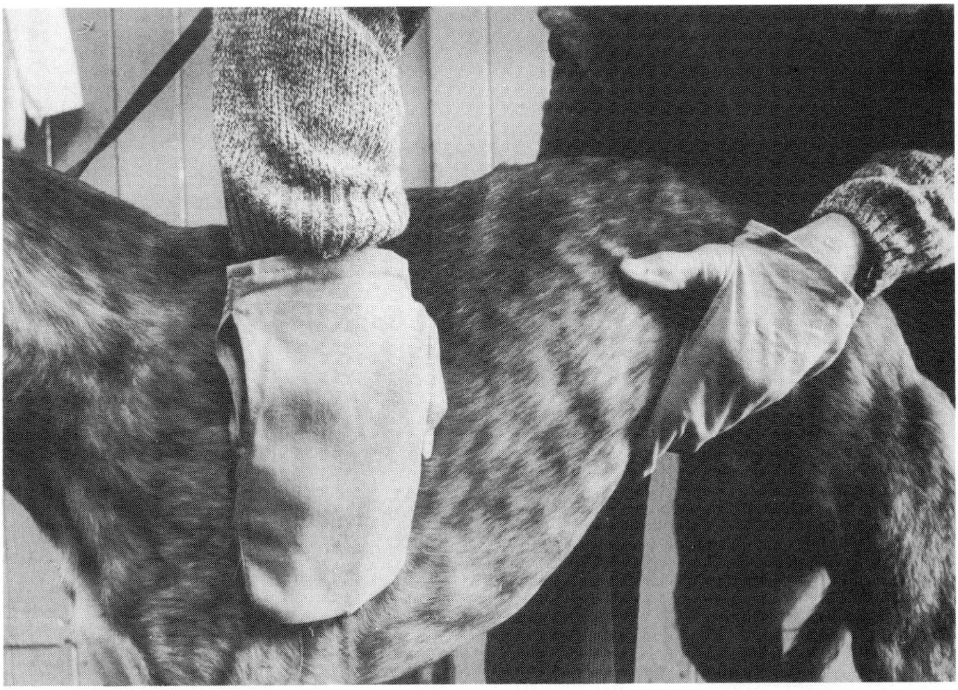

The grooming routine is completed by a polish with grooming gloves. Nothing is forgotten, not even the tail.

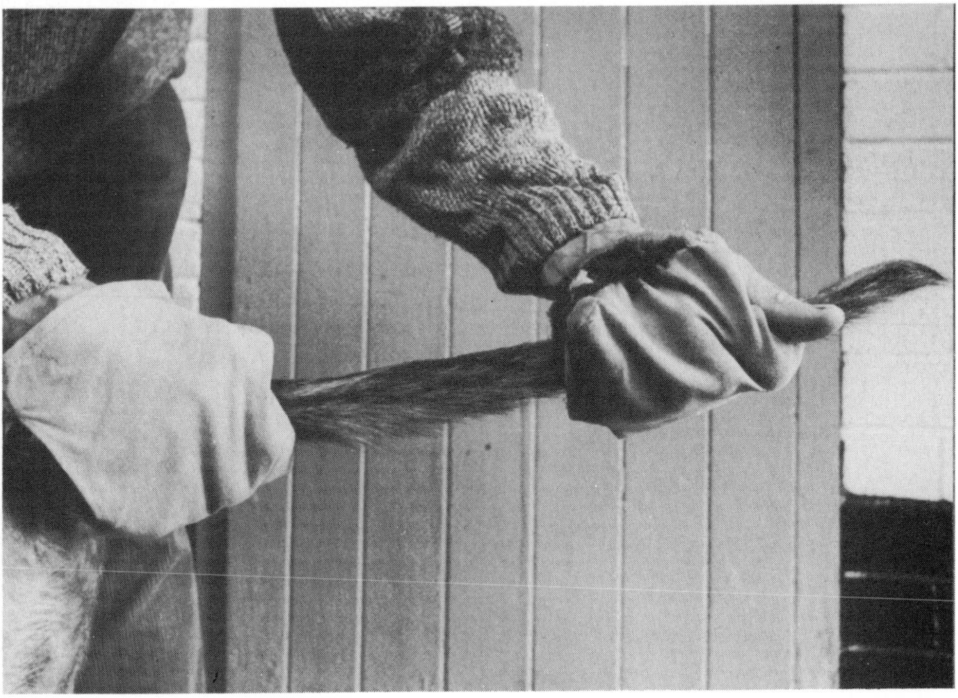

toning a dog up," said Curtis. "You should spend as long as you can doing it — it's time well spent. It takes all the stiffness out of their muscles."

The embrocation itself is not as important as the benefit received from massaging. "I think it helps you as much as anything," said Curtis. "You can use it on a dog and work it in. Then when the coat is dry again, you know you've done the job."

Curtis has very distinctive hands. They are large and long fingered and incredibly sensitive when it comes to working on a dog. He puts his whole back into the job of massaging and you can see the dog relax and tense its muscle to his touch. He recommends starting the massage at the neck and working back over the shoulders to the hindquarters. "Follow the line of the dog's body, using smooth firm movements. Always pay particular attention to the hindquarters which are the powerhouse of the dog," he said.

Many trainers frantically massage their dogs just before they go into the traps — but Curtis reckons there is little value in this. "You should have done your work before you reach the track," he said. "The only time it can be useful is with a dog that tends to cramp. It can help to get the blood flowing. But despite that, we all tend to do it. I know I always give a quick massage just before the dog goes in. It's really just out of nervousness. It makes you feel you have done everything possible for the dog before he goes out to race."

The grooming procedure is completed with a stiff brush, a polish with the grooming glove and finally a towelling. These stages need only take a couple of minutes, but the end result is a dog that positively shines with health. With a big range, grooming and massage takes up a large percentage of the workload. But there is no question of the trainer concentrating on his open racers and leaving the kennel lads to look after the graders.

"All the staff have their own greyhounds which they responsible for," said Curtis. "That is how they did it in the old days when I was a kennel lad at Portsmouth and it means that you take a special pride in your own dogs. I believe it is for the trainer and the head man to take the lead and set the pace for the rest of the staff. If you are all working hard together and trying to get the dogs looking their best, it sets up a good competitive atmosphere."

Graders and open racers get exactly the same care and attention and it is no coincidence that the famous Curtis consistency has always applied equally to the dog that is competing in the first race at Brighton and the one that is in a classic decider. Of course, every trainer enjoys his major triumphs, but there is no greater accolade than to be remembered as the trainer that got the best from every dog in the kennel.

CHAPTER TWELVE

The Kennel

GEORGE Curtis has been attached to a stadium throughout his professional career — first at Portsmouth and then at Brighton — and so he has never had to build his own range from scratch. But in the early days at Portsmouth, facilities were basic and there was an awful lot of making do. Curtis equates his move to Brighton with being promoted to the First Division.

"The facilities at Brighton are second to none. If you can't train greyhounds there — you'll never train them," he said. All the Brighton trainers are based at Albourne, Sussex, some ten miles from the stadium. Each trainer has a completely separate range and during most of Curtis's time as trainer he looked after 60-70 greyhounds. The dogs are kennelled in twos, sharing a bed, with a three foot space between the bed and the door. The kennels are on either side of a large airy corridor, which serves as the main work area for the range.

"The great advantage of the Brighton kennels is the central heating," said Curtis. "It is never a problem keeping the dogs warm in winter. And in the summer we have plenty of ventilation to keep them cool." He says he would use breeze blocks if he was building his own kennel. "They are tougher, stronger and more weather resistant than any other material," he said. "Once the basic structure is built you can line it with wooden slats — one at the back and on either side, which helps to keep it cooler.

"The most important thing is to have a kennel that is big enough for the dog to stretch out. For one dog I would have it measuring about 4 ft across coming out at least 3 ft or 3 ft 6 ins. Then I would have as much area again in front so the dog can walk about and empty if he needs to. If it is cold you can always make the bed smaller by using a bale of straw.

Or you can build a rack above the bed about 3 ft high and line that with straw or sacking. It's easy to make a kennel warmer but if it is too cramped it's virtually impossible to get proper ventilation in the summer. You must have it light and airy so you can keep the air circulating in the hot weather."

Curtis suggests building the bed 6 ft across if you have a pair of greyhounds and 3 ft 6 ins in depth. The space from the front of the bed to the gate should be at least 3 ft 9 ins. "At Brighton the kennels are not as big as that, probably only 5 ft across. But if you are doing it yourself, you should allow as much room as possible. I would go as big as 6 ft 6 ins. I'd much rather have a bed that's too big than too small — that's the worst thing in the world."

Curtis has always had a partition built across the bed so that each greyhound has its own space to lie in. This needs to be about 2 ft 6 ins high — and it can prevent a lot of trouble. "The problems always start if one dog is stretched out and there is not enough room for the other to get on the bed," he said. "With a partition this never need occur. Of course, you can get a couple that are like Darby and Joan and curl up together on the same side. But if the partition slides in and out, you can use it when you want it.

"If greyhounds are kennelled together for a reasonable amount of time they work out their own relationship and one establishes itself as the dominant partner. A lot of people always kennel dogs with bitches but I have often had two dogs in together. If the mix of temperaments works, there is no reason why it should cause trouble. Yankee Express was kennelled with his brother Copper Beeches throughout his racing career. Yankee was definitely the dominant force — Copper, who was a lovely dog, never said boo to a goose."

The NGRC stipulates that there should be a gap of at least 8 inches under each bed. Curtis suggests this should be as high as 12 inches to provide an escape route for a dog if there is trouble. "I know some people board up the gap as they feel that dirt and dust collects there. But if you have a big enough gap it is easy to get underneath for cleaning. And I always believe that if there is trouble in the kennel and one dog is being bullied he can get away by hiding under the bed. Obviously this is not going to be a common experience. But trouble can erupt in the middle of the night when no one is there. If the dog has somewhere to hide it is not going to end up being seriously bitten."

Floors should be built of concrete sloping down by about half an inch towards drainage channels. This helps when the kennel is being cleaned out. And a half an inch gap should also be left under the door so if the dog urinates it will drain out. The type of door on the kennel depends on the size of the range. "Even if you only have a single kennel you will still need some kind of walkthrough or you will get the rain coming in,"

The kennels at Brighton. Curtis believes in having a big gap underneath the bed and a partition if two greyhounds are being kennelled together. Paper bedding is piled high to make the bed as comfortable as possible. The floor slopes down to a drainage channel and the door is solid three-quarters of the way up. The gap at the top is barred.

said Curtis. "Then you can have the kennel door as open as you like. Some people use wire mesh which is lovely in the summer for ventilation but you need an additional door in the winter.

"Dogs like to see out, but this can present problems in a bigger range. At Brighton where the dogs face each other, the gap, which is barred, is at the top of the door. This has the disadvantage of dogs jumping up to see out. But if the gap was at the bottom you would have more trouble. Every time a dog walked down the range it would set the other dogs barking. They might even have a go as it went past."

Greyhounds over-heat very easily and Curtis believes adequate ventilation is a must in every kennel. "I would have a window at the back of each kennel that can be protected by wire mesh and I would fit a ventilator overhead to use on hot days. What you want is plenty of room, light and air. This creates a healthy atmosphere and if you have enough light you can keep the kennel spotless. At the height of the summer we always keep the doors open at either end of the range which keeps the air flowing."

This also applies to trainers with a single kennel. If it is built with a walk-through the outside door can be left open so the air can flow through to the kennel. "But don't forget the security aspect," said Curtis. "All windows should be covered in wire mesh and the outside door should be locked at all times when you are not there."

Understandably, security at the Brighton kennels is incredibly tight, with special alarms linked to each range. None of the kennels are numbered and there are no lists which state which dog is in which kennel. "If anyone broke in they would have no idea whether they were faced with a bottom grader of the best dog in the kennel," said Curtis. "We all carry the information in our heads."

Curtis recommends paper bedding, which he says is cleaner and more economical. "Straw is a waste of time these days," he said. "It used to be good but now they use combine harvesters it comes out very short and there is a lot of chaff. This creates dust and can be very itchy. Paper lasts much longer. We used to change straw bedding every week. It took the whole morning to do six kennels, although it was worth it when you saw how nice it looked. With paper we reckon it will last for three weeks, though you may have to cut that to a fortnight if you have a bad spell with muddy paddocks. The dogs always seem to be very comfortable on paper bedding.

"Don't economise by rationing the amount you use. I like to see a nice full bed which you can shake up every morning when you clean out."

Kennels should be kept spotless at all times. The amount of cleaning that is needed obviously depends on the dog. But every time there is a mess the area should be cleaned thoroughly with disinfectant. And at regular intervals, usually when the bedding is being changed, the whole kennel should be hosed and scrubbed out with disinfectant from top to bottom. "It helps if you have a bed you can dismantle so you can clean right into the corners," said Curtis. "And when I put a bed back together again, I always put flea powder in the cracks, they can be a fertile breeding ground for pests."

After hosing out, Curtis lets the kennel dry and then spreads sawdust on the floor which he later sweeps out. "At Brighton we have central heating so the kennels dry out pretty quickly," he said. "But the most important thing is to make sure the bed is completely dry."

In addition, the range is hosed down every day and the drains are disinfected regularly. When you are keeping 60 to 70 dogs together, hygiene is paramount and no short cuts are taken in the fight against possible infection.

Greyhounds in big ranges have to spend long periods in their kennels so it is essential to ensure that they are as clean and comfortable as possible. "At Brighton, we have the staff to consider and so we have to shut the dogs in by 4.30 pm unless we are racing," said Curtis. "I don't like to think of a dog shut in that long and many a time I have come back in the evenings just to let the dogs out."

This speaks volumes for Curtis's unique dedication to his dogs. There are few trainers who would start their day at 6 am, work straight through until 5 or 6 pm and then, on the rare occasions when there is no racing, return just to let the dogs out. But Curtis sees no special merit in this. His mind is never far from his dogs and their welfare is vital to his own well-being.

"I am a great worrier," he said. "I sometimes think I've forgotten to turn the gas out in the cookhouse — and I can't rest until I've gone back to check."

This involves a twenty minute round trip by car, "It's always been a wasted journey," he said. "But I always think to myself: 'You only have to make one mistake.' The dogs depend on you entirely — and you must never feel you have let them down."

CHAPTER THIRTEEN

The Open Racer

EVERY trainer dreams of getting his hands on a top open racer. But a fast dog in the wrong hands can end up as one big disappointment. Like athletes, greyhounds must be coached to bring out their best and the trainer must use his skill and expertise to choose the right distance and the right competition.

Some dogs such as Tico, the 1986 English Derby winner, are confined exclusively to the open race circuit. But according to George Curtis, the puppies who show their class from their first race are few and far between. "It can be very misleading when you hear of an Irish hot-shot clocking up open race wins from the moment he reaches the track," he said. "What you have to remember is that the schooling track has changed the nature of the game in Ireland. A puppy will have had so many runs round a schooling circuit, he will have had ample opportunity to show his form before he ever reaches the race track."

Curtis still prefers to see a puppy work his way up the grades and prove his ability. "I think it is very hard to make a true judgement of a puppy on a schooling track," he said. "Some people can do it. Vernon Ford who runs the schooling track at Lingfield is a very shrewd judge of pace. But I like to see how a dog performs in racing conditions. Ideally, I would start him in the bottom grade and let him work his way up, learning as he goes. Then after two or three months of graded races you can say: 'I've got something that's a bit special, I'll put him away for open races.' " At Brighton the standard of graded racing is very high and if a puppy is winning in A5, you know you've got a decent dog. "The times you are looking for from a puppy over Brighton's 515 metres is something in the region of 31.20 or 31.00," said Curtis. "That is open race time. My next move would be to try the dog in a couple of minor puppy opens. If you leave him moving up to top grade he can lose his heart running against older dogs, particularly if they try and cut him up. Safeguard a pup all you can. Don't let others dictate to you. Remember it's your pup and you should decide how often you want him to run. If you think he's a bit special, talk to the racing manager and say you want to nurse him along and just race him once a week."

Curtis recommends leaving a minimum five day gap between races unless the puppy is competing in a special event such as the Trafalgar Puppy Cup or the Puppy Derby. "Take it easy, particularly if you are running the pup over 500m," he said. "In the old days that was considered a distance race which you would never put a puppy over. But at Brighton and some other tracks, you haven't any choice if you want to run your dog."

The open racer must obviously gain experience of different tracks, different hares and different surfaces. "If a dog's a fast starter, it doesn't make much difference if he's running behind an inside or an outside hare," said Curtis. "If he's got early pace he'll be okay. But it makes a difference to the dog who relies on his break. He times it listening to the hare, crouching down ready to shoot out. The first sight is all important. And so these are the dogs that will be more affected by a change of hare."

Trapping wins or loses races and that is why the Derby roar, which deafens the sound of the hare, is always treated as such a significant factor. There have been various attempts to find solutions to the problem. Tartan Khan, the 1975 Derby winner, was taken up to the railway lines and hand-slipped on the land alongside, just as a train was roaring past. And Whisper Wishes, the 1984 Derby winner, had a recording of the Wembley Cup Final roar played over to him. "But I always think that if you want to get a dog used to noise you should take him to Romford," said Curtis. "You get trains rushing past every few minutes."

But he does not believe there is a magic solution for the bad trapper. "There was one dog in the final of the Gold Collar back in the fifties and he was a terrible trapper," he said. "The week before the decider they had him in and out of the traps about 20 times building up for the big race. But he still came out last on the night."

Curtis was brought up with grass tracks and was a slow convert to the switch to sand. "I still miss the beautiful lush turf of White City," he said. "On Derby night it was a real spectacle. But I don't miss the winter going when the ground on the inside would be bottomless. I remember Wembley being like a mud bath and at Brighton the winter going was anything up to minus 2.40 seconds. It got ridiculous. The wide runners had such an advantage that in the end, I would rather have sand. But you have to remember that greyhounds need time to adapt to surfaces. Some run brilliantly on grass and when they switch to sand their performance drops off. The owners get in a terrible state — but we always say: 'Give them time'.

"Sand certainly has its problems — like being kicked up in the faces of the following dogs. But I have never had any great worries with injuries. Turf produces more broken hocks, particularly after re-turfing in Spring, and there can be more toe injuries. On sand, muscle injuries are more frequent. In many ways I like the compromise of sanded bends — but if there is too much chopping and changing it can mess up the form for the punter."

It may confuse the punter, but constant change has proved to be the making of many greyhounds. "It works very well on greyhounds that are not entirely genuine as the change keeps their mind occupied," said Curtis. "If this type of dog has the necessary pace, open racing can prove its salvation. I have also had genuine dogs that have been moderate performers at Brighton but have turned out to be champions when they have been taken elsewhere. It was definitely the switch from Brighton that brought on Yankee Express. He won the Sussex Cup there — but he was in a different class when he went away. Brighton is a big galloping track and he liked tights bends on courses such as Harringay and Slough."

And he reckons that Lone Wolf, the 1986 St Leger winner, would not have been more than an average grader if he had stayed at Brighton. "He had that bit extra which meant we could take him open racing — and it made him," said Curtis. "He loved Harringay and although he won the Leger at Wembley, he would have won it more easily if it had been at Green Lanes."

Most greyhounds show a particular liking for a certain type of track. "Never write off a dog because he doesn't run well at one track," said Curtis. "Take the time and trouble to place your dog." This applies to graders who are failing to make their way at their home track — and to open racers when they are being entered for competitions.

"You can take a dog to a different track and can get an entirely different performance from the one you expect," he said. "That is why trialling is so important. Some dogs adapt very quickly to a new track and you know after one trial how they are going to perform. If they don't run well it is worth giving them another go — and then forget it. There's no point in running a dog if he isn't happy."

This is often easier said than done when owners are putting pressure on trainers to enter their dogs for certain competitions — particularly when big prize money is at stake. But Curtis has always stood firm on putting the dog first. The classic example of this was when he decided not to run Ballyregan Bob in the 1985 English Derby.

"If the competition had still been staged at White City, I think

Ballyregan would have taken his chance," he said. "The circuit was a fair test of any greyhound. But at Wimbledon, early pace to the first bend is essential and we would have risked serious injury."

When a greyhound is taken for a trial, the thing to look for is how he runs the track. It is just as important as the time he does. "Of course you want them to fly round," said Curtis. "But if a dog does a decent time and runs off the track, you know he will be capable of better times when he learns to run the track."

He also recommends giving a two dog trial rather than a solo. "You get dogs who don't perform well in solo trials," he said. "They do a terrible time and then come out and run an entirely different race. I've had that happen to me and the racing manager has said: 'Did you know he was going to do that?' Even if you say you are as surprised as he is, there is always the risk of people thinking you've fiddled it. In fact, all that has happened is that the dog has run much better because he likes the competition of running against other dogs. It gives him an edge."

Preparation for big competitions is all-important and it is often the timing of a dog's improvement that is decisive. All Curtis's dogs are fed a basic diet using cooked meat until after they have gone through their trials. Then when they start racing, this is stepped up in protein by introducing raw red meat to make up half the total meat content. Additional glucose is also given to replace the energy lost from racing.

"If you are just using the basic racing diet, as we do for graders, the improvement is gradual," said Curtis. "They don't suddenly fly out and do flashy times. They improve from week to week. That's all I ever did at Portsmouth and we had our dogs going right through the grades — winning seven on the trot. But it's very hard to do that now when racing managers up-grade in big jumps — sometimes hopping three at a time. In that sense, I think the art of training has been eroded. It is easier in big competitions when you have a fixed date for a final and you know what you are aiming for. With graders you are under more constant pressure."

In the week before the start of a big competition, Curtis puts his open racers on a daily dose of Orovite 7.

"This is fairly expensive and I would only use it for top open racers," said Curtis. "But when you have some of best dogs in the country in your kennel, you must be prepared to stick your hand in your pocket and give them the best. Again, the improvement is gradual. It is not going to do a dog any good in five minutes — but if you give one sachet a day along with the high protein diet and glucose, you're going to see an improvement.

"Our dogs seem to keep going longer than others — and I put it down to Orovite 7. It makes the difference when you're going through the rounds of a big competition and you've got dogs travelling up and down. It is an exhausting business and you've got to give them the best."

But Curtis maintains it is not necessarily the dog that has furthest to travel that is at the greatest disadvantage. "They are all different," he said. "Some travel beautifully and just rest themselves on the journey. Others are bad travellers, no matter what you do. Open racer She Wolf will never lie still. She stands there panting all the way there and all the way back. And that's when it's not hot! I don't like seeing it. But the fact is she still comes out and wins. It is just something in her make-up and you can't change it."

When a dog is going through the rounds of a competition, Curtis takes it fairly easy with exercise, particularly if there is a short gap between each round.

"If a dog is getting two runs a week in the competition, I would let him please himself at home," he said. " I would let him off in the paddock and he can run as much or as little as he wants to. If you have a week beween rounds, I would let him have two gallops in the week. If the race was on the Saturday, I would gallop the dog on the Tuesday and again on the Thursday. I would also dose him with milk of magnesia on the Tuesday. It never does any harm — and it can make a significant difference. I would even dose a dog on the day of a race, if he's a bit sick. I had one that was a bit sluggish and off-colour the day of the final and after I dosed him he came out and flew. Of course, it doesn't always work. But in this case the dog was probably a bit liverish and it did the trick."

Curtis admits that he gets final night nerves. Even after nearly 50 years in the game, he gets as keyed up as when he was contesting his first big competition. But he has learned one invaluable lesson. "Experience has taught me to keep everything going at the same pace when you're building up to a big final," he said. "Don't do anything different. In the old days I would try everything. I'd get in chicken or skate or extra milk. I kept thinking about all the different things I had heard. You hear that Sidney Orton feeds chicken before a big race — and you think you ought to do it. But in all honesty, I was listening to too many people. I kept changing things — and I still didn't have any luck in the big competitions. Yet the graders were doing okay, coming out and winning time after time."

The tide turned when Abbey Glade was running in the 1975 Gold Collar at Catford. "I took him through the trials and the early rounds and we got as far as the semis," said Curtis. "Then I was due to go on holiday to Spain. I rang up the kennel girl who was looking after him for me and found out that he won the final by 7¼ lengths. He beat Dancing Dolores in 34.97. That was my first classic win and I hadn't even been there to prepare the dog for it. I thought: 'That girl must know something that I don't.' But she hadn't done anything different — and that is what I eventually learnt. When you are preparing for a big final, keep everything the same. Don't try anything clever. Just trust your own judgement. If you think a dog needs a gallop, give him one. If you think he looks a bit jaded, let him rest. As soon as I started doing this, I started getting some success. Then, everyone kept asking: 'What have you done?' But the truth was I hadn't done anything. I had just kept everything the same."

Now what Curtis hopes for in the week before a final is that nothing happens to disrupt the kennel routine. "You want everything to go smoothly and then you feel that you're sending the dog out with every chance," he said. But needless to say, that does not always happen.

"I remember when Wired To Moon was in the 1977 Scurry Gold Cup final," said Curtis. "He had gone through the competition with two wins and a second and he had a good chance in the final. But the week before the decider nothing went right. The meat was fatty, everything was at sixes and sevens — and I thought we could not have given him a worse preparation. But Wired To Moon took up the running from the second bend and won at 4–1 in 26.63 beating the favourite Carhumore Speech by 1¼ lengths. I thought then: 'You're worrying too much about these dogs,' It doesn't help you and it doesn't help the dogs. You have to learn to take things calmly."

Occasionally though, a trainer is forced to make a major decision affecting a dog's welfare, in that vital week before a big final. Curtis will never forget the events that took place the week before Upland Tiger competed in the 1981 Laurels final. Wimbledon was Tiger's favourite track and he produced some flying times in the competition. Then in the final he was drawn in trap one, on the inside of five wide runners.

"He was a racing certainty for the final," said Curtis. "But the bitch he was kennelled with, Bourks Baby, came into season. To start with I thought he would be all right. But the nearer it got to the race day the more worried I got. I was frightened that he was fretting over her — so I took her away. And it was a mistake. Upland Tiger was made 4–9 favourite for the final but he didn't get out. He made up a lot of ground but from where I was standing, it looked like he was beaten a length by Echo Spark. I came back thinking that was it — but they all said it was a photo-finish and they were backing Upland Tiger to win. It turned out that he was beaten a short head. So I got two blows that night. I thought I was beat, then I thought I'd won and then we lost it by a short head. I can honestly say that was the worst I have felt in my life. I knew we should have won and I felt I had let the owner John Houlihan down and the public.

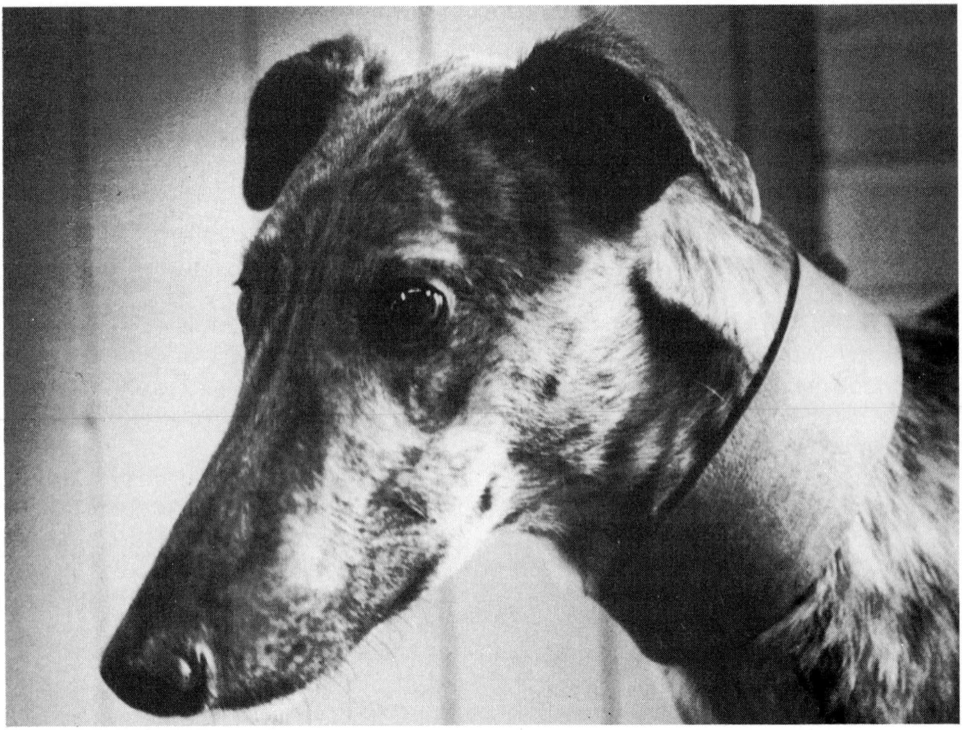

Above: Lone Wolf. It was the switch from Brighton that made him.

Below: Upland Tiger. It was the biggest disappointment of Curtis's career when he lost the 1981 Laurels.

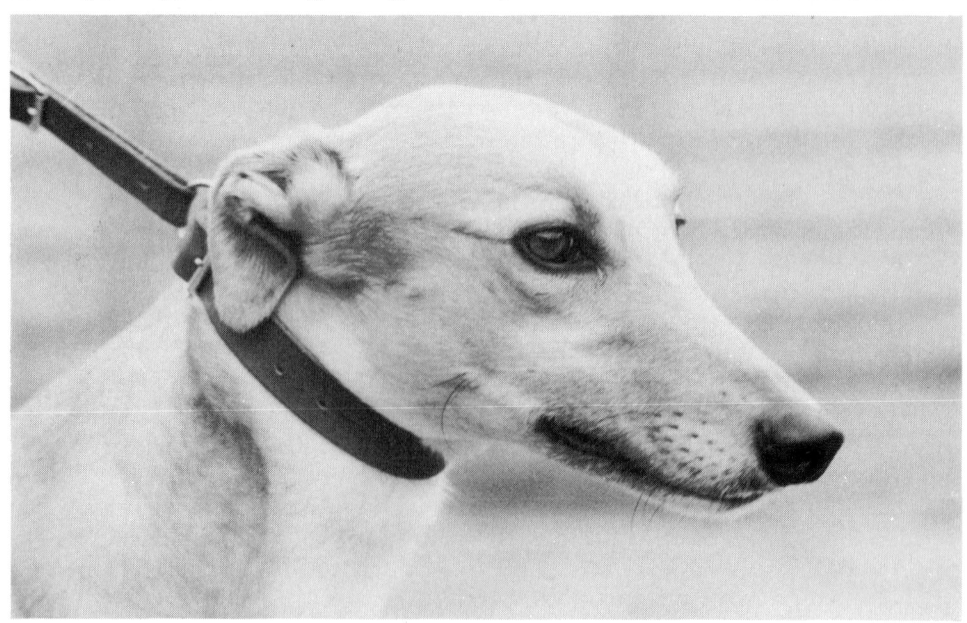

"I'm not taking anything away from Joe Cobbold who won the final. I went up and congratulated his head man as soon as the result was announced. I would always do that no matter how much it hurts. But it was very hard to swallow. I thought I was doing the right thing in taking the bitch away from Upland Tiger. But I am certain that is the reason why he lost his edge. He wasn't bothering her and it upset him more when I took her away. He certainly didn't run his best that night — and I've got to live with that."

If fact, Curtis has kept a dog and a bitch in season together until the eighth day. "Nine times out of ten the dog won't bother about the bitch," he said. "I've had far more trouble with bitches that are 12 weeks out of season. The dog will stand there barking his head off. I just worried too much about Upland Tiger."

Yankee Express had an interesting preparation for his tilt at his third successive Scurry Gold Cup. "Yankee was coming up to four-years-old and he was probably past his peak," said Curtis. "He won his first two rounds and was then beaten a short head in the semi-finals." His times had been 27.18, 26.87, and then Karina's Pal, who was also trained by Curtis, clocked 27.43 when she got the verdict.

"Bob Betts from *The Sporting Life* rang me up after the semis and said he thought Yankee had run a bit stale," said Curtis. "He had been mating a few bitches during his lay-off and I had noticed that he seemed a bit moody. I thought: 'He's probably missing the bitches.'

"He was due to mate a bitch the Sunday after the Scurry final so I rang up to see if she could be brought down earlier. Yankee did the job on the Thursday and on the Saturday he flew. He came out and won his third classic beating Karina's Pal by ¾ of a length in 27.03.

"If a dog has gone over the top and isn't very happy, there must be a reason. My old Guv'nor Bill Peters at Portsmouth always said he didn't think a mating before a big race did a dog any harm — and I remembered that. Yankee was thinking about his bitches — and he didn't have his mind on the job. As soon as he'd done the mating, he was a different dog. That night we went up to Slough he was full of himself."

This solution has worked in other cases with spectacular results. Patricia's Hope had 60 bitches following his victory in the 1972 Derby and then came back to win the classic the following year.

Curtis has always seen himself primarily as a trainer of stayers, although he reached the Derby final on three occasions — in 1969 Hard Held finished fifth, in 1970 Sirius was fifth and 1984 The Jolly Norman was fourth.

"The hardest thing about the Derby is trying to keep a dog fit over such an extended period," he said. "It used to be two weeks and it was all over. Now you've got six rounds — plus the Trial Stakes beforehand. There is a knack to it. Leslie Reynolds, who won five Derbies in seven years was the greatest of all, but everyone is good at something."

He believes the most important thing is to give yourself something to work on as the competition progresses. "You don't want a dog flying out at the start and then being burnt out by the final. If you get them on the high protein diets and vitamin supplements just before the start, you will be reaping the rewards by the final. But there is no doubt that every trainer needs his quota of luck to get through six rounds."

Graders and open racers are treated alike by Curtis and every dog is given a thorough grooming and massage every day. "I would obviously spend longer on a dog that is going to race that day," he said. "And if a dog is in a competition you keep your eyes open for sore quicks or bruising so they can be treated in time for the next round. The massage keeps the dog toned up and you can keep a check for any signs of strain or soreness. On the day of a big race, I would massage twice."

Many trainers gear a top greyhound's racing schedule specifically to the Derby. A favourite preparation is running a dog in the Pall Mall and then putting him away for the Derby. This certainly paid off in the case of 1986 winner Tico, who was incredibly lightly raced. He won the Pall Mall at Harringay and then started his Derby campaign with only 10 races on his card. He missed out only once — in the second round — and his Derby victory gave him the impressive record of 12 wins from 16 starts.

But Curtis has always paid more attention to the way a dog is running than adhering to any set pattern for lay-off periods. "I think it's a mistake to stop a dog when he is running well," he said. "If he's doing the business, you should keep him going as long as you can. Once you stop him, you are faced with the long haul of bringing him back. I strongly believe that there are only so many races in a dog — and only so much time for him to fulfil his potential. If you lay a dog up when he's running in form and then he breaks a hock when you bring him back, you're finished. I would lay the average dog off for a couple of months a year. I'm not that keen on running a dog in January or February when there is a lot of frost and snow, so that is the obvious time to rest them."

But as far as Curtis is concerned, rules are there to be broken. "We had open racer Black Spindel running right throught the worst of the weather at the beginning of 1987," he said. "We didn't think any further than his next race. But while he was running well and winning we didn't think of stopping him. With a dog like that there was a question as to whether he had the class to take on the big boys. He could have proved to be two or three lengths short when all the good dogs started coming back. So it was better to let him pick up his races while the other dogs were lying on their beds." Curtis has found that stayers keep going longer than middle distance runners. But no dog can keep on running every night of the week. "I think you can average three runs a fortnight for quite a reasonable period," he said. "But it is easy to tell if a dog is getting tired and stale. If he's not jumping out of the kennel and raring to go first thing in the morning, you know it is time to ease up."

When a dog is given a two-month rest, the biggest mistake you can make is to bring him straight back to the track, according to Curtis. "They need plenty of galloping before they get as far as their first trial let alone their first race," he said. "It is absolutely crucial to gallop them back to full fitness."

He suggests allowing a six week period from the time the dog starts back on the gallops to his first important race. "I would gallop a dog three or four times a week for at least a couple of weeks," said Curtis. "Then I would trial him over the sprint trip and then graduate to the four bends. Ideally, I would let him run in a graded race before he resumes open racing."

This may sound like a long, drawn out process but Curtis has discovered that injuries can result from bringing a dog back too quickly. "It is when a dog is returning to race fitness that he is most likely to start doing joints and muscles," he said. "The galloping ensures the dog is fit before you put him under the strain of track racing where he must travel at speed round bends. I have learnt over the years that there is no point trying to cut corners. There is nothing more frustrating that resting a dog for two months and then having him end up on the injury list his first race back."

Curtis's haul of major prizes over the years is second to none. In the classics alone he has won the Scurry Gold Cup four times, the Grand National twice, the Gold Collar, the Oaks, the Cesarewitch and the St Leger. "I have been very lucky in having some of the best dogs in the country in my kennel," he says with typical modesty. But he is undoubtedly proud of his achievement to be among the front runners of the open race Trainers Championship year after year.

He has won the Championship three times — in 1983, 1984 and 1986, he was runner-up in 1982 and 1985. "I have always prided myself on being consistent," he said. "Anyone can enjoy a good run of luck — we've all had them. And all you can do is enjoy it while it lasts, I remember going up to Wolverhampton and competing in the 1977 Trainers Championship. Ted Dickson won five of the eight races and Geoff de Mulder came up to me and said: 'We're like a lot of amateurs against a professional.' Ted had marvellous run. His head man got so used to winning, he would be on the winning line before the race had even started. That night I won the top heat race with Wired To Moon and I had to be content with that.

"But the real art of training is to consistently get the best from your dogs. In our kennel the dogs maintain their best form over a long period. And we had had a lot of success in training second season dogs into their third year."

The most spectacular example of this is the great Yankee Express who won the Scurry in 1982, '83 and '84. But Curtis has also showed a unique ability to clock up winning sequences with his dogs, which again pinpoints the trainer's art of getting a dog to the peak of his form and then maintaining it. Obviously Ballyregan Bob's world record of 32 consecutive wins stands out as Curtis's greatest achievement. But back in his Portsmouth days he won ten in a row with Crags Hope, at Brighton 1976 Golden Jacket winner Glin Bridge challenged the UK record with 15 consecutive wins, 1983 Grand National winner Sir Winston recorded an unbeaten run of 10, 1983 BBC TV Trophy winner Sandy Lane clocked up 11 wins from 12 races and Yankees Shadow, who was trained for the vast majority of her career by Curtis, notched up 20 wins from 21 races.

All these sequences were recorded against a background of major competitions, when the greyhounds were consistently taking on their closest rivals in training. It is a remarkable feat for any trainer — and although it may be Curtis's least celebrated achievement — it stands out as unmistakable proof that he is truly the master of his craft.

CHAPTER FOURTEEN

Problem Dogs

WHEN a puppy starts his racing career — the question that hangs over him is not is he fast, but is he genuine? The demands of track racing are such that there is no room for the dog that is aggressive or shows a preference for running in company. That is assuming he has shown the keenness and ability to chase in the first place. Some greyhounds are naturals from the word go and never cause their trainer a moment's anxiety. Others have initial problems that can be remedied, if the correct course of action is taken.

"There are so many stories about how to straighten iffy dogs, it can be bewildering," said Curtis. "One of the favourites was to get the rat in a gin and then let the dog bite it. It was reckoned that this put a bit of life into the dog. But I honestly believe there are only a few tried and trusted methods which are worth experimenting with."

For the dog that consistently fails to chase, Curtis recommends a trip to a coursing meeting. "If you have taken the dog to the schooling track, he has watched trials and is still not getting the idea, it is worth giving him a look at a live hare," he said. "He doesn't necessarily have to chase. It may be enough if he stands and watches for a couple of hours." For a small fee a greyhound can be given a trial at a coursing meeting and for the reluctant chaser, this can prove decisive. "Chasing a live hare can be the making of a greyhound," said Curtis. "It's all very well running after rabbits in the paddock but it does not give the dog a sustained chase. Most rabbits will have disappeared under a hedge or down a hole before the greyhound gets into his stride. But a proper chase can have spectacular results. The dog gets the scent and gets the idea of chasing. He doesn't need to kill. It's the chase that's all important.

"The best thing is to give the dog one trial — and hope it doesn't last too long. You don't want him to have a real grueller or it will tear the heart out of him. But in a fair-sized field it will do him the world of good. You don't want to do it too often or he won't chase an artificial lure. But one trial will sharpen up the chasing instinct so he realises what the game is all about."

Curtis used this remedy with Puppy Oaks and Puppy Derby winner Bad Trick when he was at Portsmouth. "She sustained a wrist injury and appeared to have lost her confidence on the track when she returned to racing," he said. "She kept checking on the bends. She had a couple of live courses and didn't get the hare either time. But she never looked back."

In fact, Curtis believes too many kills can prove disastrous for the track greyhound. "Most fast dogs will have caught a rabbit at some time in their lives — and they will be none the worse for the experience," he said. "But I think it is the worst thing in the world to keep on giving a dog a live kill to ginger him up. In the end, the dog won't run unless he's chasing a live hare and expecting a kill."

Curtis believes that puppies should be given all the help they can at the early stages. "They have got so much to learn, you have to give them the benefit of the doubt," he said. After a coursing trial, Curtis suggests taking the dog back to the track for a solo. "Watch him to see if he's getting his head down and chasing the hare," he said. "Then get a genuine greyhound to race with him, preferably an old dog that is going to start off in front and fade. Then the pup has a chance to go by and win which will give him a confidence booster. Give him a couple of easy mixed trials. You don't want a dog cutting across him or running neck and neck with him down the home straight. Let the pup have the opportunity to go past easily, so he gets the feel of the game."

Once a pup has reached the track, Curtis believes any signs of trouble should be stamped on immediately. "If puppies start messing about on the track we tell the owners immediately and advise they take them back for more schooling," he said. "There's no point ignoring it, or a bad tendency can become an ingrained habit. You can make excuses for a puppy. But if you let a dog get to about two-and-a-half-years-old and he's fighting, it's a hell of a job to get it out of him."

If a pup is showing signs of aggression or a reluctance to go past, Curtis recommends change as the most likely solution. "Don't write a dog off just because he is not running a particular track," he said. "I've had plenty of dogs that don't run Brighton and then go away and run brilliantly elsewhere. The aim is to give the suspect dog something to occupy his mind. A different hare, different track, different distances — they all give the dog something to think about.

"A lot of dogs run the noisy Sumner hare better than the McGee — or vice versa. You have to have patience and try to find the right solution.

Above: Blue Shirt on his way to victory in the Mecca Bookmakers Stayers Stakes at Hackney. As long as he kept on switching tracks, he kept on winning. (N and B)

Below: Karinas Pal winning his preliminary heat in the 1985 Derby. But he was disqualified for aggressive interference. (R. Page)

One of the best ways of straightening out a dog is to continuously swap tracks. Of course, the independent man has the big advantage there. He can go to different tracks and he has a bit more leeway than NGRC trainers.

"Few dogs have beaten us. But you've got to be realistic. If you can't eradicate the trouble, you're better off sending him to a flapper. Often owners don't know what you're talking about when you suggest a change for a dog with a string of seconds on his card. They think he's doing okay with all the close finishes. They don't see he's only running as fast as the dog in front."

Obviously fast dogs have a better chance of overcoming problems because they can go open racing and benefit from a constant change of scene. "If a dog has that bit of extra pace it makes all the difference," said Curtis. "It's very difficult to ring the changes for a grader but if the dog is fast enough for open class competitions, you should be able to get some wins from him.

Blue Shirt, winner of the 1984 and 1985 Mecca Bookmakers Stayers Stakes, 1984 Scot Grange Trophy at Henlow and 1985 Coronation Cup, was a classic example of this. "He definitely wasn't having it at Brighton," said Curtis. "I had trouble winning a race with him. Then I started shifting him around and he didn't stop winning."

The same applied to Karina's Pal, runner-up in 1984 Scurry Gold Cup. "But eventually he blotted his copybook," said Curtis. "We thought we had got him right and he was doing well. He won his preliminary heat of the 1985 English Derby and we were over the moon. But they were all shaking their heads when they came back — and that was it. He was disqualified for aggressive interference. But the owner sold him for slightly more than he paid for him and at least we had got some wins from him."

Curtis admits that he allowed his judgement to be over-ruled with 1969 Derby finalist Hard Held — and that ultimately led to the dog's downfall. The July 1966 whelp by Lisheengham Brigadier–That's An Idea finished fifth in the country's premier classic which was over 525 yards at White City. Then he clocked a new world record of 29.77 over Brighton's 550 yards.

"The owner wanted to try him in the Cesarewitch which was over 600 yards at West Ham," said Curtis. "I had my doubts as to whether he would get the trip but in his first heat he came out and did 33.01, winning by 4 lengths. I was only too pleased to think I had been wrong. But in the second round he had a much tougher race. He was tiring going down the home straight and he had a go. He was the sort of dog who liked to be out in front. When he was challenged and he was tiring he turned his head."

The repercussions were serious. Peter Shotton, who was then racing manager at Brighton, would not allow disqualified dogs to trial back. So Hard Held was expelled from the Brighton kennels.

Putting a dog over hurdles is a tried and trusted method of straightening out a 'dodger'. "Again, you are giving the dog something extra to think about," said Curtis. "Kilcoe Foxy, winner of the 1984 Grand National, used to run with the pack. His owner knew that when he bought him and we put him over hurdles right from the start. When he got the hang of it, there was no stopping him — and he really loved racing. He was a moderate dog, with suspect tendancies but he jumped like a champion. He was the best dog in the 1984 final and was a worthy winner."

According to Curtis, the troublemaker in the kennel is not necessarily going to be aggressive on the track. "You usually find they are the more determined runners," he said. "They are the type that will go through a brick wall to get to the front. The ones that turn out to be bad on the track are the sly ones. It's the sneaky one with shifty eyes you have to watch for. That's the one who will cause trouble when you least expect it."

Curtis has had some illustrious troublemakers in his kennels over the years. But true to his theory, they have put their aggression into their running. Maplehurst Star, winner of the 1980 Sussex Cup and 1980 Inaugural at Wembley, was a difficult customer. "Maplehurst Star was the second fastest I've run over 500m at Brighton," said Curtis. "Monday's Bran broke the track record and we were about ¾ of a length behind, just breaking 29.00 seconds. But he was a real bully in the kennels. He could be very nasty to other dogs.

"Ballyregan Bob doesn't like other dogs either. He gets on okay with his brother Ballyheigue Pat and the bitch we have in with him. But if he sees another dog, his hackles go up. He just seems to take an instant dislike."

The dogs that need to be muzzled in the kennel are very much the minority, though. "With 60 to 70 dogs on the strength we would only need to muzzle an average of two to three," said Curtis. "The most common reasons for doing this would be to stop kennel chewers or to prevent an injured dog from worrying at its bandage or plaster.

"But if we do have a bad dog, we don't take any risks. It's no good being soft with them. It's not fair to the owner of the dog or bitch he is kennelled with. A bite can put a dog off the card for a fortnight. Of course, everyone makes mistakes — but you should make as few mistakes as possible."

Curtis recommends kennelling troublemakers separately if there is the space, or otherwise muzzling them full-time. "We use Beaverwood muzzles which are lighter to wear and cause less trouble if the dog slobbers. The leather ones can cause irritiation if they get wet," he said.

But with most dogs, Curtis reckons you can sidestep potential trouble. "We've got one, Lomat Alec, who's a bit nervous. He would run a mile if a stranger came near him. But because he knows us, he can't resist having a nip. If he's being groomed and a dog goes by, he'll have him. But on the track it never enters his mind. There's another, First Quarter. When you walk him up the range he goes for everyone in sight. All the dogs have to be held back until he's gone past. But again, he's as straight as can be on the track."

Kennel chewers are a menace in any kennel and a muzzle is sometimes the only solution. "Some dogs will literally eat their way out of a kennel if you don't muzzle them," said Curtis. "They finish up with a quarter of a pound of wood in them. It doesn't do them any good — in fact it can be disastrous if you're trying to get them through a competition. There's nothing you can do beyond muzzling them. It is something that is in the dog. They simply don't like being shut in."

Curtis remembers one greyhound called Monty who was Houdini-like in his attempts to break out. "He would jump up to get to the bars at the top of his door — and one day he left his two dew claws up there. But it didn't stop him. I put him in a kennel with a window and he used to lift the latches up. One time I came back at midnight after I'd been open racing and I saw these two eyes glinting in the dark. It was Monty. He had managed to get out through the window.

"So I got some wire mesh and literally wired the whole kennel up. I thought he'll never get out of this. But two days later he went through the window again. He went for a rest at June Saxby's and her husband Stan said to me: 'That's a right dog you've given us. He's ruined three of my kennels. He's torn them to pieces.' When it was time for the dog to retire from racing, the owner said he would have him at home. I said: 'You're mad. You won't have a home left.'

"He started off outside in a kennel and he wasn't very happy so they brought him inside. He walked round and round trying to settle until eventually he found a place under the stairs. From that moment onwards he never caused any trouble. He is now 11 years old and is a well loved family pet. His only problem was that he didn't like being shut in."

The ideal greyhound is the dog that lies calm and happy in his kennel and saves all his energy for the track. But every trainer has his share of fretters who cause no end of problems. "Some dogs are always on the go, jumping up and down in the kennel from morning until night," said Curtis. "It is worse at the Brighton kennels where they have to jump up in order to see out of the doors."

Glin Bridge, one of the finest greyhounds Curtis trained, was a terrible fretter. When he was in the middle of his winning sequence of 15, he dislocated a toe and had to have it pin-fired. "Normally after a week to 10 days the toe is beginning to mend," said Curtis. "You hope to have them back on the track in three to four weeks. But Glin Bridge refused to lie quiet. He was jumping up and down and his toe was swollen like a sausage. The vet gave him an injection, but it didn't help.

"I was at my wits' end. I thought: 'I've got one of the best greyhounds in the country — and I can't even get him right.' Then Gunner Smith suggested that I turned the kennel door the other way round so instead of jumping up to look out he could look through a gap at the bottom. I had always resisted this idea. I was frightened that a dog might put his foot out of the gap and get hit as someone went past. But I was so worried about Glin Bridge I decided to give it a go. In a week the toe was right down. Now I always change the kennel round for fretters or for injured dogs."

The problems with most fretters begin when they are on their way to the race track. As soon as they are loaded up, they start getting over excited. "If you've got a real crackpot — a non-stop barker — it helps if you can prevent him seeing out," said Curtis. "A van is obviously the best vehicle to use but if you have an estate car the windows can be painted with whitener or stuck over with newspaper. The dog is more likely to settle if he's not seeing things shooting past." He also recommends using cages which restrict the dogs' movement. "When they are loose and you've got one panting, the heat from the body spreads and all the dogs can end up being distressed," he said.

Fresh air and ventilation are essential for dogs in transit, particularly in the summer, and Curtis suggests that the fretters are muzzled. "Most greyhounds are very calm and will settle down good as gold. But you always get the odd one moaning and groaning all the way. You can box muzzle them — and that's all you can do. In fact, I would always muzzle a greyhound when travelling, even if I only had one or two dogs. No-one expects the worst to happen — but if there is a serious accident you could be in real trouble with an unmuzzled dog. If he's in pain and you're trying to lift him — he'll go for you. He can't help himself. There are those who are against muzzling dogs in transit but I don't think it does any harm — and if the worst happens you are prepared."

The next problem the trainer faces is when the fretter gets to the race track and has to spend a couple of hours in a kennel listening to the hare and all the other sounds which he associates with racing. "The dog will get more and more excited," said Curtis. "The saliva will literally pour out and they can lose an amazing amount of weight. We've had dogs going 2 lb down — and there's nothing much you can do about it."

One solution is to chain the dog up in the racing kennel. Most will be more inclined to settle if they are prevented from jumping up and down. "I would use chain and then feed it through a length of hosepipe" said Curtis. "If you use about 18 inches of hosepipe it keeps the chain stiff and prevents it from tangling. Make sure the collar is very loose. Then if the dog pulls he won't choke himself — and if he tries anything silly the collar will just slip over his head."

Curtis leaves the dog in the kennel wearing its racing muzzle, which prevents messing around at parade time and also stops the dog from trying to chew his way out. "I have also found that putting cotton wool in the dog's ears can help, as it stops him from hearing the noise of the hare," he said. "This is particularly true when you are at a track which has a Sumner hare, which is much noisier than the McGee. Other trainers leave a radio on in the kennel to deafen the noise from outside."

But Curtis adds a cautionary note. "I remember Paddy Mullins brought a bitch to Portsmouth who was famous for her flying start from the boxes. On this occasion, she got left and I said to Paddy after the race: 'That was unusual for her wasn't it?' He confessed he had put cotton wool in her ears in the racing kennel to stop her getting too excited — and had then forgotten all about it. When she was in the boxes — the poor bitch couldn't hear the hare coming."

But Curtis is the first to admit that there is no really satisfactory solution to stop a dog from fretting. "You always feel the dog has run his race before he has got on the track," he said. "If you've got a good dog, you think how much better he would be if he saved all his energy for racing."

Upland Tiger, who Curtis rates as the fastest puppy he trained, would wear himself out when he got to the race track. "He was a lovely dog travelling and he was good in his kennel — but once you got him out on the race track he would go mad," said Curtis. "He was so strong, he would pull like a bull dog. He put years on my life."

The greyhound that keeps on running when the race is over can also pose problems for the trainer, particularly if the dog is going through the rounds of a major competition. "They use up so much unnecessary energy," said Curtis. "If they're running again the next week it can be enough to take the edge off their performance."

A lot of tracks used to use sheets just after the trip to force the greyhounds to pull up. But most trainers dislike them. "When the sheet is there, the dogs either try to jump it or pull up too fast and injure themselves," said Curtis. "In fact Ballyregan Bob injured himself at Brough Park when he pulled up too fast. It's much better to stop the hare further down the back straight, slowing it gradually to a standstill. If the hare is tripped too fast the greyhounds just shoot straight past."

There are some greyhounds who mess around after a race from pure devilment. Curtis has had dogs turning and running the opposite way at the trip — and one who would turn before he even got as far as the trip.

"In the end I advised the owner to take the dog and try him behind a different hare," he said. "I felt it was just a matter of time before he got hurt at Brighton."

He has also had dogs jumping into the centre. "Some do it because they are nervous," he said. "But most just love being chased. It always amazes me where they get the energy from after they have raced. We had one we could never catch, even when we had half the track officials after it. So in the end we would just open all the gates and he would run back into the paddock and stand there waiting to have his feet washed."

But the problem of running on has been the downfall of some good dogs. Curtis remembers competing in the 1979 Cearns Memorial at Wimbledon when he got three dogs through to the final. He ended up with a one-two finish — but it was not the way round he had expected. In the heats run on the Wednesday, Aglish Hero was drawn against Princess Glin, who was trained by Gunner Smith. "My dog could just about get 660 metres — but after the race he chased Princess Glin round the circuit three times," said Curtis. "The next day my dog was drinking gallons of water. He was exhausted."

The final was on the Friday and Curtis had Aglish Hero (5–2) in trap one, Clountie Comment (16–1) in four and Acoona Matata (10–1) in six. Clountie Comment came out like a rubber ball and won easily in 41.03. Aglish Hero finished second 2¼ lengths adrift and Jingling Star the 8–11 favourite was third. "Aglish Hero had knocked himself out," said Curtis. "He had ruined his chances with the extra running after the heats. Nowadays we use a device, which is imported from Australia. It imitates the noise of the hare and it helps to bring the dog back to you."

Some greyhounds show a distinct preference for running in daylight. "These are the nervous types who get easily distracted," said Curtis. "They don't like the artificial lights and the noise of the crowd, with people hanging over the rails flapping their programmes. You find they are taking more notice of what is going on around them than on the job they are meant to be doing. In a case like this you are better off running the dog at an afternoon BAGS meeting where there is scarcely any crowd."

But obviously, this is no solution for the top open racer. "Fortunately it is fairly rare to get a greyhound that simply won't perform in front of crowds," said Curtis. "But it does happen. I had a very good dog that came over from Ireland. The owner paid about £2,000 for him after he had clocked 29.73 at Tralee — which was a really cracking time. We thought he was something special. He was used to running in the winter when everyone was inside. But the first time he raced in the summer and there were people cheering on the rails, he just came to an abrupt halt on the home straight. We put him away and he was okay when he came back in his trials. But the first time he ran in front of a big crowd and got in front, he did it again. As soon as the cheering started he just stopped dead and trotted over the line. We gave him another chance — but he did it again. The owner had done his money on him a couple of times and so that was that. He was sold to a flapping track — and because the crowds were so much smaller he was fine."

Naturally, no trainer likes to be saddled with a problem dog. But few can afford to write off a fast greyhound because of temperamental difficulties. The advice Curtis gives is to persevere and by trial and error you should be able to find a solution. It might not prove to be the complete answer — but at least it should give the dog its fair share of wins.

CHAPTER FIFTEEN

Common Ailments

THE responsibility of running a big greyhound kennel does not begin and end with racing results. The trainer must care for each individual animal, treating injuries and illness as they occur and, perhaps most important of all, preventing the spread of infection. It is no surprise to learn that George Curtis takes this side of the job very seriously. "The greyhounds rely on you entirely," he said. "They give their best in terms of racing and it is up to the trainer to make sure they are kept clean and comfortable and that all injuries and ailments are spotted in the early stages."

A good, reliable vet that you can contact at any time is a must and Curtis has a high regard for John Baber, who looks after the Brighton dogs. "The vet is the expert and you must be guided by him," he said. "He will always put the dog before any racing considerations – and that is how it should be. But you should be able to work in tandem. When you have gained a bit of experience there are a number of treatments that you can do yourself, without the trouble and expense of bothering the vet every time. Equally, you must be able to follow through the vet's treatment. If he has stitched up a dog or set a broken hock, it is your responsibility to make sure the dog doesn't ruin his work by worrying at it or jumping up and down so the injury won't heal."

The golden rule, according to Curtis, is to keep all risks to a minimum. "I know I worry too much, but I always say: 'You only have to make a mistake once.' If a dog has been operated on in the morning, Curtis always returns to the kennels last thing at night to check that all is well. "I lost a dog once and I have never forgotten it," he said. "The dog was knocked out from an operation but he seemed okay when we left him. The next morning he was dead. The vet said it was heart trouble.

But I think he got his nose buried under the paper bedding and suffocated. It was a chance in a million — but it could have been prevented."

It is not only the greyhounds on the injured list that the trainer has to worry about. He lives in constant fear of kennel cough and kennel sickness, infections that spread through a range like wildfire, debilitating the entire racing strength. At Brighton, the situation is made worse by the fact that the six contract trainers' ranges are sited alongside each other. "We don't have the facilities to isolate infected dogs," said Curtis. "Not many people do. Even if we did, it is still debatable whether we could contain the infection. The staff have to go from block to block and they can spread it. All you can do is to keep the kennels as clean as possible. But when you have greyhounds going to track racing kennels, there is a whole new set of opportunities for infection. You can be as careful as you like, but you have to live with the fact that you are going to get an annual dose of kennel cough and kennel sickness right through the range. It is your job to spot the symptoms and take action immediately."

KENNEL SICKNESS: This term can cover a multitude of evils and most trainers have their own definition. It can vary from a dog being off-colour and refusing its food to a full blown epidemic of vomiting and diarrhoea. In Curtis's book kennel sickness covers all forms of vomiting and tummy upsets. He draws the line with acute enteritis, which is a lot more serious.

When kennel sickness strikes, you know from the moment you first open the door in the morning that you've got trouble. "It is a nightmare for the staff," said Curtis. "It is something that you come to dread. It usually starts when one of your dogs goes to a track racing kennel which has not been properly disinfected. If there has been any vomit which has not been cleared up properly, the dog will bring the infection home with him. In an ideal world you would close the range for a week as soon as the first dog went down with it. But the track needs runners and you cannot withdraw 20 dogs because one is sick."

When a dog goes sick the first thing to do is to disinfect the kennel thoroughly. "Make sure no vomit lies around," said Curtis. "The germs spread like wildfire. But the most important thing is to starve the dog for the next 24 hours. Once he has the infection everything will go through him – and that just causes more aggravation."

Dehydration is obviously a problem and he suggests keeping a supply of sterilised water readily available. "Tap water is often mildly contaminated," said Curtis. "So we boil all the water when we have a bout of kennel sickness." He fights the infection with Lectade Kaobiotic, an antibiotic which he has found very effective.

"We give two tablets three or four times a day," he said. "If you can't get this type of antibiotic, be guided by your vet. I would always keep a supply in the kennel so I can dose the dogs as soon as the trouble starts." He suggests the dog is confined to the kennel, with a coat if it is cold, and sawdust is spread on the floor to make clearing up easier. "Most dogs will feel too listless to want to go out," said Curtis. "And if you take them out, you risk spreading the infection further."

Although kennel sickness strikes a big range at least once a year, Curtis says the dogs do build up some immunity. "The dogs who had it the year before will probably only get it mildly and be off-colour for a day," he said. "You have to watch out for the newcomers from Ireland and the puppies. We always withdraw a dog, even if he only has a mild attack of kennel sickness. If you run a dog with stomach trouble you'll crease him up and he'll be off racing twice as long. If you take the risk and the dog runs off colour you've then got the owner, the racing manager and the public moaning at you, so you're not doing anyone any favours. The rule is: 'When in doubt — take him out'."

If a dog has been reported sick, he will need a trial before he starts racing again on most NGRC tracks. So by the time the dog has recovered, regained his weight and trialled back, the total lay-off will amount to around 10 days. But obviously this depends on how badly the dog is affected. The danger sign is if the dog passes blood with the diarrhoea.

"If a dog starts passing blood, take him to the vet immediately," said Curtis.

"That is acute enteritis and it is much more serious than ordinary kennel sickness, which can always be cleared up with a course of antibiotics. You can handle that yourself. But don't mess about if you see bleeding. That is a matter for the vet."

When the dog has been starved for 24 hours following sickness and diarrhoea and is showing signs of recovery he should not be rushed back to his full diet. "Only feed cooked meat," said Curtis. "If possible give white meat or cooked fish — and let him have about one third of his normal quantity. Let the dog eat this two or three times a day rather than giving one big feed. By the next day he should be ready for half feeds and a drop of milk — and the day after that he should be back to normal."

KENNEL COUGH: Kennel cough is the curse of all trainers and few ranges remain free from it for more than a year at a time. "The trick with kennel cough is to catch it in the early stages before it goes deep," said Curtis. "Never run a dog that is coughing, he will perform badly and his condition will get worse." As soon as a dog sounds husky or is beginning to cough, Curtis withdraws him from racing and doses him with glycerine and honey. "Make sure you keep the dog quiet," he said. "If he stands in the paddock barking, he'll get worse and worse." If the cough is persistent he sprays the dog's throat with a diluted solution of TCP and doses him with Terramycin tablets, giving two, four times a day.

"The cough should shift with this combination," said Curtis. "The vet can also give antibiotic injections if the cough has gone very deep. But of course, this only works if it is an infection. The antibiotics don't work on viruses."

Curtis has always kept pace with changes in veterinary treatment – but he still believes some of the old remedies are the best. "I have had a lot of success using Wright's Vapouriser with dogs who have bad coughs," he said. "What you are trying to do is to stop the dog from coughing. The more a dog coughs, the more he will aggravate the tubes. Some cough so badly they actually scar the inside of the tubes. The vapouriser comes with a candle and a canister. Stand the candle in the canister, pour the liquid round it, then place the whole thing in two inches of water inside a metal bucket. When the candle is lit the heat makes the vapours rise and as the dog inhales it helps to clear his tubes, acting as an antiseptic."

Curtis has another useful hint for the dog with a bad throat. "Get an old sock with the foot cut off. Slip it round the dog's neck and it will keep him warm and comfortable," he said.

He warns that the dog must be completely fit before he is trialled back for racing. "The problem with the cough is that it may seem to have disappeared and the dog appears well, but it can return under the stress of racing and you're back to square one."

CRAMP: Any trainer who has seen his dog stride out in front and suddenly fall back, doubled up with cramp, has every reason to feel sick. He tends to blame himself, thinking there must be something missing in the dog's diet or he hasn't given the right pre-race preparation. But Curtis says he has never found a satisfactory solution to the problem. "Stan Biss, who was training after the war, got a Harley Street specialist to come and look at one of his dogs that suffered from bad cramping. But even he failed to prescribe a remedy."

And Patricia's Hope, which won the Derby twice, had terrible trouble with cramping when he was still in Ireland. In fact coursing-king Michael Murphy bred him for Cliff Kevern, owner of the world record-breaker Ballyregan Bob. But Cliff sold him for £500 because of the cramp problem.

"You can't cure cramp," said Curtis. "But I do believe that the more you gallop a dog, the less he is likely to suffer from it. The galloping keeps him loosened up. The time you have to watch out, is when you are bringing dogs back from a long lay-off. I've seen a dog cramp so badly on his first race back that he can't finish the course. I would always advise a trainer to give a dog plenty of galloping before he even thinks about putting him back on the card. Then I would try him over the sprint before letting him go over the standard trip."

Some trainers have had success using an infra-red heat lamp on dogs that are prone to cramp. Curtis has had his best results dosing with Cider Vinegar and giving a Vitamin E supplement. "All these things are worth a try," he said. "But I wouldn't say they solved the problem entirely."

He believes the cold can be a particular menace, especially if the dog has been waiting for his race in a chilly kennel. "If the racing kennels are heated, there's no problem," he said.

"But at tracks like Hackney, where the dogs have to lie on concrete, they can end up frozen in the winter. I always put a couple of coats on our dogs when they go there and give them a blanket to lie on. The warmer they are the better. You want them to rest and they won't do that if they're cold."

But never take a dog out of a warm kennel to parade in the freezing cold. That is asking for trouble.

"Make sure you keep a coat on the dog when he comes out and keep him moving while you are waiting to go in the traps," said Curtis. "Some trainers give the dogs a rub down while they're waiting, which may help the dog which tends to cramp.

"If your dog does cramp, you must get the blood circulating again as quickly as possible. The dog is in a lot of pain and you must rub the muscles in the back legs until it begins to ease up.

HEAT STRESS: Greyhounds are very prone to overheating and if preventative measures are not taken in hot weather, the results can be fatal. In the kennel the dog will need plenty of air and ventilation and he should not be left in direct sunlight. "Cover the window with cardboard or put whitener on it," said Curtis. "That prevents the sun's rays getting through."

Although the dogs still need to be exercised, they should not be left in the paddock for too long. "We always have fresh water available in the paddocks," said Curtis. "But I have also known cases of dogs getting sunburnt. Their skins get sore and inflamed."

Far more common is the dog that gallops round the paddock in the heat and exhausts itself. When it is really hot, it is better not to risk the dog running loose at all. "I had an owner who came to see his bitch and he wanted to take her out," said Curtis. "It was a really hot day so I asked him not to take her out — but if he did, he must not take her off the lead. Well, he let her off the lead and had her galloping up and down the paddock. When he brought her back to the kennel she was in a state of collapse."

If a dog gets over-heated the most important thing is to reduce the body temperature as quickly as possible. It is a case where every second counts. "If the dog is lying there gasping, get a wet sack on him," said Curtis. "Or if you are at home, get him in the bath. The longer the body temperature is up, the more damage is likely to be done."

Travelling to the race track can also pose problems in hot weather. "It always surprises me how little people think about the welfare of the greyhound in this situation," said Curtis. "They don't realise that the harm can be done in minutes. If you leave a dog in a closed car with no shade for five minutes, he will die. One of my owners took a dog home, he went inside and left the dog in the car with the windows up. When he came out, the dog was dead."

Curtis recommends putting cardboard over the rear car windows or painting them over with whitener. "You want a good flow of air," he said. "The windows should be open, but not wide enough so the dog can poke his head out."

Heat stress is more likely to occur during daytime race meetings and this can lead to the question of whether a dog should be allowed to run. "If the dog comes out of the racing kennel panting and appears distressed, call the vet," said Curtis. "He will tell you if the dog is okay to race. He will always veer on the side of caution, but that is no bad thing."

If you are at a track where there is no vet, you must make the decision for yourself. "A good test is to pinch the dog's skin. If it doesn't go back tight, you know something is wrong," said Curtis. "But you know your dog. If he is panting and distressed and you are in doubt, don't run him."

When a dog is racing in hot conditions it helps if he is damped down with a sponge before he goes out on to the track. "When he comes off, hose him down," said Curtis. "And make sure he has access to fresh water. It is vital that the dog replaces the liquid he has lost through racing as soon as possible."

FLEAS: Fleas are a scourge in every kennel range and Curtis stresses that it is a problem that you must keep under control.

"The time to worry is between May and October," he said. "That is when the fleas breed like wildfire. And if you have a dog coming over from Ireland he will need a thorough check for ticks, whatever the time of year."

The flea's worst enemies are disinfectant and flea powder and Curtis recommends liberal use of both. "We wash and disinfect the kennels regularly and we put flea powder in between the cracks of the bed to prevent fleas from breeding there," he said. "That is where you find the eggs and if you can erradicate them, you will be going a long way towards beating the problem.

But when a greyhound is using stadium kennels or going away open racing, he is bound to pick up fleas. "We groom the dogs every day, so we are quick to spot them," said Curtis. "We use Coopo dusting powder to get rid of them."

The dogs are bathed on average twice a year. "If it is a nice day, we bathe them and let them dry off outside," said Curtis. "It freshens them up. We haven't got a special bath, we just use a bucket and sponge them all over. You can give them a good massage while you're lathering them with shampoo and then rinse them off a couple of times." But he warns against leaving a dog to dry outside if the sun is hot. "I did that once and the dogs got sunburnt," he said. "The sun reacted with something in the shampoo and their skin came out in raised lumps. You can be sure it was a mistake I only made once."

Ticks are most common on dogs from Ireland and Curtis has known a dog to be covered from head to tail with them.

"They feed on the blood and swell up," he said. "They look horrible but they aren't hard to get rid of. You must remove the head as well as the body so the easiest way is to twist them and then pull them out. Check the dog over in a couple of days to make sure there are none left. They won't come back."

Curtis started using flea collars on his dogs about seven years ago and finds them very useful. "They last for three to four months and so a couple will probably get you through the worst of the season," he said. "It is when the harvest starts that the fleas are at their worst, but I use collars between May and October. Some people think that if you are kennelling two dogs together, only one needs to wear a collar. But for the amount if costs, you might as well buy one each."

WORMING: Puppies are wormed from two weeks onwards, and it is amazing just how many worms they will have. "They can be full of roundworm, even if the bitch has been wormed when she was in whelp," said Curtis. "They can have a fantastic number, even though their tummies are not very big."

The dose has to be repeated in two to three weeks which gives the eggs time to hatch. There are a number of puppy wormers on the market. Top breeder Jane Hicks recommends starting with a type called Coopane and then switching to Panacur*.

"I would suspect a pup had worms if he was failing to develop at the same rate as his litter mates," said Curtis. "I'm not talking about the runt, who is the smallest from the start. But if they start at more or less the same size, they should grow at the same rate for the first six months."

Adult dogs are more likely to be infested with tapeworm and Curtis recommends regular worming with Scolaban or Lapitol. "Dogs pick up worms very easily," he said. "All they have to do is find an old carcase in the paddock. But if you are feeding a good diet of high quality meat, the risk is certainly reduced."

Curtis worms his dogs twice a year. "The ideal time to do it is when the dog is off injured or is resting," he said. "If you need to do it when the dog is racing, he should miss one race meeting." The typical sign of a dog with tapeworm is loss of condition. "If he's ribby and eating like a scavenger, worm him out," said Curtis. "Repeat the dose in a couple of weeks and if he doesn't improve, take him to the vet because there may be some other problem. But if a dog is walloping his food down and failing to put on weight, nine times out of ten he's got worms."

Curtis has found that worms do not always have an adverse effect on a dog's racing performance — at least not immediately. "If they lose condition, then it will affect their running," he said. "But as long as the dog looks well the worms won't be doing that much harm. I've had a dog that was running brilliantly and I've suddenly seen that he had worms. He was running in a big competition, so there was no way I was going to worm him out. I let him run on until the final — and he still won. It all depends how bad the infestation is and how long it has been there."
*(*See Whelping)*

SKIN TROUBLE: There are few sights that look worse than a greyhound parading before the start of a race with great bald patches showing all over its hindquarters. The dog looks in poor condition and that reflects badly on the trainer. But Curtis admits that he has had dogs who have failed to respond to treatment and have gone out looking terrible. "In fact it probably won't make any difference to the dog's performance," he said. "But I don't like to see it."

He attributes a lot of the skin trouble at the Brighton kennels to the paddocks. "Our paddocks are used so intensively day after day, week after week, year after year that the ammonia from the urine builds up in the soil, which makes it very acidic. When it is wet and the mud splashes on to the dog it can burn the surface of the skin and cause irritation. It's the same sort of thing as when a dog lies in its own water. When horses are put out into the paddock they dip their legs in liquid paraffin to prevent this happening. But you can't do that with a kennel full of dogs. You would spend all day doing it. We have a concrete side paddock which can be used on wet days but the dogs don't empty so well there. The best thing to do is to wash the dog's legs, tummy and hind quarters when he comes in and towel him dry."

For greyhounds with skin trouble, Curtis uses a mange skin dressing known as Benzyl Benzoate. "This comes as a powder and you make it up to a milk-like fluid and sponge it on the affected area," he said. "In most cases it clears up quite quickly. If you have a dog that is always worrying at himself, it is best to keep him in a kennel muzzle until the irritation has cleared up."

But there are some greyhounds who are prone to bald patches, particularly on the tummy, the elbows and the back legs, which is where they lie, and it can be a real problem to get the hair gowing again. "Obviously you have to clear the mange first," said Curtis. "But some dogs can be as bald as coots – and they are not even sore." For these cases he recommends the old fashioned remedy of liquid paraffin and yellow sulphur. "I had a bitch who was completely bald on her hindquarters," said Curtis. "We treated her with mange dressing but the hair just would not start growing again. We rubbed on coconut oil, which is a good cure once the mange has cleared up — but still no joy. She looked terrible even though she was running fine. I hadn't used the liquid paraffin-yellow sulphur remedy for years but I thought it might be worth a try with her. It's a very messy process, you have to mix it up as a paste and then apply it liberally to the affected area. Then the dog licks it off and it is the combination of the treatment itself, plus the paraffin and sulphur going through the dog, clearing its blood, that produces results. I don't know if I was lucky with this particular bitch — or whether it coincided with a warmer spell of weather, but as soon as she had this treatment she started to improve."

If you are running out of remedies, Curtis suggests massaging the dog dry or using surgical spirit, rather than embrocation. "It doesn't happen very often, but some dogs have an allergy to embrocation," he said. "You can massage just as effectively without using it. It helps you to massage, rather than doing anything special for the dog."

BITES: Bites occur more commonly among puppies who are being reared together than among racing dogs, but in both cases the treatment depends on how serious the bite is. "We don't get many bites in the kennel," said Curtis. "We muzzle troublemakers and when we walk them, all dogs are always muzzled. It also reduces the risk if you don't walk too many dogs at a time. The experienced staff take four out and the newcomers take two. The trouble usually occurs in the paddock. We only let them out two at a time but if they are galloping alongside each other, one might have a nip."

If the bite is no more than one inch long, there is no cause for concern. It is effectively no worse than a loose flap of skin. "With a minor bite like this, clip the hair off round the wound and bathe it in antiseptic," said Curtis. "I would use Pevedine, which is a surgical skin scrub. But diluted TCP or Detol is just as good. If you haven't got any of these to hand, use soap and water. The main thing is to clean the cut. It is also important to clip the hair, otherwise it will get caught in the skin as the cut heals. You can get curved scissors which make the job easier. Then all you need to do is dry the area and dust it with antibiotic powder — we use a type called Acramide powder."

As long as the wound remains dry and it is dusted with the powder until it heals, there should be no further trouble. "I certainly wouldn't withdraw a dog from racing if he had a minor bite," said Curtis. "If you have treated it properly with the antibiotic powder it won't do the dog any harm and it won't affect his performance."

But if the bite is more serious and has penetrated the first layer of skin, he recommends that the dog is taken to the vet and stitched up. "In the old days we used to do all the stitching ourselves," he said. "I've put 14 stitches in a dog. We kept a supply of sterilised needles and cat gut and we got along okay. But it was all very primitive. I think if the bite has gone deep, particularly if it has gone into the muscle, the job should be done properly and the dog should be given an antibiotic injection at the same time."

The nightmare that can face any trainer is if the bite catches a vein or an artery and then a tourniquet must be applied immediately to stop the bleeding. "Use a strip of bandage and tie it as tight as you can," said Curtis. "What you are trying to do is to stop the flow of blood from the heart, so tie the tourniquet above the wound. Then you get the dog to the vet as quickly as possible."

He remembers one occasion when a dog broke a leg in the paddock and the leg was literally left hanging by the skin. "The blood was going everywhere," said Curtis. "We got a tourniquet on it and rushed the dog down to the vet. He operated and inserted a nine-inch steel rod. The dog came back to the kennels and he could run perfectly well. We tried to race him, but he had only been a grader and he had lost his edge. The amazing thing was that he came back at all."

INFECTED EARS: If ears are cleaned out regularly, most infections can be nipped in the bud. "We rarely get ear canker these days," said Curtis. "We clean them out at least twice a week using a tablespoon of

Peroxide in half a pint of water. Ideally you should do it every day, but if you do it a minimum of a couple of times a week, you shouldn't get any trouble."

The problem arises when dirt gets in the ears — and this can often be an accumulation of dust from the paper bedding. If an ear gets infected, the vet will prescribe ear drops or cream. Curtis suggests saving time by ringing up and describing the problem so the prescription can be left out to be collected. "There is no need for the vet to examine the dog for something straightforward like a bad ear," he said.

"You know the ear is infected, rather than just being dirty, by the smell. But as soon as the drops or cream start to act and reduce the inflamation, it should clear up pretty quickly."

Dogs do not make the best patients and if a dog is constantly scratching his ear and shaking his head, he will aggravate the problem. In cases like this, Curtis suggests making a balaclava out of an old sock. "All you have to do is cut the foot out," he said. "Slip it over the dog's head, keeping the infected ear inside and let the other ear go through the hole. Put a lump of cotton wool next to the bad ear and that will stop the dog from flapping it. They look peculiar, but it does work — and it is far kinder to let the dog have his good ear sticking out. He will get very miserable if he can't hear what's going on around him."

SORE QUICKS: Care of the feet comes high on a trainer's list of priorities. Dirt getting into the greyhound's quicks can lead to a lot of trouble, causing swollen joints which will affect the dog's running. For this reason a thorough scrubbing of the nails is part of the daily kennel routine. If the paddocks are muddy, they may need doing a second time and they must always be done after racing. Curtis uses warm water and Pevedine for washing. Salt water can also act as a deep cleanser. If the quick is sore, he applies a zinc and castor oil cream.

"If it doesn't clear up in a couple of days I would use a kaolin poultice," said Curtis. "But I would seldom withdraw a dog from racing because he had a sore quick. I would give a good dusting with antibiotic powder and as soon as the dog had raced I would clean it up and put a poultice on."

CUT AND WORN PADS: This is a fairly common problem when greyhounds are doing a lot of road-walking. Again, early detection is essential to prevent any infection getting into the pad. Curtis suggests all road-walking is suspended and exercise is confined to the paddock. "If a dog has trouble with his pad, you should keep it covered up," he said. "Use a sock – and if it's wet, cover it with a plastic bag and bind it with tape. There are specially made boots you can buy, but I have never had much success with them."

If the cut has gone deep, he uses antibiotic powder, once it has been thoroughly cleaned. "Bind it up with lint and Elastoplast and change the dressing in a couple of days," he said. "Don't let the dog go back on the road until the pad has had a chance to harden."

If grit or cinder has got into the pads, a good soaking in warm water and antiseptic such as TCP, Detol, or Pevedine should do the trick. But if this doesn't work, the foot will have to be poulticed. Curtis recommends kaolin poultice. This should be prepared in a metal bucket or saucepan, mixed with a couple of inches of water and boiled for five to ten minutes. "Test it with your finger before you use it on the dog," said Curtis. "A dog can stand higher temperatures than we can — but even so, you don't want to take the skin off. It should be okay if it feels hot to the touch."

The poultice, which is like a paste, should be applied to the affected area a couple of times a day and this will draw out any inflammation. The pad should then heal in the ordinary way, with the help of antibiotic powder.

CHAPTER SIXTEEN

Racing Injuries

ADVANCES in veterinary science and the innovation of electrotherapy over the last decade have transformed the range of treatments available for racing animals. Injuries that would once have forced a greyhound to retire can now be treated so successfully that the dog can return to full racing. And perhaps most significantly, the length of time needed for many injuries to heal has been drastically reduced. George Curtis was brought up in the old school, when expense was kept to a minimum and trainers used to double up as 'vets'— working out treatments for their dogs, pin-firing toes and stitching up wounds. But the benefits of new technology are impossible to ignore and Curtis has been quick to utilise them.

"I have always made a point of finding out about all the new methods and treatments and then I have worked out what suited the dogs best from my own experience," he said. Fellow Brighton trainer Gordon Hodson bought one of the first ultrasound machines back from Australia and used the machine over the years to great effect. "You have to know what you are doing with ultrasound," said Curtis. "It works well but you should go to someone who is experienced in handling the equipment."

Curtis has had most success with magnetic field therapy and he acknowledges that it played a vital rôle in keeping world record-breaker Ballyregan Bob fit. He first used a Magnetopulse on the dog when he tore a muscle in his neck right at the start of his English racing career. It was subsequently in constant use in the long haul of bringing the dog back for his world record attempt following the bad wrist injury sustained in the 1985 St Leger and later aggravated at Brough Park. "I also found the Magnetopulse machine useful when Bobby was going strong in the middle of his record-breaking run," said Curtis. "He had to race twice at Hackney in four days and I have found that the machine can tone up a dog if he is a bit jaded."

In fact, he believes this is one of the most valuable uses of the machine. He has had two boxes purpose-built so the dogs can be treated without supervision, and as many as eight dogs a week receive treatment. "We use it when we are grooming," said Curtis. "We put the dog in the box for half an hour and then we can keep an eye on him without having to stand over him every second."

Curtis has found magnetic field therapy can make a big difference to his open racers when they are drawing to the end of a competition following a long campaign. "I have had dogs that I have thought were getting very tired, coming to the end of a long spell of racing when the going was heavy," he said. "You could tell straightaway when they got up in the morning that they hadn't got that bit of zip. In cases like that I would put the dog on the machine for at least five days, including the day of the race. I know many people don't agree with this but I feel it circulates the blood and takes the stiffness out. When I have done that the dog has come out and performed well — and that is what counts, rather than what is written in the instruction manual."

But Curtis warns against the temptation of seeing the machine as a miracle worker. "It cannot cure injuries," he said. "Don't put a dog on there and think it will mend a torn muscle. What it does is take the stiffness out and speeds up the healing process. That is why it was so useful with Ballyregan Bob who was racing a lot and was plagued with niggling injuries.

"It is worth using when a dog has sustained bruising after he has been baulked in a race. All that has happened is that a blood vessel has broken under the surface. Once the blood has dispersed the dog will be fully fit again. You can locate the area by the discolouration of the skin and if you test the area with your thumb, the dog will feel it. In cases like this, particularly when it happens between the rounds of a competition, a combination of massage and the Magnetopulse machine is very effective.

"All these new aids help the trainer, but I still believe that time and patience are the best healers. When a dog has sustained a racing injury, there is no substitute for rest. You can try and rush it, but unless the injury has been given time to heal and you have ensured the dog is fully fit you will live to regret it.

BRUISED TOE: This is classed as a minor injury, so long as it is spotted early and the dog is not allowed to run until it has cleared up. "The most important thing to do is to clip the nail back so that the bruising disperses," said Curtis. "You have to cut back as far as the quick so that it actually bleeds. Most dogs are fairly good when they are being treated — but it is a good idea to box muzzle them to be on the safe side. They are like children — one will stand a bit of pain or discomfort, another will scream his head off!"

When the nail has been clipped back and sealed with Vaseline, Curtis applies a kaolin poultice. This is made up as a paste with boiling water and should be applied while it is still hot. "Once you've put the poultice on, wrap a good pad of cotton wool round the toe," said Curtis. "This helps to keep the warmth in. Then bind it up around the joint with Elastoplast. This should be done twice a day until the bruising has gone and then once a day. By the third or fourth day it should be better. But I would give the dog a 10-day lay-off from racing."

PIN-FIRING: This is a simple operation which is used to tighten up the ligaments around a toe joint. With straightforward bruising, the joint remains firm. But if there is a lot of slack, further action should be taken. "If you haven't got too much movement, you'll probably get away with it," said Curtis. "But if you can swing it all the way round, you'll have to have it pin-fired."

Curtis had performed the operation on numerous occasions when he was at Portsmouth, but now he leaves it to the vet. An instrument like a soldering iron is used with a nail on the end. This is plugged in until it is red-hot. The toe is then deadened and six holes are inserted in the joint. As a result the ligament shrivels up and forms a callous. This method was very popular at one time, but now schools of thought are divided as to its benefit.

"All I can say is that we have had a lot of success with pin-firing toes," said Curtis. "You wouldn't do it unless you had to, but in most cases you can have the dog back on the track at full racing fitness within a month."

The operation proved of great benefit to 1977 Regency winner Bonzo. "He was at Walthamstow before we took him over," said Curtis. "The owners wanted him to run in the Ladbroke Golden Jacket before he came to Brighton and he did a toe in the first round. We had it pin-fired and he went on to win the Regency, clocking 40.03 for the 670m and he was runner-up behind Montreen in the 1977 BBC TV Trophy at Walthamstow. He won lots of other open races and he was never bothered by his toe again."

Some dogs are more prone to toe trouble than others and it has been discovered that entire litters can suffer from an hereditary weakness in that area. The problem first develops when too much strain is put on the outside of the foot when the dog is cornering. The toe is under maximum pressure and if the dog catches a rough edge it puts the joint

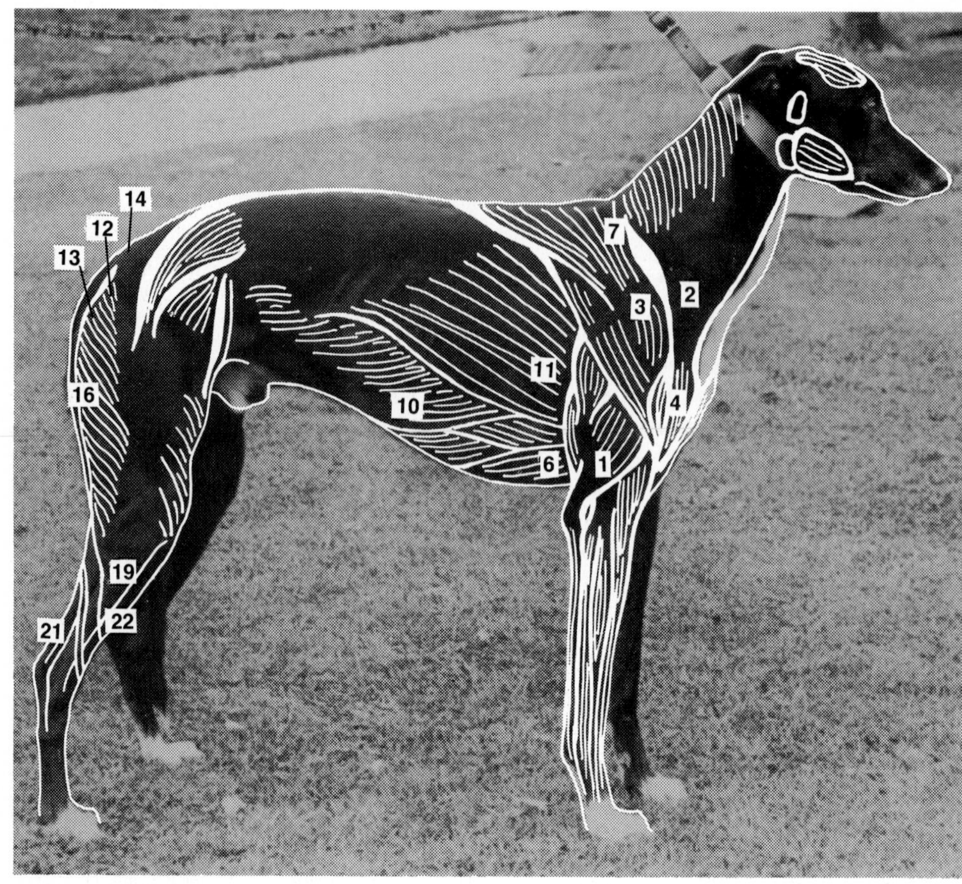

ANATOMY OF THE GREYHOUND

THE MUSCLES:

1 *Triceps (Egg Muscle)*
2 *Brachiocephalicus*
3 *Deltoid*
4 *Brachialis*
5 *Infraspinatus*
6 *Pectoral*
7 *Trapezius*
8 *Supraspinatus*
9 *Clavicle*
10 *Obliquus Abdominus Externus*
11 *Lumbo Dorsal (Fascia)*
12 *Gluteus Medius*
13 *Gluteus Maximus*
14 *Dorsal Sacroccygeus*
15 *Semitendinosus*
16 *Biceps Femoris*
17 *Gracilis*
18 *Gastrocnemius*
19 *Long Digital Extensor*
20 *Obturator Internus*
21 *Flexor Hallicus Longus*
22 *Anterior Tibial*
23 *Satorius*

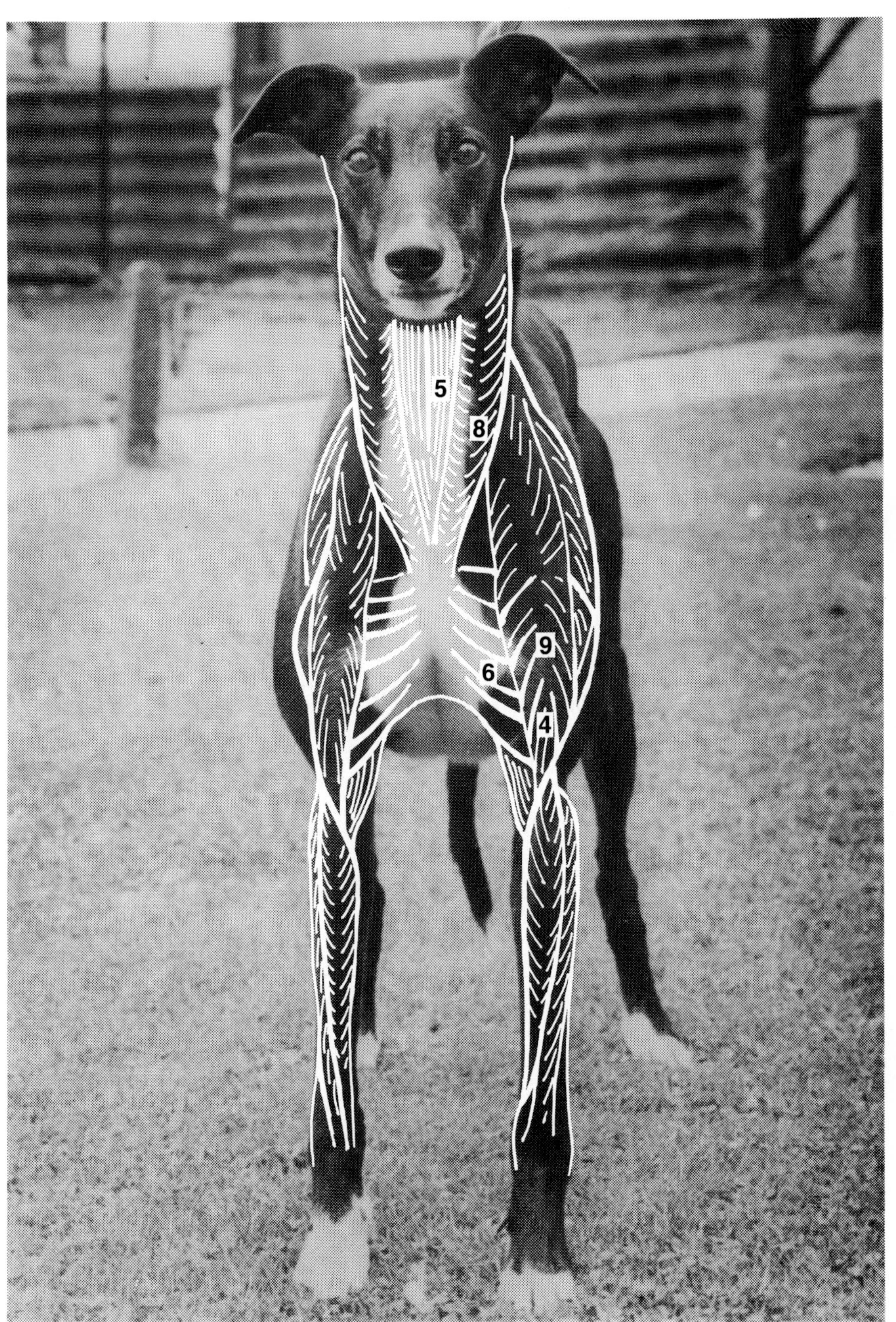
5
8
9
6
4

12
13
16
20
15
17
23
18

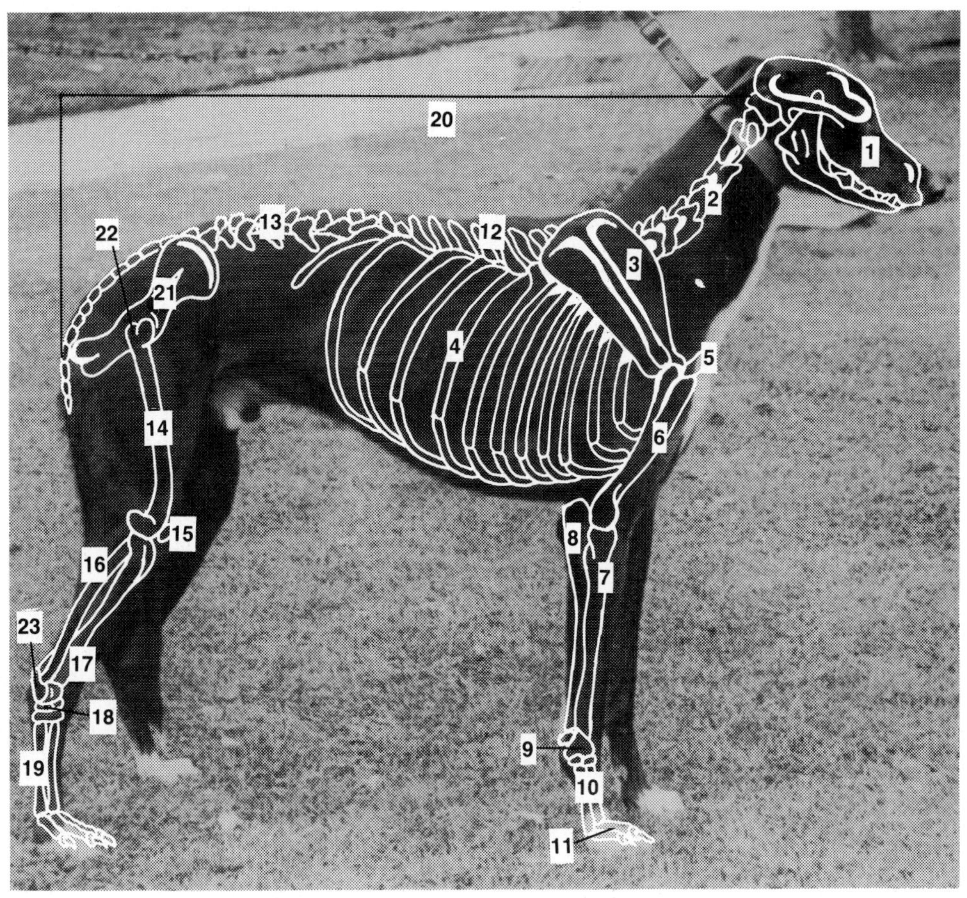

BONE STRUCTURE:

1 *Skull*
2 *Cervical Vertebrae (Neck) (7)*
3 *Scapula*
4 *Thorax (Ribcage)*
5 *Sternum (Breast Bone)*
6 *Humerus*
7 *Radius*
8 *Ulna*
9 *Carpus*
10 *Metacarpus (Wrist)*
11 *Phalanges*
12 *Thoracic Vertebrae (13)*
13 *Lumbar Vertebrae (7)*
14 *Femur (Thigh Bone)*
15 *Patella (Knee Cap)*
16 *Fibula*
17 *Tibia*
18 *Tarsus*
19 *Metatarsus*
20 *Spinal Column and Tail*
21 *Pelvis*
22 *Acetabulum (Socket)*
23 *Hock*

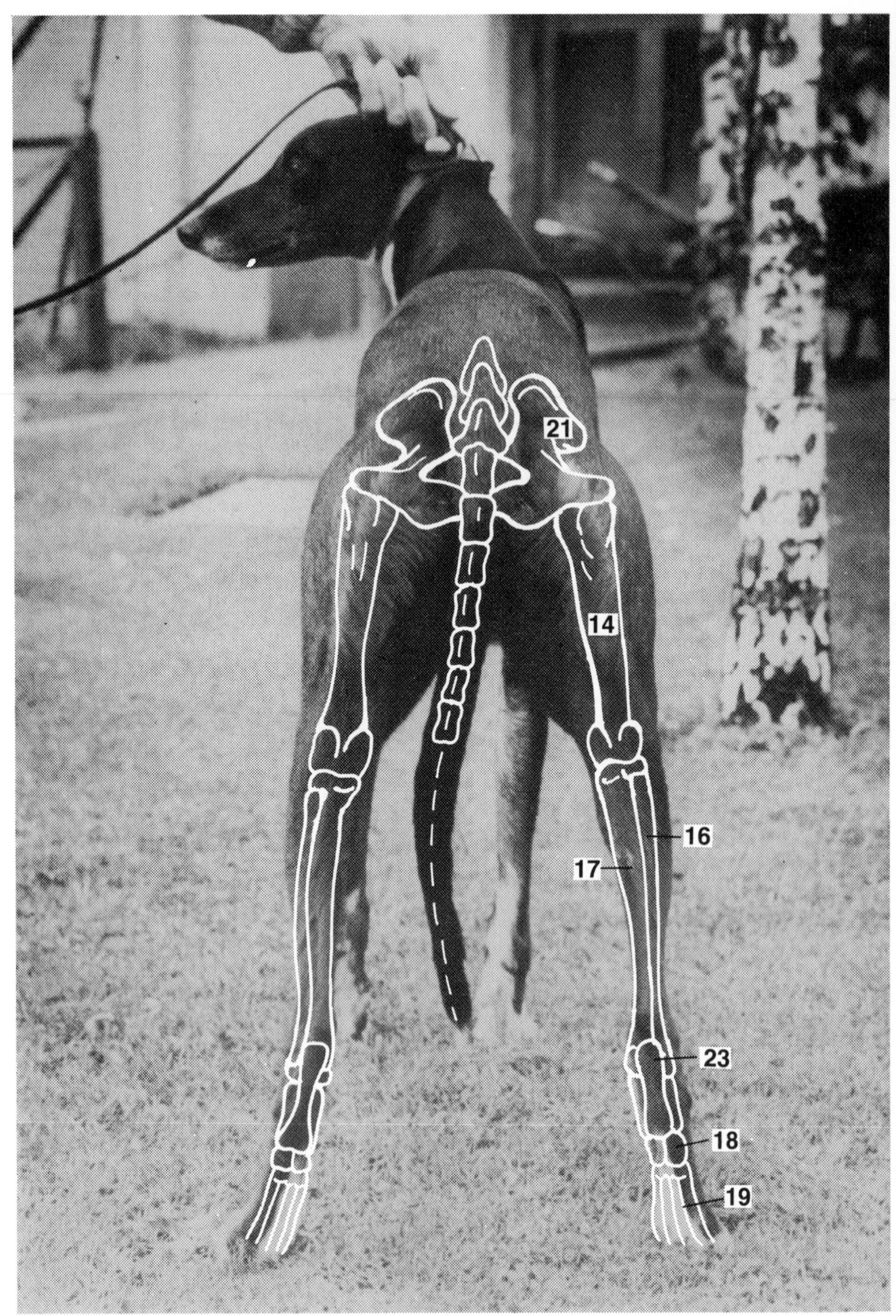
21
14
16
17
23
18
19

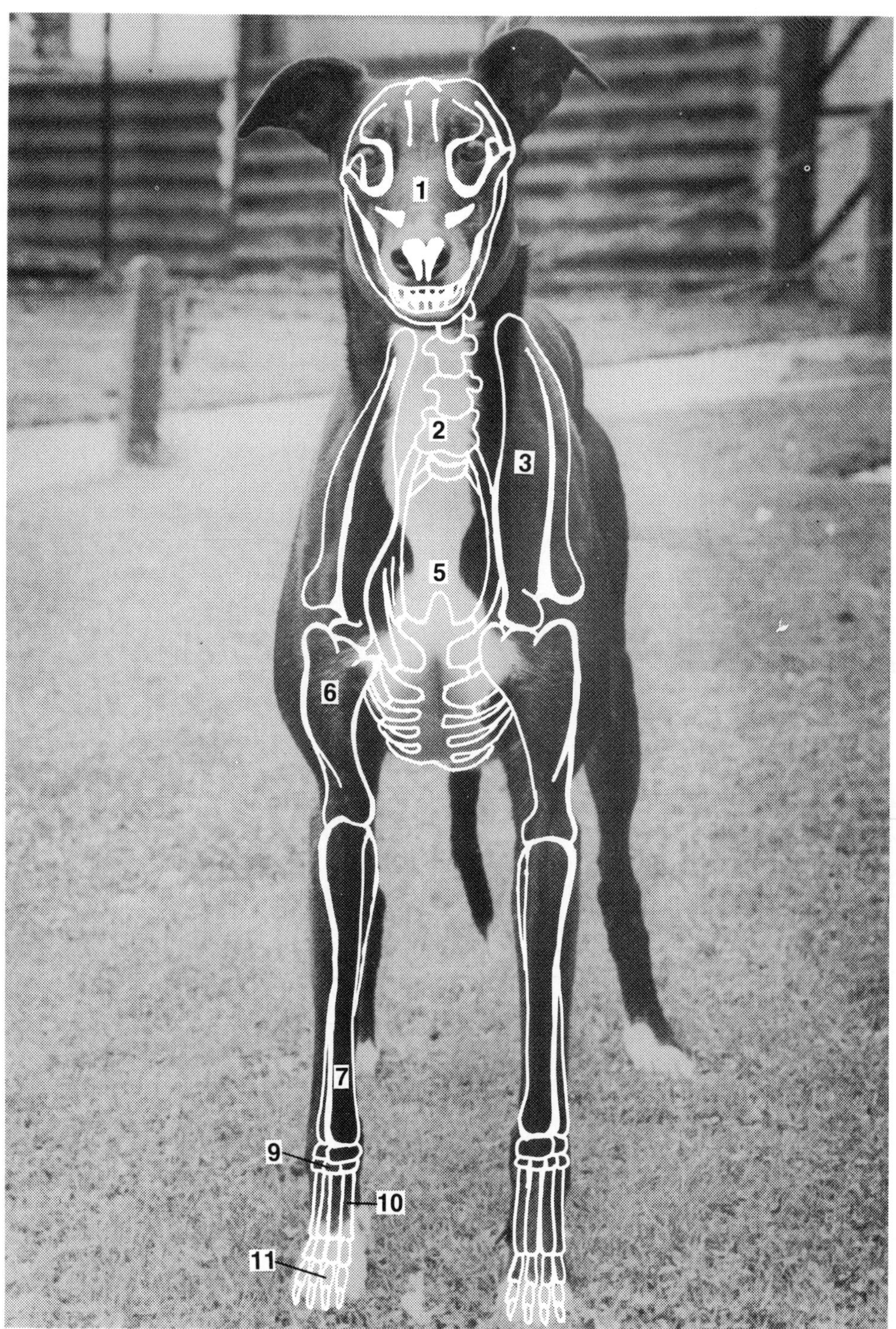
1
2
3
5
6
7
9
10
11

out. More often than not, it is the outside toes that are affected, but it can be the inside if the dog treads on a hard patch.

"It happens so quickly," said Curtis. "The dog can probably still go on and win after he's done it. But it is vital that you spot the trouble immediately. The more a dog runs with a knocked up toe, the worse it will get." It is fairly common to fire more than one toe on a foot. And again this does not appear to lead to any long term disadvantages. Curtis remembers one dog who had three toes pin-fired on the same foot — and he trained Monalee Customer, who was bought from Ireland with two knocked up toes. The August 1973 whelp by Silver Record went on to win the Cearns Memorial after having them both pin-fired.

Once the operation has been performed, the toe must be kept clean and dry. "The better you look after a dog, the quicker he will recover," said Curtis.

The other reason for pin-firing is if a toe has been dislocated. "If you know what you are doing, you can put the toe back yourself," said Curtis. "When it is back in place put cotton wool on either side of the toe and strap it up. Leave it for a week and keep your fingers crossed that it stays in place. If there is bruising and inflammation, cut the nail back and poultice it. Then when the inflammation has gone down you can get a better look. But if after doing this, it's still wonky, you should go to the vet. The danger is that there will always be a weakness in that area and pin-firing might be the only answer."

DEW CLAWS: Dew Claws are of no real value to dogs of any breed. Most will go through their lives without even knowing of their existence let alone using them. But some trainers worry that they can cause trouble for the racing greyhound. "The only time a dog uses his dew claw is when he jumps up and scratches you!" said Curtis. "Some people believe in taking them off at birth. But I don't think that is justifiable.

"The only time a problem occurs is if the claw is allowed to grow too long and it can get caught if the dog pulls up sharply. The answer is to keep the claw short. This is done by clipping or filing the nail. But I know some trainers who put sticking plaster over the dew claws when the dog is racing to prevent trouble. If the claw is hanging loose or has got twisted round, Curtis recommends box-muzzling the dog and then pulling the claw off. "If you do it quickly, the dog won't feel it," he said. "But you must clean up the wound afterwards. We use Pevedine and water, then dry it off and apply antibiotic powder. Put cotton wool inside the wound and around it. This prevents it pressing against the foot and sweating. Strap it up and change the dressing every day. It will heal very quickly because that part of the foot hardly ever touches the ground. With any luck, you shouldn't have to miss a race meeting.

TORN STOPPER PADS: This injury occurs when a greyhound pulls up sharply and hits hard ground. The treatment depends on how big a lump of skin they tear off. It it is only superficial, it will scarcely make any difference to the dog, as long as the wound is kept clean. Curtis suggests using the old-fashioned remedy of applying Stockholm Tar. "It's very sticky which makes it a messy job — but it helps to harden the skin up once the wound has healed," he said. "If the dog has only taken a layer of skin off, he should be okay to run almost immediately, particularly if you put a layer of Vaseline over the affected area. I know some track vets object to this, but if you explain the problem, most will be sympathetic."

If the wound has gone deep and bleeds a lot, the foot will have to be strapped up with cotton wool after the wound has been cleaned and dusted with antibiotic powder. "If the dog seems okay, let him walk on it within a couple of days," said Curtis. "The dressing should be changed regularly and Aureomycin Violet spray can speed up the healing. In cases like this, I would allow the dog a week to 10 days lay-off before I tried to race him again."

TRACK LEG: This can be a very difficult injury to detect as a greyhound can keep on running in the short-term without a noticeable loss of form. But inevitably the dog will be aggravating the injury, the longer he continues to race. "The problem is that most dogs don't go lame with it," said Curtis. "But if you don't catch it in the early stages, it can mean long-term trouble."

The injury is the result of a freak occurrence. A greyhound in full flight runs with its back legs on the outside. But every so often the leg is struck a glancing blow by the dog's elbow. "A dog might run a thousand times and it wouldn't happen," said Curtis. "But when it does happen the blow on the bone results in bruising and fluid forms, eventually causing a swelling."

The best remedy is to apply an icepack to the inside of the leg the moment the dog comes off the track. "If you don't have one handy, hose the dog down with cold water, for five minutes," said Curtis. "What you are trying to do is to stop the internal bleeding so that the blood congeals. If you have to leave the dog walking around on it, the blood will keep on dripping and form a swelling. In fact, this short term measure is so effective that greyhounds can continue running if they are midway through a competition.

"If you get special permission and put Vaseline on the elbow and the inside leg it will simply glide off if it makes contact with the affected area again," said Curtis. "I have known dogs run through a Derby suffering from track leg and the trainer has managed to keep them going by using

Vaseline and then applying the ice packs as soon as the dog has come off."

In the longer term, the dog will need at least a couple of weeks lay-off to cure the problem. "There have been attempts made to drain the swelling," said Curtis. "But these have never been very effective. Rest is the best cure. The dog can still be exercised as long as he doesn't gallop."

Curtis has also had considerable success using cortisone injections with this injury. "This is obviously a specialised job and the vet is the only person with the experience to carry it out," said Curtis. "He will tell you what is best for the dog". The lump that is caused by the swelling will probably stay with the dog for the rest of his life. But as long as the lump has gone solid it should cause no further trouble.

TAIL INJURIES: A greyhound uses his tail like a rudder so it is therefore an important aid when the dog is cornering at speed. But surprisingly the greyhounds that have sustained injuries to their tails have adapted remarkably well. Curtis recalls a spectacular example when a bitch called Janie recovered from distemper but it left her with a twitch in her tail.

"The vet decided to operate and he cut the tail right back until she was left with a stump about five inches long," he said. "When you consider that the average length of a greyhound's tail is 18 to 20 inches, you would have thought she would have been completely off-balance. But she learned to run with the tail she had. I don't think it makes a lot of difference if the dog is left with about 14 inches as the steering is done from the root of the tail. Of course, you would rather have the dog as nature intended, but it won't make a fantastic difference to their running."

The majority of injuries occur when a dog catches his tail in the trap or in the kennel door. If the injury is bad and bone is showing through, it is better if that joint is amputated. "If the joint is left exposed it can go rotten," said Curtis. "But if the dog has cut his tail all you need to do is clean it and then bind it up using very thin cotton wool and sticking plaster. Make sure you leave a gap at one end so that air can get through. If the tail is broken, the affected area should be encased in a three inch plastic tube."

Problems can occur with the dog who keeps banging his tail against the kennel wall, aggravating the injury and making it bleed. "Some trainers line the kennel with bales of straw so that the tail has nothing hard to knock against," said Curtis. "There is also a special shield with a zip which can be strapped around the body. But I prefer to make a loop with a bit of plaster about eight inches from the bottom of the tail. I then thread a length of bandage through the loop and tie it to the dog's back leg. You're not tying the tail direct to the leg, you're still allowing six to eight inches of movement. But it restricts the dog so he can't bang it."

MUSCLE INJURIES: A trainer must understand the physical make-up of the greyhound in order to give the correct treatment when injury strikes. But it can be difficult to acquire a basic knowledge when confronted with the complexities of veterinary text books. There is no real substitute for experience, but according to Curtis, observation comes a close second. "We groom our dogs every day so we pick up any soreness or tenderness at the earliest opportunity," he said. "A dog will always be the first to tell you if he is in pain and if you give him a thorough going over after racing as part of your daily kennel routine you shouldn't miss a lot."

Muscles make up 40–50 per cent of a greyhound's total body weight. This includes the heart muscles and the muscles which make up the stomach, intestine and uterus as well as the skeletal muscles, which are of prime importance to the greyhound trainer. Each skeletal muscle has a separate function in moving a bone one way or another as well as linking the bones firmly enough so they do not move out of place. The muscles are linked to the bones by tendons, which act as strong buffers protecting the limbs against sudden strain.

Muscle injuries can be divided into two basic categories. Strained muscles are the least serious. These can occur anywhere in the dog's body and will result in localised pain and swelling. The ligament has been injured but it has not been stretched beyond its normal limits and consequently no fibres have been ruptured. The second type covers torn, ruptured and dropped muscles where the ligaments have actually been ruptured and the injury therefore takes more time to heal.

STRAINED MUSCLES: These occur most frequently in the shoulder and they are fairly easy to detect. The first sign will be a small swelling, often no bigger than half an egg. "When you bend his leg up, the dog will be sore," said Curtis. "The first course of action is to put the cold hose on it for about five minutes. This reduces the swelling and so you can see the extent of the problem. I would always call in a vet to get an expert opinion. He is the number one man. But you have the practical knowledge and you must play your part."

Cortisone injections are the subject of some controversy and some trainers are now against using them. Curtis does not share their reservations. "You can only judge as you find and I have had good results when cortisone injections have been used," he said. "It certainly speeds up the healing process. I would only use cortisone where there is a lot of swelling — but it is for the vet to make the decision — and he must be the person to administer the injection. When you are injecting deep into the muscle it is a highly specialised business and he is the only person qualified to do it."

If the vet decides to use cortisone, he will probably wait about five days before he gives the injection. He will normally recommend a lay-off period of about three weeks. Once the fluid has dispersed, Curtis uses the Magnetopulse machine to speed up the healing process. "I wait until the swelling has gone down," he said. "I would not put a dog on the machine if there was still fluid around." But he believes the dog should be given regular exercise throughout his lay-off period. "You don't want the dog lying about in the kennel getting stiff," he said. "You must keep the dog toned up with regular exercise. The one thing to avoid is galloping. It is the sudden burst of speed that does the damage rather than a bit of gentle exercise. The vet will probably recommend a three week lay-off — but I would probably give it another week to gallop him back to fitness before letting him on the track. I would keep him on the lead until he is better. Then I would bring him back with a couple of gallops a week — perhaps even for two weeks — before he started back at the track. A dog can seem fully fit when he is galloping up a straight. What you have to remember is the additional strain the injury will be under when the dog is going round corners at speed."

The shoulder area is also prone to burst blood vessels which can appear to be very dramatic — but the treatment and lay-off period is similar to that needed for muscle strains. A large swelling develops immediately and it is important to get a cold hose on the injury as soon as possible. As soon as the swelling has gone down, rest is the only cure. "I had a black bitch called Ever Work and she burst a blood vessel when she was out on the coursing field," said Curtis. "It came up as big as a rugby ball. But after she had recovered she did all her best racing."

The bitch (Jungle Worker–New Forever) went on to win the 1967 Regency, clocking 40.95 for the 725 yards, she came third in the 1967 BBC TV Trophy at Charlton and she was runner-up in the 1967 Orient Cup final at Clapton.

OVER-STRETCHED MUSCLES: This injury is usually found in the top muscle at the front of the back leg. It is difficult to detect and the dog may run reasonably well, although he will be 2–3 lengths short of his best time. "If the dog's performance is below par and you can't find an injury, get the vet or an experienced trainer to check him over," said Curtis. "If you run your finger and thumb down the equivalent to the dog's thigh muscle he will turn his head and flinch slightly if there is any tenderness. If you put extra pressure with your thumb on the spot, the dog will definitely feel it." Curtis suggests a cortisone injection and at least three weeks' lay-off before the dog is brought back to racing.

DROPPED MUSCLE: This is a serious injury and most commonly affects the main muscles on the back leg.

"It is usually on the inside when they tear a muscle and it leaves a pocket which the fluid runs into," said Curtis. "It's purple in colour — and you can't mistake it. The dog will probably run badly and so you should be able to find the source of the trouble as soon as he comes off the track. Get the cold hose on it straightaway to congeal the blood, keep the dog on the lead and get to the vet as soon as possible." In a bad case the vet may decide to sew the muscle up. He might suggest a cortisone injection. But other than that, it is a matter of a long rest.

As the muscle heals it will knot and shrink. "You will always be able to put your finger in the sinew and feel it," said Curtis. "Most dogs will be off for at least a couple of months with this injury. Don't be in too much of a hurry to bring the dog back because if it goes again, you're in real trouble. You've got to nurse him back. Start him off with a scamper before you let him do any serious galloping and allow plenty of time before he returns to the track. There will always be a weakness in that area. I had one that went three times because the owners kept taking the dog away and trialling him. They were convinced he was okay and they wanted to bring him back in six weeks instead of eight.

"If you are patient the dog will come back and win races. He may not be quite as brilliant as he was, but he will race to the end of his time and probably never have any trouble in that area again — as long as the muscle has been given the opportunity to heal."

It is important that the dog does not make the injury worse during his lay-off period by jumping up and down in his kennel. Curtis recommends that the bed is kept directly on the floor for the duration. And if there is a gap at the top of the kennel door and the dog has to jump up to see out — the door should be reversed, with the gap at the bottom, until he has recovered.

TORN MUSCLES: This injury is like a muscle strain in that it can occur anywhere in the greyhound's body. The difference is that ligaments will have been ruptured so it will take longer to heal. Curtis recommends a three to four week lay-off and keeping the dog as quiet as possible with the bed on the floor. "With all muscle injuries, rest is crucial," he said. "The injury must be given a chance to heal completely before you think about racing the dog again."

BROKEN HOCKS: The hock is a very small bone, yet it is probably the most vulnerable in the entire greyhound's body when the dog is subjected to the rigours of racing. Broken hocks were certainly the most common injury sustained when the majority of racing was on grass surfaces. Now that sand has largely taken over, most trainers have found that the number of hock injuries have decreased.

Advances in veterinary science have meant the chances of recovery from a broken hock are very good. The hock can be operated on and many greyhounds will return to racing. But their complete recovery depends on the seriousness of the fracture. "Many greyhounds have come back and won open races after breaking a hock," said Curtis. "The dog will be almost as good as he was before. But in my experience they are never quite as good. In these cases the dog will have sustained a green stick fracture or a crack. He will probably be able to go on and finish the race after the injury has occurred. He will go within three lengths of his normal time.

"But with a real break, the dog will pull up straightaway. It's what we call a 'swinger'. The vet will have to put the bone back in place with a screw. If it's really bad he may have to use two or three screws and wire it up. In these cases the greyhound may return to racing, but he'll probably be half a second short of his best time."

If a hock is cracked or chipped, the lower half of the hind leg is put in plaster. In time, a callous forms, which will hardly be visible. The lay-off period is around three months and then the dog will have to be galloped back to fitness before he returns to the track. "When a vet has to screw the bone back into position, the lay-off will be more like four months," said Curtis. "The test comes when you take the plaster off and you see how straight the leg is. Obviously the callous will be much bigger and you have to hope that will reduce as the healing process continues. I had a dog in the kennel with a very bad broken hock — Jason Be Lucky. He had three screws inserted and it was also wired up. The vet said it was the worst break he had operated on. We got as far as galloping him, but it was obvious the dog would not be good enough to race again, so he was retired. But that is the exception. I would say that only one dog in ten won't return to racing after a hock injury.

WRIST INJURIES: These have become more common as the number of sand tracks have increased — and they are the injury that all trainers fear the most. When Ballyregan Bob injured a tendon in his wrist, many people thought this was the end of his world record challenge. Curtis nursed him back to fitness, but it took five long months. "If it had been a break, we could never have done it," said Curtis. "Wrist injuries of all types are the worst a greyhound can suffer — and the only real cure is rest and patience."

The wrist has so many small bones that it can go back or front. A hairline crack or a chip can go undetected — and this can become one of the worst problems for a trainer. "A callous will form in a remarkably short length of time," said Curtis. "If you are running a dog once a fortnight, a chip could go unseen, but every time the dog runs he will be lame. The friction of bone against bone will cause more trouble and the injury will get worse and worse. You can tell if it's nothing worse than a strain if it starts to go right day by day. But if it's broken, even just a hairline fracture, there will be a swelling behind the wrist and the dog will be reluctant to put weight on it. In a case like that you should have the dog X-rayed straightaway."

If a dog has broken his wrist, it will be put in plaster. But there is little chance of the dog returning to racing. If it is a crack or a chip, the only cure is rest. The dog should be put in a kennel with his bed on the floor and care must be taken that he doesn't aggravate the injury by jumping up and down.

There are more options available with a tendon injury. Curtis used a combination of cortisone injections and electro-therapy on Ballyregan Bob. But he admits that rest was the most important aspect of the dog's recovery. "We could have had the tendon pin-fired but we rejected that in favour of rest," he said.

Once the injury has healed, the long haul of bringing the dog back to racing fitness begins. "I think after a serious injury, your attitude should be that any racing is a bonus," said Curtis. "Realistically, I would estimate that only one dog in four will return to racing after a wrist injury."

Occasionally a dog will lose his confidence after he has been badly injured. "You get the odd dog, maybe only one in ten, who won't fancy racing again," said Curtis. "But the other nine will come back and win races. The majority are so tough and determined they will go through a brick wall to chase. If there is a reluctance it is probably because there is still something wrong. If a dog keeps checking, there must be a reason for it. But if confidence is the problem, you shouldn't force the pace by putting him behind live courses. The dog has been through enough and if he is forced to race he may run awkwardly and put more weight on another leg and sustain another injury.

"You know the vet has done his best — so there is no point messing around with a dog hoping for miracles. Use your commonsense and if the dog turns out okay it's a bonus. If it doesn't come off, it's simply bad luck and you have to start looking for a home for the dog."

CHAPTER SEVENTEEN

A Star is Born

FOR nearly 50 years one greyhound remained more famous than any other of his breed. Ask the man in the street to name one dog and the answer would be Mick The Miller. But in 1985 two remarkable animals changed all that . . . Scurlogue Champ and Ballyregan Bob.

After decades of decline, when little was heard but the all too familiar story of falling attendances and tracks closing, greyhound racing suddenly produced two superstars who revitalised the sport. The glory days were recaptured as crowds flocked in their thousands to see these brilliant animals race — and the tarnished image of greyhound racing receded as their triumphs caught the imagination of the public.

Comparisons are odious. Scurlogue Champ was the best marathon runner in the history of greyhound racing and anyone who saw him will never forget his unique style. Ballyregan Bob was the best six-bend specialist there has ever been and with George Curtis behind him, his talents came to full fruition. The most amazing aspect of the situation was that these two extraordinary greyhounds emerged at the same time — and between them set the sport on a new course.

George Curtis, always the man to play a situation down, does not gloss over this final chapter in his career. He said: "Ballyregan Bob was remarkable. He was the greatest stayer in history and there will never be another dog like him."

But you don't have to probe very deep to find the inescapable Curtis modesty. "I was so lucky to be given a dog like him to train," he said. "His unique ability was in him before I got him. It was nothing to do with anything that I did, or didn't do. All I did was look after the dog." Anyone who knows the agonising history of Ballyregan Bob's fight for fitness, will understand that there was a lot more to the world record-breaking success story than this. In fact, soon after Bobby arrived from Ireland he had the desperate look of a brilliant puppy who would never make the big time.

His exceptional pace was spotted in the first trial he ever ran, when he clocked 30.60 for Limerick's 525 yards. The brindled dog, by Ballyheigue Moon out of Evening Daisy was only two weeks past his first birthday. Cliff Kevern owned the sire and he had asked friends in Ireland to look out for any decent pups from Ballyheigue Moon's first crop. "Moon was a good dog on the track, although he never proved it in England," said Cliff. "He won the Puppy Derby at Limerick in 1981 and I bought him for £4,500. I brought him over for the English Derby, but after doing a very good trial time he split his web which ended his chances. He never seemed to settle after that. It seemed as though he was pining. I took him back to Ireland and he won eight top-class open races on the trot. That was enough to make him a viable proposition at stud."

In June 1984 Cliff got a telephone call from Ireland to say that a dog from a May 1983 mating between Ballyheigue Moon and Evening Daisy had gone round Limerick in a good time. His name was Ballyheigue Pat. Cliff agreed to buy him for £1,250. Then, a few days later the contact from Ireland rang again. "Forget Ballyheigue Pat," he said. "I've just seen his brother run. He's got the same early pace — but he stays on."

"I've always liked stayers," said Cliff. "Most of my dogs race at Brighton, so they have to get 515 metres. I immediately agreed to buy Ballyregan for £1,500." Ballyregan Bob justified his purchase price from day one. He did a 525 yards trial round Tralee in 30.56 and then won his first race by 12½ lengths in 29.48. "The dog was only 13 months old and he had already proved himself open class," said Cliff. "As soon as he ran that race I had offers coming in to buy him."

Cliff, a retired builder, was not tempted. After 40 years involvement in the sport, he knew a good greyhound when he saw one. "I shipped him straight over to George at Brighton and told him I had something special," he said. George Curtis decided to reserve judgement.

Curtis said: "When Cliff told me the time he had won the race in, I took it with a pinch of salt. You hear of these spectacular times so often and I thought: 'How can he be 13 months old?' But sure enough, he was. Then I couldn't wait to get my hands on him. They brought him over and kennel lad Alan Taylor went to the airport to collect him. He said to me: 'He looks the part.' When I first saw him I thought he looked marvellous. But he was still only 14 months old, so we had to wait a month before he was old enough to run. I gave him a couple of trials. In the first one he came from behind on the inside to win by 7 lengths. He did 30.77 for the 515 metres. Then I said to Cliff: 'That's the fastest dog I've seen since Upland Tiger.' Cliff knew that I rated Upland Tiger as one of the best I had ever trained. In his next trial he did 30.44 and then in a solo he flew round in 30.30. He was only 15 months old and he was doing top heat time at Brighton."

Everyone was amazed — particularly the hare driver, who had been doing trials around the 31.50 mark. "Suddenly he got this dog who was over a second faster and he couldn't get the hare away," said Curtis. "At one point Bobby was actually running with the hare and he turned, almost as if he was saying: 'What's happening?' " No one thought any more of the incident and a week later Ballyregan Bob made his English racing debut. On the strength of his trials, Curtis had decided to make him a railer and he was drawn in trap three for a puppy open over 515m.

According to Curtis, the dog ran a bit green and finished an unspectacular fourth. But it was not until he was back at the kennels that they found the cause of the trouble. "He came off a bit lame on his off-hind but he also had a lump at the back of his neck," Curtis said. "He had pulled a muscle and I think it dated back to the solo trial when he virtually pulled up because the hare wasn't going fast enough.

"I thought: 'That's a good start.' Anyway, we had to lay him off until the start of the Puppy Derby at Wimbledon." Curtis took him to the Plough Lane circuit and put him in a three dog trial. "Bobby was drawn in trap one and he ran right off the track," he said. "It was after that run that I decided he was no railer and from then on he was always seeded wide."

But the change did not appear to help as Bobby, berthed in trap five in the opening heat, was third all the way round and then finished in second place 1½ lengths behind Lord Jim. In the second round he got into all sorts of trouble and finished fifth. "He was virtually crucified round Plough Lane," said Curtis. "At one stage he was almost brought down."

Things were no better when he returned to Brighton and got beaten into third place in an A3 race. "It was a disastrous start," said Curtis. "He had run four races and had been beaten four times." Fortunately, Ballyregan Bob was soon to make amends and ran unbeaten through the three rounds of the Cosmic Orbit Young Puppies Trophy. In the opening heat he beat Keeper Tom by 1¼ lengths in 30.24. He went on to win the £1,000 decider in 30.04, again relegating Keeper Tom to second place.

At last Ballyregan appeared to have settled down and was fulfilling his early promise. After a couple of top heat wins at Brighton he went to Hackney to contest the William Hill Lead. In the opening heat Bobby soon took command and stormed round the 523m course to notch up his first track record when he beat Hot Primrose by 7½ lengths in 31.23. He won his semi-final in 31.47 and then led all the way in the £1,500 decider to knock 16 spots off his own track record.

This completed a run of eight wins on the trot and Curtis decided to give his dog a couple of months rest before bringing him back to contest the Pall Mall at Harringay. He was well fancied for the event and his progress through the early rounds seemed a formality. But disaster struck. In the opening round he got to the first bend, a dog moved off wide and put him on the floor.

"I thought he was very lucky not to be seriously hurt," said Curtis. "The marks where he screwed round in the sand were there all night. When he picked himself up, he was 12 lengths behind and although he was eliminated in fifth place, he was 4 lengths ahead at the trip. Philip Rees and Geoff de Mulder were there and they said: 'You've just lost your price for the St Leger.' I spoke to Cliff Kevern after the race and of course, he was disappointed. But I said to him: 'This is the fastest dog anyone has seen for years. He'll do times they've never seen before. But we've got to be careful with him. He could have been finished tonight. We don't want any more of that.' "

Curtis's head man Bill Masters was also very upset by what had happened. On the face of it, it seemed as though the dog had failed when he was first tested in top-flight company. But Curtis's long experience in the game stood him in good stead. "I remember talking to Bill afterwards and I said: 'The main thing is that we've still got a dog that we can work on tomorrow. He could have come off carrying his leg. Forget about tonight. We've got to nurse him along. But whatever we thought he would do — he will still do.' "

The next event on the calendar was the John Power Trainers' Championship which was staged at Walthamstow. Bobby was drawn against Ken Linzell's Ballintubber One over 475m. "The two dogs came out level and Bobby swung out wide and gave him 3 lengths," said Curtis. "Then he picked up Ken Linzell's dog and beat him by 2 lengths. Ballintubber was a very fast dog, he went on to be Dog Of The Year in Ireland and he won two classics, but Bobby picked him up. It was a two-dog race and both had every chance."

While Bobby was running like this, there was no cause for concern and Curtis entered him for the Blue Riband at Wembley. But again, Bobby ran into trouble and ended up on the hare rail. When he came off he had split the web of his toe. Despite a number of spectacular runs, a pattern seemed to be emerging. Over four bends Bobby stood a real risk of running into trouble at the first bend. His early pace was indisputable — but there was no guarantee that he would clear the first bend trouble.

"After the Blue Riband race I spoke to Cliff and I said I thought we were asking for trouble," said Curtis. "Bobby simply did not have the pace of a classic dog to the corner. He always stood the chance of getting into trouble and that could finish him off. He was on his knees at Wimbledon in the Puppy Derby, he ended up on the floor at Harringay in the Pall Mall and finished lame at Wembley. I thought we stood a very real risk of ruining a brilliant dog."

To Curtis, the dog had the unmistakable look of a six-bend specialist. The problem was that everyone has assumed Ballyregan Bob was a natural for the Derby. In fact, Cliff Kevern had backed his dog to win £7,000 for the kennel. Now Curtis was telling him it was a waste of time to take the dog to Wimbledon. To his credit, Cliff accepted Curtis's judgement and scrubbed his bet. This was particularly laudible considering that Cliff had been a greyhound owner for over 30 years and in all that time he had only had one Derby dog. Sirius reached the classic final in 1970 and his chances were destroyed when he was drawn in trap five. For many years Cliff had his own breeding establishment in Ireland and he has spent a great deal of money on his dogs. To find an outstanding dog, and then discover it was not a Derby type must have been a blow. But Cliff has always put his dogs first and he supported Curtis wholeheartedly.

"I fully agreed with George," said Cliff. "He was a length short of Derby pace to the bend. If the Derby had been at White City, make no mistake, we would have won it. But at Wimbledon it's a lottery to the first bend and there isn't the width of track to keep out of trouble. The dogs run into each other. At a big track like White City there is plenty of room and Bobby would have used it because he had a lot of trackcraft."

It was decided that Bobby should specialise in six bend events with the St Leger as his main objective. This was a decision that baffled the Press at the time. "I came under a lot of pressure," said Curtis. "The Press has been good to me over the years but I have learnt not to listen to what is said. My concern is with the dog, first and foremost and with the owner. I tried not to worry too much about the criticisms for withdrawing Bobby from the Derby. In the end, they all came round to my way of thinking. Cliff was 100 per cent behind me. That's what made it so easy for me. He was an ideal owner."

Curtis agreed to let Bobby go for the Olympic at Brighton, even though it was over 515m, and his dog made it all look easy with an unbeaten run through to the final. Bobby was only one spot outside the track record in his heat and in the final he beat House Hunter by 1½ lengths. But his performance confirmed Curtis's decision to concentrate on six bend events.

"In the final Bobby missed his break and found a bit of trouble," he said. "He was giving House Hunter 5 lengths going down the back straight and then he picked him up. If it had been a shorter distance he would have been beaten. But by the trip he was 5 lengths ahead. He had been very impressive in his heat and semi but that was only because he had a clear run."

Two champions . . . Curtis and Ballyregan Bob together at the Brighton kennels.

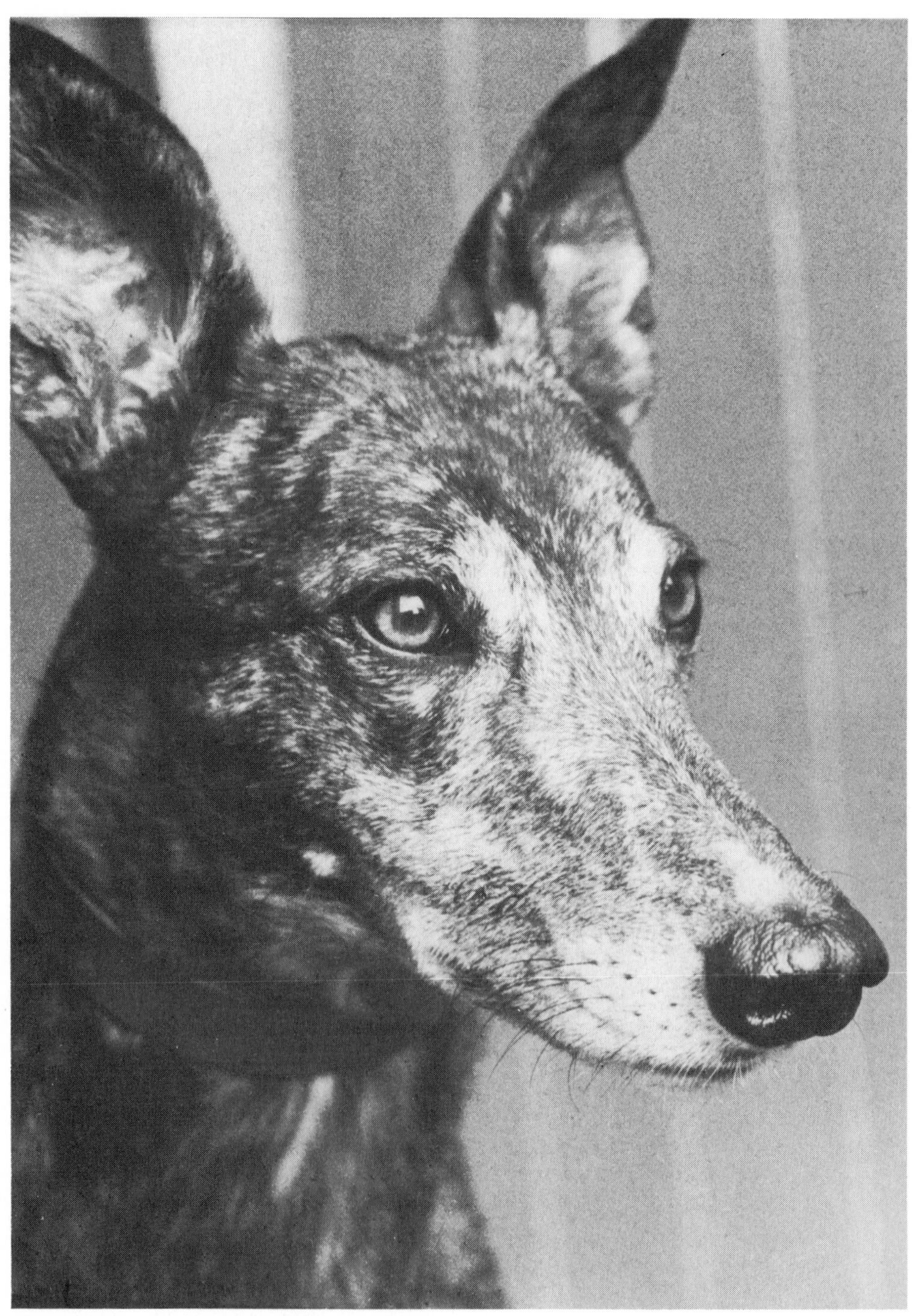

Ears pricked . . . world champion Ballyregan Bob in classic pose.

Curtis took Bobby up to Walthamstow for his first attempt over a six bend course and he took his chance in the E. Coomes Test over 640m. It was almost as if Bobby knew that the famous Curtis reputation was riding on him. He came out second and was second at the turn but then he flew round the 640m course to win from Air Drama by 9½ lengths in a new track record of 39.40. As if that was not justification enough, Bobby went on to win his semi-final by 13 lengths from Embassy Sailor and then took the £1,200 decider by 9¾ lengths from Air Drama.

"The track was running 60 slow in the semis and 40 slow in the final," said Curtis. "But each time Bobby came out and won by big margins — and the dogs he was beating were track recordholders. It was then that I felt completely justified in switching him to six bends. It was a wonderful thing for me. I'd been under a lot of pressure and I knew I had to make that decision. To be honest, I did it for the dog. I love the dog and I didn't want to see him getting hurt. He was an exceptional greyhound — and it was a dream for me to get hold of him. But he needed the extra distance.

"If I had been younger, I don't think I could have made the same decision. You are so keen to show everyone what a good dog you've got and show off that you are the trainer. It takes a long, long time to realise is that it is not so much the trainer but the dogs you've got in the kennel. I've trained all sorts — fast dogs, slow dogs, dogs that wouldn't go. But when I got to Brighton, I got into a different class. Then Jane Hicks came along and helped to make up a terrific kennel. And finally Cliff came along with the greatest dog I've ever seen in my life — and he was only a puppy. You know you've got a fast dog, the question is what do you do with him? At Harringay he was the luckiest dog ever. He came off the track sound and I was given the chance to nurse him along until we found out what he needed. From Walthamstow he just went from strength to strength. He proved he was the best stayer in the history of greyhound racing. I'm not saying he was the best greyhound — he wasn't a Derby dog. But over six bends there has never been a better dog."

On Derby final night, there were no regrets in the Curtis camp as Bobby proved to a crowd of over 12,000 that he had finally found his niche. He was invited to compete in a supporting open race over the 660 metre course and the line-up for the Mirror Punters Club Plate was outstanding. It included St Leger winner Jet Circle, Lord Jim, Oakwood Lady and Lisas Girl. Bobby in trap five, was one of five seeded wide runners. Jet Circle was ideally berthed in trap one. Curtis's dog was second out of the gates and then he found his extra gear and led all the way to beat Lord Jim by 12 lengths and set a new track record of 40.43, despite the going which was calculated 30 slow. Cliff Kevern, who saw every trial and every race that his dog competed in, reckoned

Ballyregan Bob could have won the Derby that night. "People were standing there with their stopwatches and they were amazed at his time," he said. "On his showing that night he could have beaten any dog in the country over four bends. But I had no hard feelings. I knew he would have to have got through five rounds to have reached the final."

The St Leger was the competition that Curtis and Cliff Kevern were aiming for. But before the start of the classic, Bobby was entered for the Essex Vase at Romford, which was worth £3,500 to the winner. The event was staged over 575m — and despite a nerve-wracking start, Bobby showed he was more than equal to the task. In his opening heat he was slow away and tailed the field until the three-quarter stage when he moved into fifth place. Amazingly he made up ground to finish first, beating Special Bran by a short head in 35.48. In the semis, he murdered the field and won by 11½ lengths from Plough Bawn in 35.21. But after the race he was lame.

"I rang up Cliff and said I wasn't happy with the dog," said Curtis. "I wanted to withdraw him. Cliff said: 'Is he walking lame?' He wasn't, but I just felt he wasn't right in himself. There was only three days between the semis and the final and I didn't think he had enough time to get over it. If it had been left to me, I would have taken him out. But Cliff said he thought we should go ahead because everyone was expecting the dog to run and they would be disappointed. I said: 'They'll be a lot more disappointed if he gets beaten.' But I agreed to let him run.

"I couldn't be at the final and when the telephone went I asked Lily to answer it. 'I know who it is,' I said. 'They'll be ringing to tell me Bobby's been beaten'. The next thing I heard was Lily saying: 'Did he? . . . Did he? . . . Well Done!' I couldn't believe it. Not only had Bobby won — he had equalled the track record."

Ballyregan Bob had come out second with Gunner Smith's Aitch Bee taking the lead. By the third bend Aitch Bee was some 6 lengths ahead but Bobby had collared him by the fifth. Then he flew by to win by 2¼ lengths in 35.15 on going estimated .20 fast. "That showed the sort of dog that Bobby was," said Curtis. "He could run a race like that and he wasn't even fit. He was not only one of the fastest dogs I have ever handled, he was one of the toughest. He was the strongest and most determined runner. When he was on the track, nothing could stop him."

This took Bobby's winning sequence to ten. But Curtis disclaimed rumours that he was going for the UK record of 20 consecutive wins set by Westpark Mustard. The St Leger was the prime target and the dog was to be rested in preparation for the classic. The Gold Collar at Catford was dismissed as Curtis felt the circuit was too tight for his dog.

As soon as Bobby was fully fit, Curtis trialled him around Wembley.

He was rewarded with a 39.30 run, which was inside the track record, on going estimated 45 fast. But a last minute hitch nearly sidelined his star. Curtis's range was affected by the dreaded kennel cough and Bobby went down with it. Fortunately, he made a good recovery and after a trial round Brighton, he was able to take his place in the Wembley classic. Bobby was quick to show that he was back to his best. In his opening heat he was in third place until the three-quarters stage when he moved up the field to finish 3¾ lengths in front of Evening Light recording 40.15 for the 655m course. In the second round he took the lead from the first bend and powered round in a record-breaking 39.46, 8 lengths ahead of Skidrow Black. Everyone expected the same relentless progress through to the final. But the semi-final turned out to be a race that Curtis will never forget.

Bobby berthed in trap five, came out second but all six runners reached the first bend together and there was the most appalling pile-up. Skidrow Black, Ben's Champion and Bright Jester came off worst, with Bright Jester ending up on the floor. Ballyreagan Bob was forced to jump over the fallen dog before he could race on. He finished first, beating Evening Light by one length in 40.56. But the race had taken a terrible toll. Bobby had landed awkwardly when he was forced to hurdle Bright Jester and his wrist swelled up like a balloon. "We took him for an X-ray to check that nothing was broken," said Curtis. "But it was nearly as bad. He had done a tendon in the back of his wrist. That is one of the worst injuries a dog can suffer and we should have withdrawn him straightaway from the Leger final. But we kept on hoping against hope. We took him down to the physiotherapist at Brighton Football Club and we had him on the Magnetopulse machine. But I think we knew all along it was no good. The most amazing thing was that Bobby had been able to run on and win his semi-final with an injury like that. He was at least 7 lengths adrift but he still kept going. You could see the poor dog was suffering but he wouldn't give in. He was determined to win."

Curtis and Cliff Kevern were faced with the inevitable decision of withdrawing Ballyregan Bob from the classic final. It was a bitter blow for both of them. Curtis had waited all his career to train a St Leger winner and on form Bobby was a certainty for the final. All he had to do was turn up. Cliff Kevern had waited almost as long to own a classic winner and after his selfless behaviour over the Derby, he deserved the Leger reward.

"I was upset for myself," said Curtis." I have always seen myself as a trainer of stayers and I knew I had a dog that was more than capable of winning the St Leger. I had waited all those years and there wasn't a dog to live with him. The final was a foregone conclusion. At Walthamstow Bobby had run against the same dogs and murdered them. But that was how it was meant to be. I felt shattered for Cliff. He had the prize in the bag and then he found out his dog was not going to run."

Cliff admits that the St Leger was a major disappointment. But to an extent, time has softened the blow. "I knew how much George wanted to win it," said Cliff. "It was the worst kind of luck because it was certainly ours for the taking. Ballyregan Bob was head and shoulders above the rest. But the dog was hobbling. There was no way he could run." Now the drama lay in in whether the dog, who was just over two-years-old, could regain his racing fitness. "Wrist injuries can go either way," said Curtis. "We had the option of pin-firing or rest. We decided to rest the dog but we knew it was going to be a long job." In fact it was not until November that Ballyregan Bob was ready to race again. "We tried everything," said Curtis. "I worried myself sick over the dog. I put his foot in hot water, in cold water, we used poultices to take the stiffness out. He had hours of treatment on the Magnetopulse machine and he had cortisone injections. I think everything helped but the main thing was rest. What you need is the patience to let the dog get over the injury and then even more patience to gradually bring him back to racing fitness." As soon as Ballyregan Bob was sound again, he was allowed to exercise in the paddock. "There's no point in keeping the dog confined to the kennel indefinitely," said Curtis. "He had to get used to using his foot again. To start with I used to walk him down the gallop just to keep him happy. Then I started giving him gallops. But injuries can be very deceptive. The dog can seem as right as rain when you gallop him. But when you get him on the track, going round the bends, the adhesions around the site of the injury break down and the dog can go lame again."

Curtis gave Bobby three trials round Brighton as he bought him back to fitness and in the third solo he recorded an unofficial track record, clocking 40.73 for the 695m course. The dog's comeback had been timed to perfection. In his first race back he stormed round Brighton to win by a massive 14¾ lengths, setting an official track record of 41.13. This was Ballyregan Bob's fourteenth consecutive win and following Scurlogue's failure to break the UK record when he stumbled at the seventeenth hurdle, Curtis's dog was now on target.

In his next three outings he broke the track record each time he ran. At Nottingham he clocked 41.87 for the 680m, at Hackney he beat Teeling by 8 lengths in 42.24 for the 683m and at Wimbledon he recorded 40.35 over 660m.

Curtis had always been determined that if Ballyregan Bob went for the UK record, he should run against the best in training. He knew he had the best dog and he wanted to prove it fair and square. This became increasingly difficult as the opposition shyed away from taking on the staying star. His races had to be arranged and the prize money for the runner-up had to be guaranteed. This put increasing pressure on Cliff Kevern, who had to bear the expense of a dog that was virtually unbackable, and on Curtis who had to keep the dog's interests in the forefront at the same time as satisfying an expectant public. This situation came to a head in Ballyregan Bob's next race when he was scheduled to run at Sheffield. Two days before, the dog came down with kennel sickness.

"We had been a bit reluctant to go up there in the first place," said Curtis. "Then Bobby went off-colour. I knew what everyone would say if I tried to withdraw him. It was not only the bad publicity, it was also the fact that everyone was looking forward to seeing him run. On the Friday, Bobby wasn't too bad, so I thought we'd be okay to risk it. He seemed better on the Saturday so we let him go, although naturally I thought he would have lost his edge. Sue Warner took him up to Sheffield for me and the next thing I knew she was ringing up to say that he had won by 20 lengths!" Ballyregan Bob led from half way and recorded 44.21 on going estimated 20 slow for the 715m course leaving Hot Primrose trailing home in second place. "I think this run showed that Bobby was a different dog to most," said Curtis. "I knew he wasn't 100 per cent and yet he won by 20 lengths."

Ballyregan Bob had now won 18 races in succession and Harringay was set as the venue for the next race number 19 over 688m. Again, he showed he was a class apart when he came out second and then beat Glenowen Queen by 14 lengths in a record-breaking time of 41.94.

Curtis's dog had achieved the incredible feat of breaking five track records in seven runs — as well as being one race away from equalling Westpark Mustard's UK record of 20 consecutive wins. At long last he was poised for major recognition. He had overcome big setbacks and was ready for the race the greyhound world have been pleading for . . . against Scurlogue Champ.

CHAPTER EIGHTEEN

World-beater

BALLYREGAN Bob had proved himself a great dog, but there was one race in which he was clearly several lengths adrift . . . the popularity stakes.

Marathon superstar Scurlogue Champ was still the people's favourite, he had notched up 16 successive wins in his record-breaking attempt and despite his failure at Peterborough, the public adored him. The black dog with the late, late run and Curtis's contender were constantly compared, and the question on everyone's lips was 'Which of the two brilliant greyhounds was the better?'

In a sense it was a question which should never have been asked. The two dogs were entirely different. One was phenomenal over the marathon distance and had a unique style of running, the other was a six-bend specialist with classic pace. The only thing they had in common was that they were both exceptional animals and happened to be running at the same time. But it soon became clear that what everyone wanted was to see the two dogs run against one another.

Bookmakers John Power were quick to see the potential in the situation and Wembley put in a strong bid to stage a match. The result was the John Power Showdown in December 1985. It was certainly a great event for the sport, but Cliff Kevern and George Curtis were reluctant to get involved. In the first place, they were the ones with everything to lose. Scurlogue Champ had failed in his record-breaking attempt and he did not have his reputation on the line. Ballyregan Bob was on the brink of achieving the UK title and his entire future was at stake.

"Everyone wanted us to do it and in the end we agreed," said Curtis. "But there was one thing I stood firm on. I wouldn't let Bobby go further than 710 metres against Scurlogue Champ. I felt I had to bear his potential stud value in mind. Breeders do not want marathon dogs and I did not want to devalue Bobby by running him over too long a distance. I also knew we could not get the same class of dog to compete with over the extended trip.

"Scurlogue Champ was the great crowd-puller. He was going full blast before Bobby ever made a name for himself. He was going over 800m and winning by a distance when Bobby was going over 523m at Hackney. But the public were desperate to see the two dogs run together. I could understand that — but there was no way I was going to let Bobby take on Scurlogue over the distance and see him get beaten by 10 lengths. I would have been a lunatic to even think about it. I wasn't afraid to take the dog on and although people said we had the advantage because of the distance, they tend to forget that Scurlogue had run unbeaten six times at Wembley. In the aftermath, they said it was the wrong distance for Scurlogue. But we let him have 750 yards — how much further did he want?"

Cliff Kevern also had mixed feelings about the event and, not for the first time, he felt there were those who were anxious to exploit his dog. The race was to be for four greyhounds — Scurlogue Champ, Ballyregan Bob, Track Man and Glenowen Queen and the connections were asked to put in £3,000 each to make up a first prize of £12,000. The sponsors John Power put in an additional £3,000 for the runner-up and Wembley were left to provide nothing but the trophy.

Although everyone was expecting a match race between Scurlogue and Ballyregan, the two other runners were no slouches. Glenowen Queen in trap one was on offer at 25–1. Dickie Hawkes' bitch came to the race with a record of 30 runs and 14 wins including two track records. Adam Jackson's Track Man, a 12–1 chance in trap three, had 19 wins from 43 runs with four track records to his name. This compared with Ballyregan Bob, the 4–9 favourite in trap four who had 29 wins from 35 runs and eight track records and Scurlogue Champ, 9–4 against in trap six, who had 40 wins from 49 races and 17 track records.

Scurlogue was proclaimed the People's Champion at Wembley and his supporters sported his rosette and chanted his name in the electric run-up to the off. But the verdict was never in any doubt. Ballyregan flew out and established a long lead from Glenowen Queen by the first bend. Track Man kept the leaders in his sights but Scurlogue Champ walked out and seemed even more disinterested than usual. He checked at the first bend and just before the finishing line first time round he turned back. Ballyregan had built up an unassailable lead and crossed the line 11¾ lengths in front, recording 42.48 for the 710m. Behind him Track Man caught Glenowen Queen and dead-heated for second place.

Above: Scurlogue Champ. (W. A. Lewis)

Below: Scurlogue pulls up in the John Power Showdown. (Stephen Nash)

After the race Ken Peckham reported that Scurlogue Champ was lame — and this was the reason for his turning back. But Curtis believes there was another side to the story. "Dickie Hawkes said before the race: 'I hope they have plenty of stewards round the track, because Scurlogue Champ could give up racing.' I think that is exactly what happened. Ken Peckham said he was lame and I'm not disputing that. But in the showdown he came out walking, like he usually did. Bobby shot out and by the home straight the first time round Scurlogue was about 30 yards adrift. The crowd was going crazy and the hare was 30 yards in front. He couldn't hear the hare and he couldn't see it and I think he just packed it in. That's how it seemed to me. He was such a brainy dog, he was almost human. This time he didn't understand what was happening so he simply gave up. I have never seen a dog stop like that through lameness. I've had dogs with green stick fractures of the hock and they've still run on to win their race and Bobby kept going after he did a wrist in the St Leger. I think that Scurlogue was just too intelligent.

"I would never try to take anything away from the dog. I rate him as the most extraordinary greyhound I have seen in 50 years. I would say that six out of every eight rosettes at Wembley were for him — he had a following that far exceeded Ballyregan Bob's. If he had gone within four or five lengths everyone would have been happy. As it was, a lot of people were disappointed. After the race Ken Peckham was so sick he just took the dog away. I didn't speak to him. But we have always remained the best of friends. And when Bobby got the world record, he sent a congratulations card signed from The Champ."

But after all the post mortems were over, the fact was that Ballyregan Bob had equalled the UK track record in breathtaking style and was ready to go for win number 21. The race took place 10 days later at Brighton over 740m and again, every effort was made to ensure a top-class line up with £3,000 going to the winner, £1,000 to the runner-up and £250 each to the others.

The six were in trap order: Disco Clipper, Glenowen Queen, Track Man, Wyoming Ivy, Ballyregan Bob and Lady Opinion. Bobby's starting price was 30–100 which completed his record of starting at odds-on throughout his 21 race sequence. As the traps went up Track Man was the first to show, but Ballyregan Bob came out of the first bend just in front and then went on to increase his lead until he was 9 lengths ahead at the winning line, recording a time of 44.62. Tom Johnston, the trainer of Westpark Mustard who had held the UK record for 10 years, was at Brighton to present the prize.

Ballyregan Bob was now the undisputed king of stayers and he had earned a place in greyhound racing history in the best possible style. At all stages he had taken on and beaten the best and proved himself more than worthy of winning the 1985 Greyhound of the Year title. But Cliff Kevern and Curtis knew that there was more running left in their superstar. They announced that the dog would be aimed at the world record of 31 consecutive wins recorded by the American greyhound Joe Dump. The plan was to give Ballyregan Bob a six-week rest and let him mate a few bitches. Then he was to return to the campaign trail. Curtis said at the time: "I will not duck races with him. I want him to take on the best every time he runs. But I will look at him after every race and if there is any sign of recurring lameness from his wrist injury, we will retire him to stud immediately."

From the time of the showdown onwards the publicity surrounding Ballyregan Bob started gathering momentum and every race became a major event watched by thousands. "We were lucky in that Bobby was the perfect dog to handle," said Curtis. "The pressure might have got to us, but it never got to him. He loved his exercise. I've never known a dog that loved to gallop more, except perhaps Yankee Express. But with Bobby, we didn't even need to whistle him up the gallop, he came of his own accord. He has always enjoyed his grub and he travelled well. When he was at the race track he lay calm and quiet in his kennel and when you came to get him out, he just shook himself and then he was ready to race. You could see his heart pumping and his ears would prick when he got out on to the track. He was excited, but he never got hysterical."

Ballyregan Bob was in such hot demand he mated 16 bitches before he trialled back at Brighton, ready to contest the Burroughs Regency at his home track. This proved no obstacle and he won by 11¾ lengths from Swift Breeze in 41.81. The dog was now a star attraction and all the tracks were anxious to stage a race for him. But according to Cliff Kevern, the job of organising Bobby's race schedule was becoming increasingly difficult and in the end he employed greyhound agent Danny Baker.

"We had to get a sponsor for each race in order to get enough prize money to attract other runners," he said. "At this stage there was no money in it for me. The dog was always odds on, so he couldn't be backed. The tracks couldn't come up with decent prize money and yet I had the expense of transporting him up and down the country. When he was 10–1 on we also had the security aspect to worry about. That involved even more expense."

Bobby won by 9½ lengths at Wembley before travelling up to Nottingham, where he beat Teeraha by 3 lengths in 41.99 over 680m. Then it was back to the south for an invitation race at Wimbledon over 660m. Bobby flew out and scorched round in a new track record of 40.15. He beat Fergus Rock by 13¾ lengths. Powderhall was the next venue and Bobby was away from home a week. "He was running for

£1,000 prize money," said Cliff. "That sounds like a lot. But I was out of pocket by the end of the trip. We had to take up two kennel staff plus a security man and pay their hotel bills for a week. In a sense, I didn't mind doing it because Bobby was doing such a good job for the sport. You could see that by the reception he got at the tracks. But I blame the tracks themselves for giving so little back. The promoters didn't have the first idea about where to go for sponsors and I could see the opportunities passing them by." The trip to Powderhall proved worthwhile as far as Ballyregan Bob was concerned. He notched up another win — and another track record. This time he led all the way to beat Shandon Beggar by 14¼ lengths in 39.60 over 650m.

A fortnight later Ballyregan was back on the road, travelling up to Brough Park for a £500 race. This was race number 27 in his winning sequence and the dog appeared to be warming to his task. At the Newcastle circuit he did not take the lead until the fourth bend but then he set the track on fire with a lightning 41.15 for the 670m beating Humes Nest by 15 lengths. The problem was that Bobby was still in top gear at the trip. At Brough Park they use a sheet to stop the dogs running on and Curtis's dog was forced to pull up sharply as he sped up to the obstacle.

"When we got him home we found he had aggravated the old wrist injury," said Curtis. "It was the worst thing that could have happened, though at the time we did not fully realise how bad it was. He was booked to run in the Anglo-Irish International at Wimbledon just over a week later and there was a top-class line-up ready to take him on. I wasn't keen to run him, I knew he wasn't right in himself. But in a situation like that, you feel you can't withdraw the dog unless he is on three legs."

The line-up in trap order was: Oughter Brigg (10–1), Low Sail (6–1), Glenowen Queen (10–1), Glenivy (50–1), Ballyregan Bob (1–5), Lady Opinion (20–1). It says something about the phenomenal toughness of Ballyregan Bob that he made this race look as easy as the others. Glenowen Queen came out in front but it did not take Bobby long to get her measure. He took the lead and despite a late burst from Low Sail he crossed the line 5¾ lengths in front of Natalie Savva's dog, recording 40.23 for the 660m. Oughter Brigg got up to take third place, a further 3 lengths adrift. Ballyregan Bob was only four races away from the world record, but he was in a bad way when he came off the track at Wimbledon. "We knew it was a matter of resting him and then trialling him back," said Curtis. "To be honest, I had my doubts whether he would ever be fit to race again. The dog had been through so much and to me, he had nothing left to prove. I would have been quite happy to stick with the 28 wins. Then the NGRC gave a special lunch for Cliff Kevern and me to honour the UK record. They kept saying what a marvellous thing it would be for the sport if Bobby could go for the record. We felt after that, we should at least have a go."

So it was back to familiar routine of rest and treatment on the Magnetopulse machine. After six weeks the dog was given a solo trial around Hackney's 247m with no ill effects. A week later Curtis took him up to Wimbledon. It was Derby final night and Bobby should have been the star attraction on the supporting card. Instead he was relegated to a fitness trial. He went round the 480m course but when he came off his wrist had swollen up and he was hobbling. That night the glories of 12 months ago when Ballyregan Bob smashed the track record on Derby final night seemed a long way away. Both Curtis and Cliff Kevern knew the dog was in serious trouble.

"The only hope lay in rest and patience," said Curtis. "We knew it would be fatal if we tried to force the pace." But even with all his long years of experience, Curtis could not have envisaged that it would take Ballyregan Bob five and half months to get back to the track. "We knew it was going to be a long job, so we put Bobby on a rester's diet cutting out the raw meat," he said. "We allowed him to rest completely until the swelling had gone down and then we let him have light exercise. Then it was a question of galloping him back to fitness. We galloped him and galloped him until we thought he was okay. But when he first went back on the track three months later, he still went lame.

"We took him to Harringay and just tried him round the 272m course. Even though he was obviously feeling the injury, he did 16.29 which is an open race sprinter's time. He made a good recovery so a couple of weeks later we put him round the 475m. That time he did a 28.57. Tico had just gone round in 28.43, so he was only 2 lengths short of the dog who had just come back from doing the clock in Ireland." The problem was that Bobby was still coming off lame after every trial.

"We decided to trial him around Brighton, which is an easier track to run," said Curtis. "We put him over 515 metres and a week later over the 695 metres which was a really stiff test — and on both occasions he took off. But I was still worried. I wanted one more trial to convince myself that the dog really was all right. Everyone kept saying: 'When are you going to make up your mind?' But I wanted one more trial just to see if he could do the time. Bill Masters had worried about the dog all the way along and I said: 'If he can just reproduce something like his best time, he will prove to us that he's okay.' "

Bobby was taken to Harringay and put in a three dog trial round the 660m course. He flew out and led all the way to beat Winsor Ann by 9 lengths and set an unofficial track record of 39.99.

"The dog had been through so much and yet he could come out and do a time that had never been seen before," said Curtis. "They said the record of 40.14 would never get beaten and yet here was a dog with a serious injury problem who could do a time like that. Bobby had the heart of a lion. If anyone had seen him come off the track after that trial, they would have thought he was not fit to race. But with a wrist injury like his, he was always going to come off lame. Harringay's vet Bruce Prole saw him and said: 'I only wish I had treated him — he's made such a fantastic recovery.' "

At long last Ballyregan Bob was declared fit. There were only four races between him and the world record but Curtis was well aware that the dog's wrist could go again at any time. Racing manager Jim Layton suggested that the superstar was eased back with a graded race at Brighton. "I always wanted Bobby to race against the best," said Curtis. "But Joe Dump's record had all been done in graded company. I thought we were justified in giving Bobby a comeback race before we finally made up our minds if the record bid was on."

Ballyregan Bob was entered in a top heat race over 695m in what was effectively open race company. He was slow away but by the first quarter he had taken the lead and pulled away to beat Mines Kango by 9 lengths in a calculated 42.16.

"I knew then that we were all right to go for the record," said Curtis. "But I was terribly worried all the time. I only ever took one race at a time — I knew it would only take one wrong turn for him to do the wrist again." In fact the tension got so much that Cliff's wife Jessie could hardly bear to watch the dog race. "I couldn't bear to miss a race, but I hardly dared to watch in case he stumbled and hurt himself again," she said.

But according to Curtis, it was almost as though fate had taken a guiding hand. "After all the trouble, everything suddenly started going so smoothly for us. It was like it was meant to be," he said. Harringay was chosen for race number 30, a circuit that Curtis always believed was ideal for Bobby's style of running. "He was always strong at Harringay," he said. "It was a nice long run to the first bend and it was a good, safe track to run."

By now the publicity machine was in top gear and a huge crowd came to see the dog race. Bobby did not let his supporters down. Running from trap four, he was third to show but he soon worked his way into the lead and came home 10 lengths in front of Sacha Bran in 42.00 for the 688m. With one race to go to equal the world record both Curtis and Cliff Kevern were besieged by the Press. "We lost count of the number of interviews we gave," said Curtis. "It was almost impossible to get a day's work done. The other trainers at Brighton said they would never have put up with all the fuss and the disruption. But I thought: 'It isn't going to last for ever' — and I wanted to give everything I could for the sake of the sport."

Cliff Kevern virtually moved into the Brighton kennels so he could field the incessant phone calls. "The whole business was incredibly time-consuming," he said. "George could get nothing done so I went down to relieve the pressure. But it was also very exciting. We went along with the whole thing and never refused a single interview. It was the sort of thing that happens once in a lifetime — and we knew it was bringing greyhound racing to a far wider audience. I remember coming into the range one day and a TV crew were cowering in the corridor. They thought greyhounds were vicious animals that had to be kept in cages. But by the end of their visit they were complete converts. They had Bobby jumping up and licking them. He was a marvellous advertisement for his breed."

A week later Ballyregan Bob returned to Harringay in a bid to equal the world record of 31 consecutive wins. The TV cameras were there and again, a massive crowd turned up to see if the brilliant brindle could do it. Bobby took the lead early and then stormed home in a record-breaking 41.71 for the 688m, beating Wheelwright Arms by a massive 16 lengths. It was an incredible achievement for a dog which was so badly injured that he went lame every time he raced. But Bobby had proved that he was a totally exceptional animal. His determination and will to win were matchless.

The week before his world record bid was unforgettable for both Cliff Kevern and Curtis. There was not a person in Britain who did not know who Ballyregan Bob was — and American journalists and video crews came over to see the challenger for Joe Dump's crown. "At the time, I thought I was taking it all in my stride," said Curtis. "But when I look at the pictures that were taken then, I look years older. I have never liked a lot of public attention and I was never very good at going in front of the cameras. I could just feel myself go stiff. But we had to go through with it."

Everyone wanted to talk to the trainer of the country's most famous dog — and according to Curtis, they all asked the same question. "Without exception, they asked me for my secret formula for success," he said. "They all thought I was doing something special with the dog — and that included people inside the greyhound racing world as well as the ordinary news reporters. No-one seemed to believe that I treated him just like all the others in the kennel. All our dogs have the very best diet and I think that builds up a strong constitution. I think in Bobby's case it gave him the strength to get over his injury problems. But apart from that, the only extra thing I did was to gallop him. That was not so much because he needed it, he just loved going down there. We were always so busy in the kennel I would take him down in my lunch hours. I maintain that any trainer could have got the same from him. Whatever was special in Bobby, was in him when he was born. Maybe he's got bigger lungs or a stronger heart. But to me, it was his determination to win that made him great."

Cliff Kevern takes nothing away from Ballyregan Bob's undisputed greatness. But he believes Curtis's training skills were crucial in guiding the dog to his world record. "With athletes you can tell them what you want and gee them up for the big race," he said. "But with an animal you have to get their trust, which you can only do through your actions. George transmits love and affection for a dog through his hands. He talks to his dogs all the time and gets on their wavelength. I've seen dogs arrive at his kennels who are nervous and cringing and within hours they are a different sort of animal. Every dog is an individual and George appreciates that. While other trainers will just stick to a routine, he will take the time and trouble to discover the secret of every dog in the kennel and adapt their training accordingly. An animal must be in the right frame of mind to give its utmost — and George is truly gifted in being able to produce this in his dogs. Ballyregan Bob would never have got over his injuries and achieved his success without George."

The world record attempt was scheduled for Tuesday, December 9 — and right up to the last minute there were newsmen at the kennels. "Other trainers thought I was asking too much of Bobby to have him in and out of his kennel all the time, posing for pictures and going through his paces on the gallop," said Curtis. "But I knew that he could take it. He thrived on all the attention. The Sunday before the big race an American video crew came to shoot a film of him. We had him down the gallop and I whistled him back for them. Then the director came up to me and asked me to go through the whole thing again. That time I had to draw the line and say 'No'. He might have been an exceptional dog, but I didn't want him exhausted before the race."

Curtis had asked Cliff Kevern if the world record race could be staged at Brighton. Twelve months previously he had decided to step down as trainer at the end of the year. This was the decision of a highly principled man, and Curtis has never had any regrets. As always, he was totally honest and straightforward in announcing his intentions. He could not know that the climax of his career would fall in his last few weeks of being a trainer.

Cliff did not hesitate in agreeing to Curtis's request. "After all George had done, it was the least I could do," he said. "I also thought we owed it to the Brighton racegoers." Obviously the track that was to host the event was going to attract a huge crowd and massive tote takings. The race was going to be televised on both the BBC and ITV and the Press was going to be there in force. There was considerable speculation about potential sponsors but in the end, the *Racing Post* got the race for putting up £2,000 first prize. In view of the size of the event, this again seemed a wasted opportunity. It was a unique occasion, yet financially it was being treated little better than a senior open race."

Endless trouble was taken to ensure that the best possible line-up was produced for the *Racing Post* World Challenge. There was not the slightest suggestion of making things easy for Ballyregan Bob and Low Sail was flown over from Ireland especially for the race. On the night of the world challenge, Brighton was packed to capacity with a crowd of some 10,000. There was a carnival atmosphere with posters and banners galore. Representatives from every national newspaper were there as well as TV cameras and video crews. In all the excitement, there was one chance meeting that sticks in Cliff Kevern's mind. "A boy called Liam Kennedy came to introduce himself to me," he said. "He had bought Bobby as a nine-week-old puppy for £100 and he had reared him. He and his friends had travelled all the way from Newcastle West in Ireland to see the race."

Curtis is well-known for being a bag of nerves on final nights — but on this occasion it seemed as though nothing could go wrong. "I knew the dog was fit and I knew he would give his best," he said. The line-up for the world challenge in trap order was: Low Sail (4–1), Kalamity Kelly (20–1), Burnt Oak Tony (66–1), Swift Breeze (40–1), Queen's Comet (66–1), Ballyregan Bob (1–4 fav). The crowd erupted as the traps rose and Bobby came out in third place behind Swift Breeze and Queen's Comet. It stayed that way going round the first and second bends but by the home straight Bobby had moved into overdrive. He closed the gap and despite steering an incredibly wide course past Queen's Comet he strode into the lead by the halfway stage. He crossed the line 9¼ lengths in front of Swift Breeze recording 42.04 for the 695m.

The staying superstar had kept the tension going right to the last second — and the celebration cheers at Brighton Stadium were enough to lift the roof. Ballyregan Bob had proved himself the best six bend specialist ever and had won a world record for Britain. Once again, greyhound racing was a sport to be proud of. Events the next day proved this beyond doubt when Bobby's victory was proclaimed from the front pages of every national newspaper.

For Curtis and Cliff Kevern a dream had come true. All the agonising months when the dog looked as though he would never race again were forgotten. Ballyregan Bob had taken on the world and won. For Curtis, the final act was even more like a fairytale, for he was within two weeks of his retirement. "It was the most wonderful thing for all of us. But what pleased me most was when I saw the newspapers the next day," he said. "I really felt we had done something for the sport."

It took many weeks for the ballyhoo to die down — and offers for promoting the dog poured in. "To begin with, everyone wanted to

Above: Ballyregan Bob equals Joe Dump's world record. (Stephen Nash)

Below: National celebrity. Cliff and Jessie Kevern with George and Lily Curtis when Bobby is presented on BBC TV's Blue Peter.

TODAY

Bob to prove the hottest dog of all

THE Sun

The face of a champion one race from greatness

Once more, Bob—please

The Daily Telegraph

Bob's last run sets the record

Bob's date with history

DAILY EXPRESS

BOW WOW!

Bob tops the world

A dog's life—at £300,000

NOW BOB CAN EARN A FORTUNE

THE INDEPENDENT

HEADLINE NEWS
The national papers gave massive coverage the day after Ballyregan's world triumph.

HOTDOG
THE STAR
DOG OF THE CENTURY!
BALLYREGAN BOB'S RECORD See BACK PAGE
He's the Bally greatest!
Bounding Bob gets world record all to himself
Daily Mail
A FEW BOB MORE
Ballyhoo has cost a packet
BOW WOW WOW!
Sun Sport
Ballyregan Bob, pedigree champ of the world
Bob does the job for world record
Bob's fair lady!
CHAMPION GREYHOUND IS A WINNER AT LOVE TOO
Bob bob bobbin' along to a record
'This dog loves going on the podium. He is a true star'
THE TIMES
DAILY Mirror
Super Bob-the world's top dog
STANDARD
Bob the dog that defies belief

Above: Press and TV cameras surround Bobby after his world record victory. (Stephen Nash)

Below: Celebrations following the world record.

know if we were going to carry on racing Bobby," said Curtis. "I knew that he was good enough to carry on until he had 40 wins — he was that much better than any other greyhound around. But both Cliff and I decided to retire him to stud immediately after his 32nd race. If it had been a different time of year we might have been tempted to carry on. But with the bad going of January and February approaching, there was no possibility. We had been so lucky to keep the dog fit so he could get the record, it would have been greedy to ask for more. My only regret was that Bobby did not win a classic. He was clearly more than capable of it. But we had our compensations.

"To me, his value from then on was going to be at stud and I thought we should concentrate on getting his new career underway." This did not stop the offers coming in. Curtis was invited to take Bobby over to the States for a season's racing, which would have been very lucrative for both trainer and dog. But Curtis was not even tempted. "Everything is so different over there we would have been at sea from day one," he said. "All we could do was devalue the dog."

Cliff Kevern was equally adamant that Ballyregan Bob had retired for good. He signed the dog up with a sponsorship agent and there was a lot of talk about the money that could be made from promotions. "Bobby has made a lot of TV and public appearances," he said. "He was on BBC's Sports Personality of the Year, Blue Peter, Saturday Superstore and the Animal Roadshow. He went up to Aintree to pose with Red Rum and he has done pub openings. But there was no money in any of it." In many ways, the opportunities in the aftermath of Ballyregan Bob's triumph were wasted. The dog was a household name and he could have been used for promoting products such as petfoods. But the greyhound racing world was taken off-balance. It had never had anything on that sort of scale to deal with — and no one knew how best to exploit the situation. Promoters outside the sport talked in telephone numbers, but then failed to come up with the right sort of package.

Cliff Kevern admits that he was mildly disappointed that this side of Ballyregan Bob's career failed to take off. "But I knew I would get my financial rewards when he went to stud," he said. "The great thing about Bobby is that he has it all ways. He is brilliantly bred, he has terrific early pace and classic staying power. I used to say to my agent in Ireland: 'Find me a dog that's broken the 300 yard track record at Tralee and stays on for 700 yards.' That was asking for the impossible — but with Bobby we virtually had it."

There was a lot of interest in Ballyregan Bob from America and Cliff had numerous offers to stand the dog at stud over there. Ireland wanted him, too. But at the time Cliff wasn't interested.

So Bob returned to stud with George Curtis at the Albourne Kennels at a fee of £600, the highest ever asked in Britain for a sire. It did not put breeders off. Bob had a few problems adapting to the requirements of his new career and a number of his early visitors failed to produce pups, but the 1987 stud book lists 27 litters registered to the world champion, with a further 32 in 1988.

True to his word, Curtis stepped down as trainer at the end of 1986 and his right-hand man Bill Masters took over. The two swapped positions, with Curtis working as head man. It would not be an arrangement that would suit many, but it worked out extremely well. Curtis had the involvement — but not the responsibility. Never a man to go in search of glory, he was quite content to stay at the kennels, getting his satisfaction from giving the best possible care to the dogs.

The year ended with Ballyregan Bob winning the Greyhound of the Year award for the second year in succession and Curtis winning the Trainers' Championship, for the third and last time in his astonishing career. "It meant everything to me to go out on top," he said. "I feel I have nothing left to prove."

CHAPTER NINETEEN

Last goodbyes

True to his word, Curtis stepped down as a trainer at the end of 1986, swapping roles with his right hand man, Bill Masters. The name on the racecard may have changed, but otherwise it was very much business as usual at the Albourne "winner factory".

In 1987 Masters sent out more than 100 open race winners. His biggest success came with Yankees Shadow in the Regency at Brighton. She also won the Canada Dry Marathon at Walthamstow, and other top class winners included that grand campaigner Lone Wolf (Pat Daly Gold Vase, Sid Hooper Spring Cup and Surrey Cup), and Black Spindel (Wingspares Invitation).

More success followed in 1988. Masters claimed the Regency for a second time with Silver Mask, the Olympic with John Doe, the Test at Walthamstow with Fryers Well and the Etherington Golden Sprint with Round The Bend. The following year John Doe landed the Super Trapper at Hackney, White Island won the Olympic and finally Nans Brute brought Masters his own taste of classic success by winning the Scurry Gold Cup at Catford. The partnership seemed as strong as ever, but while George was happy to take a back seat and get on with "doing his dogs", Bill Masters was finding the demands of training at a busy track like Brighton an increasingly heavy burden. A regular BAGS contract meant four meetings a week had become the norm, and so there was precious little time to contemplate regular raids on the open race circuit. As a consequence, the supply of open race ammunition began to dry up and the kennel slowly ran short of greyhounds with the ability to compete for the top prizes.

But Masters and Curtis were still to enjoy one more night of success together. The 1990 Trainer's Championship was held at Brighton, bringing together Britain's leading handlers — John McGee, Linda Mullins, Ernie Gaskin, Ken Linzell and Phil Rees — in pursuit of a £2,500 prize. Masters had not qualified, but when Geoff de Mulder pulled out, the Brighton trainer was invited to take his place as the sixth trainer. Freely available at 16-1 to land the title, Masters pulled off a remarkable victory, beating McGee by a single point. That night of glory was to prove the swan song for Masters, who by now had a young family and was thoroughly disillusioned with the lifestyle of a greyhound trainer. That autumn, he quit.

For Ballyregan Bob the late Eighties were to prove equally traumatic. Once his honeymoon period at stud was over, the flow of bitches gently ebbed as breeders stepped back and waited to see if the world record holder could reproduce his own magic in his offspring. Early results were not encouraging. Decoy Regan Lass (Ballyregan Bob x Decoy Boom) proved a smart middle distance bitch, winning the £10,000 Produce Stakes at Wembley and the North East Cleaners 2,000 Guineas at Brough Park, but she alone among Bob's early pups showed real class. There were soon plenty of decent pups about, top graders at good tracks, but no chips off the old block. Very soon, Bob was getting no bitches to speak of.

Cliff Kevern cut the stud fee and took Bob home, but gradually became more and more disenchanted with British breeders. The 1989 stud book shows just eleven litters registered to Bob, and finally, in October that year, Cliff bowed to pressure from America to stand his great champion across the Atlantic. He went to Louise and Jackie Ryan in Abilene, Kansas, amid enormous razzamatazz. Brian King, a well-known greyhound owner who accompanied Cliff on the journey to America to deliver Bob, recalls: "When we got to Dallas we had to change planes for Witchita. Bob was given the red carpet treatment and whisked away to the other plane. We were not so lucky . . . we missed our connection. By the time we finally checked into our hotel Bob had been tucked up in his kennel for hours. Then at one o'clock in the morning there was a call from reception to say a "wedding present" had arrived for Cliff. I went down and there was a hug box tied with ribbon, and a card which read:

To Bob on our wedding.

I know I'm not your first, and I won't be your last, but I hope I'm your best. Love, Gabby Marilyn.

The box was filled with dozens of Kit-Kat bars . . . Bob's favourite.

The gift had come from Gabby Marilyn's owner, Bill Fullerton, who had driven hundreds of miles to ensure that his bitch was the first to be mated to Ballyregan Bob in America. Cliff returned home without his beloved Bob and, ironically, within a matter of weeks, Ballyregan Bob's pups were beginning to make headlines back in Britain. A September

1987 litter out of Chocolate Satin produced Shropshire Lass, Carlsberg Champ and Chocolate Chip, who between them dominated marathon open racing for much of 1990.

The biggest success of all came when Shropshire Lass carried off the TV Trophy. It was a moment that Cliff Kevern would have savoured almost as much as the triumphs of Bob himself but, tragically he was not destined to witness it. Long before Ballyregan Bob was making headlines Cliff was fighting a continuing battle against cancer, and in March 1990 it finally beat him. He died just a week before that TV Trophy Final.

Ballyregan Bob stayed in America until October that year, serving a total of 34 bitches, but Cliff's widow, Jessie, was itching to have him home again.

"Cliff always said he would bring the dog home after two years. I was worried about Bob, not being able to see him, and I decided to cut it short. I knew that was what Cliff would have wanted," she said.

Bob returned via Holland and Germany and entered quarantine kennels in January this year. He was due out within a few weeks of this postscript being written. But as the book went to press his future was still uncertain. He may well return to stud duties, his reputation considerably enhanced since he left these shores. Carlsberg Champ went on to win the Cesarewitch, the Ron Bazell Silver Collar, the Kent St Leger, the Courage Marathon and the Stow Marathon, while his sister Chocolate Chip won thirteen opens. Meanwhile a second litter out of Sandy Gem was beginning to impress. The best was Bob's Regan, winner of the Ladbroke Golden Jacket and the Regency in 1991, and no fewer than six other members of the litter have won open races.

George Curtis, of course, would love to be reunited with the finest greyhound he has trained. But George and Cliff did not always see eye to eye on Bob's abilities as a sire and it seems unlikely now that Jessie would allow Bob to return to what many would consider his natural home.

For a man who "retired" more than four years ago, George shows remarkably little sign of stopping work. While Bill Masters was still pondering his future at Albourne, George was looking forward to new pastures and new challenges. Brighton property developer John Regan, a Curtis owner of long standing, had bought Lowlands Farm near Burgess Hill and was in the process of turning it into a top class training establishment. When he invited George to move in alongside trainer Eric Jordan it was, in George's own words "an opportunity too good to miss."

The arrival of Curtis may well have been a factor in Jordan winning a contract to replace Masters at Brighton. And it wasn't long before the new partnership was in the limelight. Jenny's Wish, trained by Eric Jordan, landed the 1991 TV Trophy . . . yet another big race winner associated with George Curtis. Not that he has anything left to prove.

Starting at the age of 14 with no money and no education, Curtis made his way to the very peak of his profession. And that success was achieved with the unmistakeable Curtis hallmarks of hard work, dedication and total honesty. He has joined the ranks of the sport's all-time greats. But he should also be remembered as the man who reached the heights with his reputation unblemished.

PEDIGREE OF BALLYREGAN BOB

bd d May 1983

BALLYREGAN BOB	Ballyheigue Moon	Yellow Band	Lively Band	Silver Hope
				Kells Queen
			Monalee Peg	Prairie Flash
				Sheila At Last
		Heather Suzie	Newdown Heather	Printers Prince
				Pardee
			Susie Gaye	Kerry Wonder
				Palfium
	Evening Daisy	Here Sonny	Monalee Champion	Crazy Parachute
				Sheila At Last
			Handbag	Odd Venture
				Goodish
		Airdrie Hill	Spectre	Crazy Parachute
				Supreme Witch
			Yurituni	Pigalle Wonder
				Rather Fancy

PEDIGREE OF YANKEE EXPRESS

bd d October 1980

YANKEE EXPRESS	Pecos Jerry	Annexed	Venerated	Ample Time
				Viewed
			Amber Annette	Kosher
				Amber Ann
		Classy Babe	Spec Harmony	Tell You Why
				April Nancy
			Dr Nell	Great Valour
				Penny Bobs
	King's Comet	Cobbler	Monalee Champion	Crazy Parachute
				Sheila At Last
			Yurituni	Pigalle Wonder
				Rather Fancy
		Robin's Silver	Oregon Prince	Knockhill Chieftain
				Burleigh's Fancy
			Cheekie Brownie	Quare Customer
				My Daffy